I *Believe* IN
HEALING

REAL STORIES FROM THE BIBLE, HISTORY AND TODAY

CECIL MURPHEY
& TWILA BELK

Chosen

a division of Baker Publishing Group
Minneapolis, Minnesota

© 2013 by Cecil Murphey and Twila Belk.

Published by Chosen Books
11400 Hampshire Avenue South
Bloomington, Minnesota 55438
www.chosenbooks.com

Chosen Books is a division of
Baker Publishing Group, Grand Rapids, Michigan

Chosen Books edition published 2014
ISBN 978-0-8007-9689-1

Previously published by Regal Books

Printed in the United States of America

The Library of Congress has cataloged the original edition as follows:
Murphey, Cecil.
    I believe in healing : real stories from the Bible, history and today /
Cecil Murphey and Twila Belk.
        pages cm
    Includes bibliographical references.
    ISBN 978-0-8307-6553-9 (trade paper : alk. paper)
        1. Healing—Religious aspects—Christianity. 2. Healing—Biblical teaching.
I. Title.
BT732.M88 2013
234′.131—dc23   2012051451

Cecil Murphey and Twila Belk are represented by The Knight Agency Inc., 570 East Avenue, Madison, GA 30650.

16   17   18   19   20   7   6   5   4

Contents

Part 2

QUESTIONS ABOUT HEALING

HOW TO READ THIS BOOK

In Part 1 of this book, after a personal introduction by Cecil Murphey to explain his belief in divine healing, we present documented and witnessed examples of healings that have occurred during the nearly 2,000 years since the last pages of the Bible were written. Many of these stories are contemporary and written by those who actually experienced healing.

If you're unsure about whether healing is still available and valid for Christians today, or if you would like biblical proof and theological rationale for healing, start with Part 2. In this section of the book, we provide answers to many of the most commonly asked questions about healing. In providing this material, our purpose is to prove healing in the past was part of the work of God's Spirit; show that the widespread belief in healing today is part of the ongoing work of God's Spirit; and prove that modern healings occur by medical documentation and the words of credible eyewitnesses.

I Believe IN HEALING

REAL STORIES FROM THE BIBLE, HISTORY AND TODAY

INTRODUCTION

I *Believe* in Healing

CECIL MURPHEY

It's easy to say, "I believe in healing." The statement by itself doesn't mean much. But when I write, "I believe in healing *because . . .*" I'm not only stating what I believe, but also giving a reason for it.

I have two reasons for my belief in healing.

First, I believe in physical healing because we've experienced it in our family. Many Christians would make that the second reason; however, I had to see it happen before I was able to grasp that God was still the divine Physician.

I grew up outside the Church and hadn't thought seriously about divine healing. My wife, Shirley, grew up in Zion, Illinois, a city founded by John Alexander Dowie and based on a belief in healing as part of the atoning death of Jesus Christ.

Here's the story of the experience that led me to become a firm believer in physical healing.

"I'm sorry," the doctor said and stared at the floor, "but we don't expect her to live through the night."

I had already been talking to him for a couple of minutes when he made that statement.

"Sir, we're Christians and we're not afraid of death," I had said. "I ask you to be honest with me."

That's when he told me they didn't expect my wife to live. I was shocked, and yet I was able to accept the doctor's pronouncement.

He led me into a small room, where Shirley lay on a gurney, and told me I could stay there. Although he didn't say it, the tone of his voice added, "until she expires." Our two daughters were sleeping in another small room just down the hallway. Wanda was two, and Cecile was seven months old. A nurse said I'd be able to hear them if they awakened.

I sat on a chair across from the gurney, laid my head against the metal bars, and prayed. As I prayed, I mentally replayed the accident in my mind.

It was the night before Thanksgiving. We were on our way from our home in Zion, Illinois, to spend the holiday with my parents in Davenport, Iowa. The night was cold and overcast. We were about halfway there, and I was behind a large semi. He must have had quite a heavy load, because every time we went up an incline, his speed went down to less than 30 miles an hour.

I pulled out and it looked clear ahead, so I started to pass the truck. I was just even with the hood when a car came from the opposite direction at an enormously fast speed. I couldn't pick up any additional speed, and I couldn't throw on my brakes. I did the only thing I could think of doing—I turned the wheel and headed toward the left shoulder.

Just as I pulled onto the shoulder, so did the other vehicle—and it hit the front passenger's side of our car.

The next part is blurred, but I remember that when I got out of the car, I had only a few bumps. Wanda, our older daughter, was in the front seat with her mother. Shirley had thrown her arm in front of Wanda to protect her. Our younger daughter, Cecile, was in the back seat. She had been thrown to the floor and bruised her right knee, which seemed her only problem. Both girls were crying, and I tried to calm them before I turned to my wife.

Shirley had taken the brunt of the accident. Her head went through the windshield, and her door was caved in and pressed against her body. I couldn't get her out; however, by then two men were at my side. (I don't know where they came from.) They ripped off the door, and I was able to touch Shirley. Her face was filled with blood, and pieces of glass were everywhere. Blood poured out of her neck.

We were less than two miles from a hospital, and someone must have called them. One man held a cloth against Shirley's neck and pressed it tightly. She moaned several times.

The ambulance came and carried her off. One of the onlookers gave my daughters and me a ride to the hospital. I learned that the people in the other vehicle—a Cadillac—were unhurt, and that the vehicle had been racing at 85 miles an hour. A police officer at the hospital told me the other driver would be charged.

After sitting in the room with Shirley for a while, I thought of our families. This was before cell phones, so I called my parents collect from a telephone in the hospital. Next, I called Shirley's mother, who lived with us in Zion.

"We've been involved in a head-on collision," I said, "and Shirley's badly hurt." Even though the doctor didn't give me any hope, I wasn't willing to give up—and I didn't tell either set of parents that part.

"I'll tell the church people," Shirley's mother said.

We were members of a small congregation in Waukegan, Illinois, which was about 100 miles from the accident. Being part of the membership meant a commitment to be called at any time of the night or day for prayer. When called, we agreed to pray until we felt a sense of peace. Things were set up so that Mom Brackett had to make only 3 calls. Each person she called in turn called 3 or 4 others. Within minutes, the 40-plus members of the church were praying.

Shirley survived the night. On Thursday, she remained unconscious and was hanging on to life. The doctor was surprised she hadn't "expired." I didn't know what to do about our daughters. Mom Brackett and Shirley's uncle drove out to the hospital that afternoon.

"No change," the doctor said. "She's not worse and she's not better." He said X-rays showed that most of the bones in her body were broken. He gave me an extensive list of her injuries, but I could hardly take in the information.

When the doctor learned that Shirley's mother was there to pick up our daughters, he urged me to go with them.

I didn't know what to do.

After the doctor left us, Mom said, "I want to tell you something." As I had expected, she had started the prayer chain working. "Gus called about 20 minutes afterward," she said. Gus was a golf pro and one of the leaders of our congregation. He heard only that we had been in an accident and Shirley was badly injured. Nothing else.

Gus said that when he prayed, he saw the car. He described the injuries in Shirley's body, including the broken bones. By this time, Mom, a former nurse, knew about Shirley's injuries. She told me, "That's exactly what Gus saw."

I believed what she said. If God hadn't revealed it to Gus, how did the man know?

Mom added, "Gus also said the Lord assured him that Shirley will be healed and we're not to worry."

I didn't understand, but I felt a deep peace after hearing those words.

Mom wanted me to return to Zion with her. I was torn. I felt I belonged at Shirley's side, but I also needed to be with the girls, who were shaken up and cried easily. I went back to see the doctor.

He said, "You need to be with your daughters, and you can't do anything here. I promise you that if there's any change, we'll call." I didn't tell him about Gus; I gave him our telephone number, as well as that of Shirley's sister, who lived next door, and the number of Beach Park Elementary School, where I taught.

I called the hospital Thursday night, and three times on Friday, and three more times on Saturday. There was no change. Shirley was alive, but no better or worse. I called on Sunday morning before church, and again that evening—and still there was no change.

On Monday morning, I went to school. By noon I couldn't keep my mind on the class, so I went to the office and called the doctor.

"I was just going to contact you," he said.

"How is she?"

After a long pause, he said, "If you want to come back tomorrow, you can take her home. She's—she's all right."

"What do you mean?"

"There are some things we can't explain, but she's fine. She's lost a lot of blood and she's weak, but I think she can handle the ride home."

I have no recollection of my response. I do remember that the principal told me that he would cover my class and I should go.

My brother-in-law drove me to the hospital. Minutes after our arrival, Shirley and I walked out together. She was healed.

There is one other significant thing about this healing. Twenty-five years later, Shirley developed what we assumed was arthritis all through her body. She went to see a rheumatologist.

After he examined the X-rays, he asked her, "Were you ever in a severe accident in which you suffered a number of broken bones?"

"Yes, years ago," Shirley said.

He showed her the X-rays and pointed to the various places in her body where there had been breaks. "Those places have calcified," he said, "and your system has gone rheumatic."

God healed Shirley a few days after the accident, as Gus had assured us. God did not heal the arthritis, and Shirley lives with it today. But she is still alive.

My second reason for believing in healing is because it's in the Bible.

As an adult convert, I studied my Bible daily for more than three years before we experienced healing in our family. During that time, I read stories of Jesus touching the blind and the lame, and of the apostles setting people free of various diseases. I knew about the healing of Naaman the leper and the lame man at the temple gate. I didn't doubt these stories, but the biblical accounts kept healing on an impersonal level. That is, these miracles had happened to other people. Even more significantly, these stories of God repairing people's bodies took place in the ancient past.

Shortly before I married Shirley, I joined the congregation where she was already a member. Pastor Walter Olson, a godly man, agreed that miracles in the Bible were true and that God healed. "However, all supernatural activity stopped—totally—at the end of the apostolic era." Those were his words from the pulpit one Sunday morning.

After the service, I asked him how he could be sure that miracles ended after the time of the first apostles.

Pastor Olson quoted 2 Timothy 4:20: "I [Paul] left Trophimus sick at Miletus."

He said, "If Paul could still heal, why did he leave Trophimus unhealed?" He also mentioned Timothy's stomach ailments and said that obviously Paul hadn't been able to do anything for his protégé.

As a new convert, I learned so much from Pastor Olson that it never occurred to me to question him further on this matter. He was the scholar and the teacher, and I was an eager disciple.

We moved from the area, and I realized that our pastor wasn't alone in his beliefs about healing. What he had told me seemed the commonly accepted position among Baptists. I heard the same assertions from ministers of the Evangelical Free Church. In those days, only Pentecostals dared to stand firm and say, "I believe in healing *for today*."

No statement in the Bible says healing or miracles ceased

If the great theologians of the past were around today and insisted that healing ended at the end of the first century, I'd ask for an authoritative, biblical proof, which I don't think they could provide. At best, they could tell me their observations. At worst, they would announce their prejudice against spiritual things they didn't understand or had no experience with.

God's Word says, "I am the LORD, and I do not change" (Mal. 3:6).

Without intending to insult my old pastor or anyone else who held or holds to the cessation of healing, I would say that it's easy to declare such a doctrine. If we don't see healing taking place on a regular basis, we assume:

- God dropped that phase of compassion;

- Something is wrong with the modern Church; or

- Widespread healing has not been part of God's sovereign plan throughout human history.

One purpose of this book is to show the Spirit of God working in healing bodies through the centuries.

A. J. Gordon published *The Ministry of Healing* in 1882, and for many years it was *the revered book* among Pentecostals and others who believed in healing. The book begins with this paragraph:

Have there been any miracles since the days of the apostles? To this question the common answer has been, in our times at least, a decided no. A call recently put forth in one of our religious journals, asking the opinion of ministers, teachers and theological professors on this point was very largely answered; and the respondents were well nigh unanimous in the opinion that the age of miracles passed away with the apostolic period. *The statement contained in several of these replies gave evidence indeed that the question had never been deeply investigated by the witnesses.*[1]

PART 1

STORIES
AND TESTIMONIES OF
Healing

A Shattered Dream

Alyssa Barlow loved to sing and dance. She envisioned a life on Broadway after she graduated from high school. At the age of 17, she stumbled on the stairs and turned her ankle. Excruciating pain in her ankle caused her to think it was broken, and she had to use crutches. Then her foot turned ice cold, and that cold feeling, coupled with intense pain, spread up her leg. Because her leg hurt so much, she couldn't even put a sheet on top of it.

After two months of doctor visits and special tests, Alyssa was diagnosed with reflex sympathetic dystrophy (RSD), a rare, chronic neurological syndrome that causes nerves to overreact and fire constantly. "There's no cure for it," the doctors said. "It will eventually spread throughout your entire body."

Not only were Alyssa's days filled with pain, but her dream of being a dancer was also shattered.

The doctors didn't offer encouragement of recovery; they simply gave her medication to help with the pain. They discussed clipping the nerve on the back of her heel, which would leave her with foot drop. "You'll never walk normally again," they said. Alyssa would need to use crutches and would eventually end up in a wheelchair.

Alyssa's mother, who strongly believed that God had a different plan for her daughter's life, said, "We will not accept that."

"You heard the doctors," Alyssa said. "My life is ruined."

After the doctor's prognosis and her mother's refusal for surgery, Alyssa became bitter. Her negative thoughts and bad attitude intensified as she lay in bed most of each day.

She questioned things she'd learned about God over the years and grew angry. *You say You have all these great plans for me, God, yet You allow this to happen. What about Your promises?* She thought about everything she had worked for up to this point. *If You loved me and had plans for me, I wouldn't have to go through this. I've served You all this time and this is what I get.*

Throughout Alyssa's process of dealing with the diagnosis and wrestling with God, her parents didn't lose faith that God would take care of her. They refused to accept the doctors' prediction that their daughter would never walk again and rejected their plan to clip her nerve. Instead, they prayed with her and for her and trusted God for her healing.

Gradually, Alyssa changed. Supported by the love of her family and others, she made her peace with God. She thought about her dreams and realized that maybe she had been missing God's dreams for her life because she couldn't see beyond her own.

One day after praying, Alyssa's parents urged her to walk in their pool, regardless of the horrific pain. Reluctantly, she tried it with her dad's help. Despite the pain she felt as she walked, she sensed God with her, encouraging her to push through it. She focused her attention on God and with each step she praised Him.

She walked in the pool a second day, but on the third day it rained so hard she decided to try walking inside. She put one crutch down and took a step. It hurt horribly, but she wanted to trust God. She put down the second crutch and began to walk.

The pain didn't go away, but she kept walking without her crutches. For the next year, she remained determined to walk and push through the pain while claiming, "God said I was okay. He said I would be healed."

Eventually the pain was gone—and Alyssa Barlow exchanged her dreams of Broadway for the dream God had for her: being on stage, singing, playing instruments, and recording music with her sisters in a group called BarlowGirl.[2]

"He Will Not Die"

As a gifted upperclassman at Liberty University, Charles Hughes traveled with Dr. Jerry Falwell across the nation to participate in his "I Love America" crusades. He also preached as a member of an evangelistic team that included Mark Lowry, David Mussel and Richard Bernier.

On March 17, 1978, as the team was traveling up a snowy mountain road to a crusade in Harrisburg, Pennsylvania, an out-of-control 18-wheeler crashed into their van and crushed it against the mountainside. The impact smashed Charles's skull and put him in a coma.

After Charles arrived at the hospital, a group of surgeons opened the top of his skull to relieve pressure on his brain and to allow it to swell outside the cranium. They wanted to prevent his going into a vegetative state.

The doctors did what they could for him, but Charles remained unresponsive. "We don't expect him to live," the doctors told the Hughes family. "Will you allow us to harvest his organs to help someone else?" The doctor held out papers for them to sign.

Despite his son being in a coma and all signs indicating death, Robert Hughes, founding dean of Liberty Baptist Theological Seminary, insisted, "He will not die."

Jerry Falwell stood at his side and didn't try to change his mind. Robert went to the hospital's prayer chapel to beg God for healing.

Meanwhile, Falwell called the university and talked with Liberty co-founder Elmer Towns: "Charles is in a coma. He's about to die. Gather everyone in your department and pray." Falwell didn't stop there. "Alert the heads of every department to pray."

Falwell flew back to Lynchburg, Virginia, to hold a prayer meeting at Thomas Road Baptist Church. He updated those in attendance about Charles's condition, emphasizing that he was on life support and that the doctors had little hope for his survival.

He instructed the congregation to divide into small groups to claim healing for Charles. "Pray in faith because God has promised to hear and answer." Then he made a bold announcement: "I believe Charles will be healed, and he will be our commencement speaker in May."

After intense prayer, Falwell returned to the pulpit and encouraged everyone to hold a one-day fast on behalf of Charles.

Charles was released from the hospital on June 17, 1978, exactly three months after the accident, and in May of the following year, Jerry Falwell's prediction came true. The expected-to-die man was present to give the commencement address.

The audience might not remember what Charles said that day, but they won't forget what they saw: Charles refused the offer of a wheelchair. He stood and walked with the others. He climbed the stairs to the platform. That—along with his scars, scattered tufts of new-grown hair, and stitches that circled his scalp—sent a powerful message: God is a miracle worker.

Charles's general surgeon said, "He progressed further than any of us ever expected. We refer to him as a miracle case."

Charles went on to earn his seminary degree and his doctorate degree. At present, he enjoys his position as Care Pastor at Liberty University, where he supervises the prayer room. He also serves as pastor of Truth Baptist Church in Lynchburg, Virginia.

A Singer's Throat Disease

(DAVE CLARK)

My physical problems began with canker sores in my mouth and throat when I was 12 years old. The sores healed, but they returned frequently. Each time they came back, they hurt more and stayed longer.

After multiple visits to the doctor provided no relief, my parents finally took me to the Mayo Clinic. They diagnosed a severe case of aphthous stomatitis, but learning terms like "deteriorated esophagus" didn't make my throat feel better. In the days and years that followed, I relied on a numbing solution called Viscous Xylocaine. One sip before each bite allowed me to swallow food—but I couldn't taste it.

At age 17, with my parents' hesitant blessing, I moved to Nashville to write music. Eventually, I became a guitar player with the Speer family. The famous singing group accepted me even with my physical difficulties and gave me the opportunity to flourish as a songwriter. I continued to pray and to ask others to pray for my healing. After five years, I left the Speers to pursue writing full-time.

I wrote out of my pain, and I saw God use those songs to minister to others who were hurting. Even though God was blessing the songs, my physical condition continued to worsen. I prayed, my family prayed, and people across the country prayed on my behalf, asking God to touch my life and heal me.

In December of 1990, I told David Graves, the new pastor of our church, about my physical problems. He said my condition sounded similar to that of Martha Wilson from his former congregation. After years of pain, being anointed with oil, and people praying for her, she hadn't gotten any better.

Martha went to Guatemala on a church mission where she met Dr. Castillo, a Guatemalan. He prescribed a new treatment, and Martha improved immediately. However, the medicine wasn't available in the United States. (My understanding is that the medicine provided short-term relief while Martha was in Guatemala. I never learned anything else about her.)

On Christmas day, I called my good friend Roger Pacholka. He mentioned that he was going to Guatemala within the next few weeks.

I told Roger the Martha Wilson story. As a medical student and now as a doctor, Roger had always been discouraged that he couldn't do anything to help me. He asked me for the doctor's name and address. I could give him only a last name—a common name in a country of 11 million people.

When Roger arrived in Guatemala, he asked one of the host missionaries if she knew of a Dr. Castillo. "That's my family doctor," she said, "and I have an appointment with him tomorrow."

Roger sent a note to Dr. Castillo explaining my situation and asking for the treatment plan. After Roger returned home, he found a version of the drug available in the United States under a different name, and he gave me instructions about how to take it. "It might work in as little as 14 days," he told me, "but if it does, you'll probably need to be on it the rest of your life."

I started treatment but wondered how something that tasted like water could do anything for my throat. And in 14 days? It didn't make sense to me, but there had been too many signs pointing to a miracle.

Each day people asked how I felt; each day I answered, "No change." My throat didn't get worse, but it was already at the point of being as bad as it could be. People finally stopped asking.

On the thirteenth day of my treatment, I flew to Houston for a writing project. That night, frustrated and discouraged, I called my wife, Cindi, and poured out my heart. I had thought I was on the brink of a cure, but nothing had changed. We prayed for strength.

After 19 years of incessant pain because of the ongoing throat disease, I came to a crossroads where I finally surrendered everything to Jesus Christ. I committed myself to serve the Lord as fully as I could, no matter how much I had to endure. I would trust God even if I had pain the rest of my life.

I had a peaceful sleep. The next morning, May 1, 1991, I awakened and swallowed. *There was no pain.*

I stared in the mirror at my throat. No ulcers. The night before, my throat had been lined with open tissue, and now there was not one trace.

At first I wondered if the reprieve would be temporary. But after more than 20 years, I still enjoy the evidence of God's complete healing—and during that time, I've gone without a drop of medicine.

Many top Christian artists have recorded Dave Clark's songs, including Phillips Craig & Dean, CeCe Winans, and 4HIM. Clark has written 25 number one songs, including "Crucified with Christ," "Strange Way to Save the World," and "Be the One." ASCAP awarded him their Lifetime Achievement Award in 2009. Donna Clark Goodrich wrote his story in *Healing in God's Time* (Washington, DC: Believe Books, 2009).

Call It a Mystery?
(CHERYL COLWELL)

On Friday afternoon, my brother, Bob, sat on his lawn, next door to my house, sobbing. He had taken his wife, Janet, to the hospital for bronchitis, but her condition had turned out to be much worse. X-rays and a CT scan revealed two masses in her left lung: a lemon-sized shape in the upper lobe and a quarter-sized form in the lower lobe. Further tests confirmed her doctor's suspicions.

My brother wept as he told me, "Cancer. They've given her two months to live." Our father had died of cancer, and so did our aunt, an uncle and our older brother. To us, the word "cancer" was a death sentence.

My aunt was visiting us that week. She wasn't a believer, but as she watched television late that Friday night, an ad for a healing service rotated through the programming. The idea niggled in her mind all night.

Early Saturday morning, she said, "I don't know what this means, but I'm supposed to tell you to take Janet to that healing service."

That was strange. Even stranger was that as I listened, I knew Janet would be healed.

Bob picked Janet up from the hospital, wrapped her in a blanket, took along a lawn chaise lounge, and we drove 45 minutes to the service. My husband, mother and aunt accompanied us. We entered the tent, and Bob made Janet as comfortable as possible, while the rest of us began to sing with the congregation.

When the preacher began to speak, I felt confident it wasn't a sham. He was a humble, sincere man, who told us that he was not the healer—Jesus was. God had given him a gift of knowledge to know what He wanted to do. In his next sentence, the preacher said, "There is a woman here with a diseased left lung. Come forward. God wants to heal you."

Janet gasped. Tears flowed down our faces as Bob took her forward for prayer. Janet told us later that she felt as if she had floated down the aisle, and that when the man prayed for her, she felt her body wrapped inside the arms of Jesus.

When Janet told her doctor, "I've been healed," he was skeptical. Not wanting to be irresponsible, Janet decided to proceed with the scheduled surgery.

After Bob had waited for a while outside the surgical room, a perplexed surgeon met him. "I've checked the upper lung and didn't find anything. Do I have your permission to make a larger incision and go into the lower section?" Bob agreed.

Not long afterward, the surgeon returned. "I'm sorry, sir, but I have been through every centimeter of her lungs. There is no growth there."

Afterward there was a buzz around the hospital and in our community about what had happened. No one could deny that the cancer had been present—it was documented. And no one could deny that it was gone—a respected surgeon vouched for that.

People were left with a choice: They could call it a mystery, or they could believe the truth that Jesus healed my sister-in-law.

Cheryl Colwell enjoys crafting stories, filled with mystery and romance, about ordinary people who find supernatural help from God when plunged into insurmountable circumstances. See www.cherylcolwell.com.

Healings IN THE MINISTRY OF
Charles Haddon Spurgeon
(1834–1892)

Charles Spurgeon's ministry in London began with remarkable incidents of healing that took place on his visits to the sick during his first year at New Park Street Chapel.

✦

In 1855, a man with a fever rose from his bed the same day that his doctor had declared his case critical. He appeared at the evening meeting and told the congregation that Mr. Spurgeon had prayed with him that morning, and he had been divinely healed.

✦

Another account is of a man who walked firmly down the aisle in church to a front seat. For years, he had limped. He was quoted as saying, "Glory to God!" giving praise for God's having used Mr. Spurgeon to bring about his miraculous recovery. He threw away his cane, assured he wouldn't need to use it again.

A man from Wales who was visiting London "had been sadly afflicted mentally" and pleaded for his family to get Mr. Spurgeon to pray for him. Spurgeon came to the man's bedside, and returned the next evening. During the following night, the sick man awakened and cried out. He said he had dreamed of meeting the Savior, who assured him that the devils had been cast out.

A few days later, he was able to leave the house. Afterward he moved to Canada, where he became a successful businessman.

A child was sick with a fatal, contagious disease. The family invited Spurgeon to the house. He knelt with them in a circle around the bed, and offered up a prayer for their daughter's salvation, adding a petition for her recovery.

The father and mother both prayed. When they arose from their knees, the child, just becoming conscious, asked for water. "I feel very much better," she said.

Afterward the girl told her mother that during the prayer she felt a "strange sensation running all over her, as though the fever began to decline at her head and gradually passed off at her feet."

With reference to the healing of the sick by prayer or by the laying on of hands, Mr. Spurgeon ever maintained a very careful reserve. It was difficult to secure from him a direct expression of his convictions in this matter.

Reverend Russell Cornwell, a contemporary of Mr. Spurgeon's who eventually wrote his biography, worked as a correspondent for a prominent American newspaper. He once asked Spurgeon whether he believed all persons could be healed by the use of sincere prayer by persons who believed in Christ and whose lives were righteous. Spurgeon answered that his experience in the matter had been quite extensive, but that he needed to look further before he would be able to answer such a question without reservation. Yet although he was not a physician and never wrote prescriptions, he felt that there was unexplainable mystery about the whole matter. He asserted that there was some power connected with prayer that ought to be used when persons were in pain and could be relieved by it.[3]

The Faith of a Few Good Friends

(MARSHA ROBINSON)

"Don't you want to go to the emergency room?" my husband, Bryant, asked. His face showed his concern.

"I guess so," I mumbled.

I had been ill for two weeks with what I thought was a bad case of the flu. I ran high fevers and was unable to enjoy the Christmas holidays. I was not getting any better, so that Sunday morning, Bryant helped me to the car and drove me to the ER. I was assessed by a triage nurse and taken to an exam room. Several doctors saw me and ran tests to determine what was wrong with me.

At the outset, they said it was the flu and that I would be able to go home in a little while. Later, as test results began to show some troubling numbers, they told us they wanted to keep me overnight for observation. Bryant went home.

The phone rang at 2 A.M. "Your wife has been moved to the ICU. She is on a ventilator and her condition is critical."

Confused, Bryant dressed quickly and rushed back to the hospital.

Later that morning, the lead physician called for my family and friends to meet him in a hospital conference room. Bryant thought the doctor was going to give them good news—something like, "This is what's wrong with her, here's what we're doing about it, and this is when she'll go home."

Instead, the doctor informed my family and friends that tests confirmed that my kidneys had failed, and I was in septic shock because of a large atypical kidney stone. A raging klebsiella infection had taken over my body.

The doctor went on to say that my condition was so grave that I had a zero percent chance of surviving the night. "On a scale of one to 10, with 10 being the worst a person could be, she's a 12." He paused and added, "We have her on a variety of machines, but sometime tonight, her heart is going to stop. We can revive her, but her heart will stop again and we'll have to revive her again. You need to tell us how many times you want to put her through that. There is nothing else we can do."

He left the room. The click of the door shutting behind him was followed by stunned silence—and then spontaneous prayer burst forth. That conference room became a fervent prayer meeting. Word spread to friends who were in waiting rooms and hallways. They began praying as well.

While they were still praying, the doctor returned and said that, as he was walking down the hall, he remembered a dangerous and rarely used treatment for sepsis patients. The medication he suggested, Xigris, was only recommended for patients who had been deemed near death. It was known to cause severe abdominal and cerebral hemorrhaging. He further stated that it only helped 1 in 13 people.

Our 12-year-old daughter said, "Mommy could be that one."

Bryant gave permission to use the drug.

The doctor said, "I've already ordered it. I figured, what did we have to lose?"

The FDA has since taken Xigris off the market. Studies revealed that more people died from having it administered to them than those who were given a placebo. However, I had no side effects, and the Lord protected me from the poor outcome Xigris is known to have. I also believe that the doctor's suggestion of a treatment—any treatment—bolstered those praying people's faith and encouraged them to keep praying.

When I did not die that first night, the lead physician updated his prognosis: I now had a one percent chance.

Over the next few days, the incredulous doctors told Bryant they could not explain why I was alive. They added that he should not expect great strides. My body could not recover from such an ordeal completely. They said I would more than likely be in the hospital for months.

For the first few days in the hospital, I was on continuous dialysis. My family was told that if I did survive, I would continue to be on dialysis for months—or years. When the treatment was stopped four *days* later, Bryant was told that I would need intermittent dialysis—possibly as often as three times a week—for the rest of my life.

God had a different idea. He not only spared my life but also accelerated my recovery. I was released from the hospital after 28 days. More than one doctor and several nurses called me "the miracle lady."

I had dialysis treatment only three more times in the hospital and have not required it since. My kidney function is normal.

That is what praying people did for me. They ignored every difficulty and tore away every barrier with their prayers.

God reversed even the effects of the sickness. After my release from the hospital, I was so debilitated by the month of being immobile that I needed inpatient physical therapy. The rehab facility's goal was to train me to function in a wheelchair. I astonished them every day with how I regained my strength and my ability to walk.

I left the program earlier than expected. Today, I remain well. I work full-time as a magazine copyeditor, speak in churches, teach writing workshops, have obtained ministerial credentials, take care of my family, and live an abundant life because people prayed and God healed me.

Marsha Robinson is a staff writer and copyeditor for the *White Wing Messenger*. She serves on the development board of the Southeastern Christian Writer's Conference and CreateCon, a conference for creatives (mrobinson@cogop.org).

"This Is Real!"

Felito Utuie, a 22-year-old evangelist, sought permission from the Moslem chief of a village in Mozambique to do evangelism.

"If you come, will I see that happen?" the chief said.

Felito assured him that he would and received permission to have a meeting. Felito preached and asked, "Who recognizes their need of a Savior?"

Many people came forward. After that, Felito said that he and his team would pray for the sick. They prayed and there were many healings, such as a deaf boy who was instantly healed.

The healing convinced the chief, who stood before the people and said, "This is real! Only God can do this!" He urged all the sick to come forward.[4]

Healings IN THE MINISTRY OF
George Fox
(1624–1691)

The Quaker healer George Fox began his ministry at the age of 19, and continued for nearly 45 years. Based on Fox's journals and other writings, historians estimate that approximately 170 divine healings took place through his ministry.[5]

In 1655, Fox went to see a Baptist woman who they said was dying. Those who called for Fox asked him to say some comforting words to her in her final hours. Fox wrote, "I was moved of the Lord God to speak to her and the Lord raised her up and she was well to the astonishment of the town and country."[6]

On January 25, 1683, James Claypoole was so sick with kidney stones he couldn't stand or lie down. Fox went to him, prayed for him, and asked the Lord to rebuke his infirmity. "As I laid my hands upon him the Lord's power went through him." The man went to sleep and "presently after his stone came from him like dirt and so then he was pretty well."[7]

In 1653, Fox was in Bishopric, and people brought to him a woman who couldn't speak or eat. Fox ministered to her and she was healed.[8]

In 1659, a woman had palsy and little use of one side of her body. She often fell and couldn't get up. Fox visited her and saw her fall down. He took her hand, and immediately the disease left her.[9]

—⁕—

In his journal, Fox wrote about his 1672 visit to the Carolinas of America. After he heard that a woman in Cumberland had been sick for a long time and the doctors hadn't helped, he sent a friend to lay his hands on her and pray for her. Fox's friend did as he was told, and God healed the woman right then.[10]

—⁕—

In his own journal, John Banks (1638–1710) wrote that his shoulder hurt, and the pain became so intense he could hardly use his arm or hand for three months. The hand also began to wither. He tried doctors but found no help.

One night he dreamed he was with George Fox, and in the dream he said to Fox, "My faith is such, that if thou seest it thy way to lay thy hand upon my shoulder, my arm and hand shall be whole throughout."[11] The dream stayed with Banks, and he believed it was a vision from God.

Fox held a meeting one Sunday at Swarthmore. John Banks attended and afterward showed Fox his arm and hand. Fox "turned about and looked upon me, lifting up his hand, and laid it upon my shoulder, and said, 'The Lord strengthen thee both within and without.' And so we parted."[12]

That evening, Banks sat down to eat, and his arm was healed.

New Skin

Author Don Stewart was present at a crusade led by A. A. Allen in Paramount, California. A woman covered from head to foot with a sheet was also there. Allen pulled the sheet off her body. The ministry leaders on the stage said the odor was terrible. Her whole body was a mass of blood and puss, and an open wound went "from her chest down to her intestines."

As soon as Allen prayed, the color and texture of that mass around her face and chest began to change to that of normal skin. It kept changing, and the transformation moved down her body. At last, the entire wound closed.

Stewart wrote, "We had all seen healings every night for years, but we had never seen anything like this."[13]

Crippled from Birth

A mother brought her young son to a meeting. The boy had been born crippled; his arm and hand were paralyzed.

Carey Cramer knelt beside him and prayed with compassion. After holding the boy's hand and continuing to pray for about five minutes, Cramer felt a twitch in one finger.

As he prayed, Cramer felt God urging him to pray as he would for his own son, who was about the same age. God healed the boy completely—his arm, hand and fingers became fully functional.[14]

"I Want to See!"

The late Linda Riesberry was among those who heard Father Matt Linn and his brother, Dennis, teach about healing. At the end of each worship service, those who needed physical healing stood, and the others surrounded them. Father Linn asked them to explain their needs, and the others were to pray for five minutes for those individuals. The Linn brothers urged them, "Be Jesus to the person."

Riesberry was part of a group that surrounded a woman named Jane. When asked about her need, Jane said, "I want to see." She told them she had been born blind.

The group prayed silently for five minutes. During that time, Riesberry felt God tell her to lay her hands on Jane's eyes. At first she resisted, but the impulse was so strong that she finally laid her right hand across Jane's eyes.

After they finished praying, Jane was able to read only Riesberry's nametag, which was in large print. She said to Riesberry, "When you put your hand on my eyes, it was not your hands I saw. . . . I saw the hands of Jesus . . . as soon as you touched me."

Jane wasn't completely healed, so the group prayed for five more minutes. Then Jane was able to read even small print. They marvelled that a woman born without sight could now read words.

The late Reverend Linda Riesberry, R.N., B.Sc.N., M.Div., was ordained by The Evangelical Church Alliance and served as chaplain to The Avalon Retirement Centre, in hospital chaplaincy, as a trainer in pastoral care, and as a minister in palliative care and pastoral care.

A Malformed Ear

God has healed a number of deaf people through the ministry of Chad and Julia Dedmon. One mother came to Chad as he was leaving a meeting and asked for prayer for her 13-year-old daughter, whose ear was malformed. The girl had no eardrum, and had only about 35 percent hearing in one ear and none in the other.

After prayer, the mother whispered in her daughter's deaf ear. The daughter, born deaf in that ear, said, "I love you, too."[15]

Healings IN THE MINISTRY OF
St. Francis of Assisi
(1181–1226)

St. Francis of Assisi, founder of the Franciscan Order, had an incredible healing ministry. A vast number of miracles took place during his public ministry and are widely reported by scholars.[16]

Once, in the city of Toscanella, a soldier offered St. Francis lodging at his home. The godly man saw the soldier's young son, who was lame. The father fell at the feet of Francis and begged for healing for his child.

Though reluctant at first, considering himself unworthy to exercise such power, Francis eventually put his hand on the boy, blessed him, and lifted him up. The boy was completely healed.

In the city of Narni, a man named Peter had been paralyzed for five months. He had completely lost the use of his legs and arms, and could move only his eyes and tongue.

When he heard that Francis had come to Narni, Peter sent a messenger to the bishop of that city to ask him to send the servant of God to him, confident that he would be freed from the illness. Francis came and made the sign of the cross over him from his head to his feet. Peter was immediately restored to his former health.

A beggar boy who was completely deaf and mute from his birth lived in Citta della Pieve. One evening he came to the house of a man named Mark, and by means of signs, the beggar asked for shelter.

Mark took him into his house and willingly kept him with him. The boy was a good servant and understood by signs what was commanded him.

One night, Mark said to his wife, "I would consider it the greatest miracle if the blessed Francis would give hearing and speech to this boy." He also promised that if Francis would heal the boy, he would "hold this boy most dear and provide for him as long as he lives."

Immediately after Mark made this vow, the boy was able to speak and said, "St. Francis lives."

＊＊＊

One day at San Gemini, a man pleaded with St. Francis to heal his demonized wife. Francis and his coterie prayed for her and she was set free. The report was that the evil spirit left so quickly, Francis didn't initially believe she had been freed.

Later, passing through the same city, he met the woman again. She ran up to him, fell at his feet and kissed them, because she truly had been set free.

Testicular Cancer

(MICHAEL E. WRAY WITH JOANN RENO WRAY)

When I tried to get out of bed on Monday morning, July 2, 1990, pain pinned me down. *It's worse. Something's wrong.* Later I was able to get out of bed and limped into the living room. Mom sensed my embarrassment, so Dad talked to me in my room.

"I'm scared; my left testicle is enlarged and painful."

"Why didn't you tell us sooner?" He hugged me and said, "Let's get you to the doctor."

An hour later, I was in Dr. VanSchoyck's office. After examining me and taking X-rays, he said, "You need to see the urologist immediately."

At the urologist's office, I endured another exam. Finally, the doctor called us into his office, motioning to the seats in front of his desk. He closed the door.

"Mike has testicular cancer. The left testicle is four times normal size. It's caused from a tumor that must be removed." He paused before he said, "Do you want the operation Thursday or Friday?"

Mom and Dad held tightly to my hands. Mom's face was ashen, and she was crying. Dad spoke only in broken syllables.

"If the cancer hasn't spread," the doctor said, "Mike has an 80 percent chance of recovery."

Mom composed herself enough to speak. "I know you're trained as a surgeon," she said, "but you aren't the Healer. God is. He'll answer our prayer and heal Mike."

The urologist silently nodded, and then he wrote something in my chart.

The next day, Mom handed me an open Bible and pointed to Isaiah 58:8, which she had highlighted in orange.

I read the words slowly. "Your wounds will quickly heal. Your godliness will lead you forward, and the glory of the LORD will protect you from behind."

"Read those words every day, out loud," she said. "Memorize them. That's God's promise for you."

I did as she told me, and the family prayed. They spread the word to friends around the country. I received cards from all over the United States, Canada, Central America and Europe. In my fear and weakness, some days I could barely recite the words of Isaiah 58:8.

I had the surgery, and my survival chances dropped to 50 percent. The cancer had spread into my lymph nodes. Thirty-six spots of cancer dotted my lungs. Six tumors, each the size of a large man's fist, crowded my lower abdomen. I went to an oncologist, Dr. Vicki Baker, to start chemotherapy.

A few days later, Dr. Baker talked with my parents.

The night before, a woman who led a prayer group in Poland had called Mom. With her thick accent and in broken English, she had said, "We pray for your son. God gave us word. He will live. He will not die."

Dr. Baker and Mom came into my room. I didn't know it, but my survival odds had again decreased, now to less than 20 percent.

Five days of chemotherapy began on Monday, July 16. Each day, three chemotherapy drugs and four blocker drugs to quell side effects dripped into my veins. Despite nausea and vomiting, I did better than expected and went home with an appointment to return in 21 days for round two.

Mom and her parents drove me to the cancer center. There would be more X-rays and blood tests—and then the chemo.

Shortly after the tests were completed, Dr. Baker joined us. She put a set of X-rays on the light board. "Here are Mike's first X-rays before chemo." She pointed to several films. "You can see the cancer on his lungs and the tumors in his lower abdomen."

It was the first time I'd seen these images. My hand went to my stomach. *How could so much cancer hide in my skinny body?*

Dr. Baker started crying. Mom placed her hand on her shoulder and said, "Doctor, please, what's wrong? We need to know how to pray. God will answer our prayers for Mike's healing."

"It's just—I don't see miracles very often," Dr. Baker said. "Look at today's X-rays." She slapped the new films into place. "The cancer on his lungs is completely gone. Blood tests show a massive drop in cancer markers."

She wiped away tears and said, "Chemotherapy doesn't work in 21 days, but God does."

Today I am alive and well and, at age 40, have fulfilled a dream I'd had since age 4—going to China, where I taught spoken English and met my wife, Grace. Together we parent her teenage son. We both teach and lead music at our church and have taught Bible studies in China.

JoAnn Reno Wray is a freelance writer, editor and graphic artist. Since 1974, she has operated EpistleWorks Creations. JoAnn's writings have been published in newspapers, magazines, online, and in book compilations. See http://epistleworks.com.

Waiting for Healing

(WANDA ROSENBERRY)

My husband, Randy, was cutting wood, and I was splitting and stacking it, as it was our only source of heat in the winter. I picked up a huge log and placed it on the splitter, and suddenly my right shoulder felt as though someone had yanked my arm off my body.

I could barely use my arm, but I finished splitting that log and then told Randy I had to stop. Even though it hurt worse than previous attacks of bursitis, I figured that's all it was. So I treated it the way I had treated the bursitis in the past. But the pain became worse. I finally went to the doctor about it.

"It's not bursitis," said my doctor. "You've torn your rotator cuff and will have to have surgery to repair it. Maegan [his nurse] will contact the surgeon and set up an appointment with him for you."

"May I call you later about that?" I asked. "I don't have the money for the surgery, and I can't afford the time off work. I have to think and pray about this."

"All right, but don't wait too long; it'll only get worse."

This was on Thursday. I prayed for healing repeatedly and nothing changed. Yet I continued to pray.

Sunday morning during the worship service, the pastor called for those who needed prayer to come to the front. I went down and told him about my torn rotator cuff. He and his wife laid hands on me and prayed for healing. Nothing happened, and I sat back down.

By the end of the service, I was still in a lot of pain, but it wasn't as severe as before. I had faith that God would heal me, and I was going to wait on His healing.

The next day the pain had lessened considerably, but it still wasn't gone. I continued to pray for healing. Tuesday morning I woke up, got out of bed, and without thinking about it raised my arms up and stretched.

"My shoulder is completely healed!" I yelled to my husband. I showed him the full movement of my arm.

To this day, my right shoulder has not given me any more trouble.

Wanda Rosenberry lived with her missionary parents in Africa for six years during her childhood. She is a self-employed typist and copyeditor. She has previously published two articles (wandarose38368@hotmail.com).

A Healed Heart
(MARTHA HENEISEN)

My sister-in-law, Glenda, had been sick for several weeks with flu-like symptoms, such as fatigue, shortness of breath and a cough. Thinking her illness would soon run its course, she delayed going to the doctor until it was almost too late.

One Sunday, she was unable to walk because of weakness and swelling in her feet. She couldn't bend her arms, and her once-flat abdomen was a rounded mound under the covers. She slept propped up on pillows.

Perry, her husband, drove her 20 miles to the emergency room in a small town in Kentucky. She was admitted and diagnosed with flu and an enlarged heart. At Glenda's insistence, Perry left early that afternoon to go back to work in Lexington, Kentucky.

On Wednesday, Perry received a call that Glenda was no better and had been diagnosed with congestive heart failure. That night he stayed at the hospital with his wife.

Early in the morning, Glenda went into cardiac arrest. The hospital staff performed cardiac resuscitation.

After she had stabilized enough to be transported, the doctor arranged for Glenda to be taken to Central Baptist Hospital in Lexington. With a new diagnosis of cardiomyopathy, the doctor gave the family no hope. He suspected Glenda's heart muscle was so damaged that she would require a heart transplant. They would keep her in intensive care while they ran additional tests.

That evening, I received a call. "Glenda's so sick she might not make it." I lived too far away to get to the hospital, but I could pray.

Before Glenda's illness, I had always prayed before I got out of bed in the morning and before falling asleep at night, sometimes even falling asleep while praying. During her illness, my prayers were different. I prayed almost without ceasing. I had never experienced anything like that: I *had* to pray.

I felt that if I relaxed or stopped, I would break a connection with God that was keeping Glenda alive.

There was no improvement in Glenda's condition after her transfer to Central Baptist, so the doctor scheduled a biopsy for the following day. If it came back positive, he would recommend putting her on the heart-transplant list.

On the day of her scheduled biopsy, I was at my desk when I felt a weight lifted from me. Worry, stress and fear evaporated. I sensed that I no longer needed to pray for Glenda.

That evening, when I couldn't reach family members in the hospital's waiting room, I rang the intensive care unit.

To my surprise, Glenda's nurse answered the phone. "She's much better."

"I understand they were doing a biopsy today . . ."

"She's much, much better."

"And if the tests were positive, you'd put her on the heart transplant list . . ."

"Don't you hear what I'm saying? She's better. She started getting better before we gave her the first dose of medicine."

Relieved, I hung up the phone. Later that evening, I called again.

This time, a family member answered my call to the waiting room and confirmed the nurse's report. "She's better. It's unbelievable. We could almost see her getting better right before our eyes. The last time we were back there, a nurse was combing her hair and getting her ready to move out to a room."

I remembered what I had felt earlier that day. I knew that was the moment God answered my prayers.

Glenda went home with a lightweight implantable defibrillator. The FDA had only approved the device eight weeks earlier. She was never put on the heart transplant list.

Martha Heneisen has won awards for inspirational writing, children's books and short stories. Since retiring from nursing, she does volunteer work, writes, travels, and enjoys her family (mheneisen@comcast.net).

Healings IN THE MINISTRY OF
Kathryn Kuhlman
(1907–1976)

An article in *Redbook* magazine in the 1950s brought Kathryn Kuhlman into prominence. To the surprise of investigators, they found "verifiable examples of actual healings."

After that, Kuhlman's books of documented miracles became best sellers. In 1970, *TIME* magazine dubbed her a one-woman shrine of Lourdes and admitted that healings "seem to be happening."[17]

In 1947, Kuhlman held services at the Gospel Tabernacle in Franklin, Pennsylvania. She had just begun to lay hands on the sick for healing.

Although doubtful about healing, she searched the Bible for guidance.

At one Sunday service, a woman stood to give a testimony of healing. She said that at Kuhlman's service the night before, without anyone laying hands on her or Kuhlman being aware, she had been healed of a tumor. She went to her doctor, who confirmed her healing.

The following Sunday, a World War I veteran who had been declared legally blind following an industrial accident was healed. He had 85 percent of his vision restored in the permanently impaired eye, and perfect eyesight restored to his other eye.

The crowds grew. Auditoriums filled hours before Kuhlman was scheduled to speak. Countless miracles took place, most without anyone laying hands on the afflicted or Kuhlman praying for them.

The evangelist walked the platform and called out healings as they took place where people sat. People in wheelchairs started to walk. In one service, a five-year-old boy who had been crippled from birth walked up to the stage. In Philadelphia, Kuhlman laid hands on a man who had received a pacemaker eight months earlier, and the scar from the operation disappeared. X-rays would later confirm that the pacemaker was also gone.[18]

⊹═◈═⊹

Many consider Delores Winder's story the most outstanding healing in Kathryn Kuhlman's ministry. Although Winder had been skeptical about healing, after she was freed from her sickness, she became a healer herself.

At 48 years of age, Delores Winder was dying of a rare bone disease. Her esophagus was ruptured, a fractured bone was poking through her skin, organs were failing, and the doctors said they could do no more for her. She was granted permission to leave the hospital so that she could die at home. A friend asked her to watch a televised Kathryn Kuhlman meeting. Winder did—and said she wasn't impressed. She was quoted as saying, "I was just revolted by what I saw. I did not believe in divine healing at all, and I felt at the time that these television ministries were making a mockery of faith."

Certain that she was going to die, she prayed intensely about who would care for her children after her death. As she prayed, the name Kathryn Kuhlman came to her.

Although still skeptical, Winder, very sick and in a body cast, went to hear the evangelist. During the service, while Kuhlman spoke, Winder had a vision of Jesus Christ and felt assured about her children.

That assurance was enough for her, and she was at peace. Because she didn't believe in healing, she wanted to leave. As she prepared to go, a man stood next to her and said, "Something is happening to you."

"My legs are burning like fire and I am dying, and I need to get out of here right now."

The man was sure that she was being healed (and she was), so he urged her to go to the stage, where Kuhlman prayed for her.

Winder said that she walked off the platform. She didn't need the cast or a cane. What happened was medically impossible.[19]

At another of Kuhlman's meetings, Nick Ittzes and his wife sat a few rows in front of a teenage girl with a terrible skin condition. Kuhlman summoned the girl to the stage, describing her condition as she did so. In Ittzes's words, the girl's skin looked like the hide of an alligator.

The young woman rose, and as she walked forward, Ittzes and others watched a miracle take place. By the time she reached the stage, her skin condition had totally cleared up.[20]

Gallstones Be Gone

On May 21, 2012, after an ultrasound test, Gail Manizak's doctor called her cell phone before she reached home. She was diagnosed with gallstones, a possible mass on her pancreas, and a two-inch cyst on her kidney.

Her doctor was concerned because the cyst was two inches long. A specialist wanted to do a CT scan because the pancreas was swollen and inflamed. Two days later, a surgeon set a date for a CT scan to look for a "mass" on the pancreas.

Gail had never been to the Bethel Church Healing Rooms (Redding, California). She wouldn't have gone then except a friend had invited her several days before the diagnosis. The friend wanted to be at Bethel on her birthday, and not wanting to attend alone, she had invited Gail to go with her.

Five days after the initial exam, on May 26, Gail went to the Healing Rooms at Bethel and received prayer.

On May 29, Gail had her CT scan. Two days later, she received a call with the results: The scan found nothing irregular—no gallstones and no mass on the pancreas.[21]

Healed of a Blood Disorder

In a letter dated May 18, 2012, Robin Miller of Colorado Springs, Colorado, wrote to Bethel Church (Redding, California) to thank them for praying for her healing. The miracle had taken place at their church on March 24.

Robin said that after she had a deep-vein thrombosis and a pulmonary embolism seven years earlier, her doctors told her she had an incurable blood disease with clotting disorders. Her hematologist said she would need to be on blood thinner for the rest of her life.

Robin and her husband went to the Healing Rooms for prayer. She believed she had been healed, but because it was a blood disorder, she wouldn't know until her physician again examined her.

When she asked her doctor to run another test, he told her that her condition was genetic and it would never go away. But he did the test again.

In her letter, Robin reported that all seven vials of blood came back normal. She was healed. She sent a picture of herself holding the document that showed her original diagnosis and the document that proved she was now well.[22]

The Family Reunion
(MARY CANTELL)

Ken embraced my husband, Jeff, and me one Sunday morning after church and asked, "You think you might want to go to my family reunion?" Ken and his wife, Ginger, and their daughter, Abbie, were longtime friends.

We said, "Sure, why not?"

I didn't have any idea why we accepted the invitation, but it felt right, and I was oddly excited about attending someone else's family reunion.

The following Saturday, we packed cheese, crackers, olives and fruit, along with bottled mineral water, for the reunion outing.

"Will you need your ice pack today?" I asked Jeff before we left.

"I'm okay now, but you'd better bring it. Just in case."

Jeff had injured his back as a teenager. Then, a year or so earlier while helping a friend with yard work, he severely strained it again. A physical therapist said the X-rays showed a problem with two of his discs. One was herniated, and the other was bulging.

The scenic drive through the countryside to the campground in New Holland, Pennsylvania, took about an hour. When we arrived, we saw a crowd of people milling around checkered-topped picnic tables in an open-air pavilion. Large quantities of soda, hot dogs and beef patties, along with mounds of Tupperware containers, lined the front tables. The temperature bordered on sweltering.

Just then, my mood changed. What prompted me to agree to attend a family reunion where I was clearly not part of the family?

Realizing that I had the wrong attitude, and determined to make it a pleasant time, I suggested to Jeff that we go off somewhere to pray. We moved toward a cluster of trees where we could be alone. Afterward, my husband began to get one of his back twinges of pain.

"I'm going to need the ice," he said.

We headed back to the pavilion. As soon as we stepped inside the shady interior, a tall man standing next to Ken beckoned for us.

"Be right there. Just have to get some ice," I called out as I pointed to our ice chest. "It's for my husband's back."

The stranger shook his head while motioning with his hand. "No, no ice. Come over now."

I was perplexed, but we went to him.

Ken introduced his cousin, Silas, who pulled out a chair and gestured for Jeff to sit down. "You're in pain, aren't you?"

"How could you tell?"

"God leads me to situations like this," Silas said. "On a scale of 1 to 10, what's your pain like?"

"It's not a chronic pain but more intermittent. Right now it's about a 6."

"Take off your shoes."

Silas, whom we learned was a reflexologist, asked Jeff more questions. He began in a conversational tone, but then his voice rose with passion. He quoted Scripture and talked about God's purpose for our lives. He placed his hands on Jeff's shoulders, stating that he felt strongly that God didn't make him to be in this situation.

Several others gathered around us.

Silas knelt in front of Jeff and grasped his feet. "Do you see how his feet are not evenly lined up?" Silas asked. "They're not the same length."

I noticed the slight difference.

"Watch closely," Silas said. Then he began to pray aloud.

Focusing on Jeff's feet, there was no mistaking what I saw as Silas's hands passed in a quick, circling motion above them. Something was causing Jeff's left foot to move.

Had I just witnessed a miracle? I'd never believed the so-called miracles on TV, but I couldn't deny what happened before my own eyes.

When Jeff got up, Silas asked, "How do you feel?"

"Pretty good."

"On a scale of 1 to 10, tell me about the pain in your back."

"One. Actually zero. There's no pain."

"None?"

"None. I feel fine."

It's now been more than three years since that day in New Holland, Pennsylvania. My husband's pain never returned.

I am humbled by God's healing.

Mary Cantell is a professional journalist and published freelance writer of various genres including fiction, non-fiction and poetry. See www.marycantell.com.

Healings IN THE LIFE OF
Henrietta Mears
(1890–1963)

Henrietta Mears, a woman God used in extraordinary ways, shaped some of the most influential Christians of our time. Because of her guidance, Billy Graham, Bill Bright and 400 others went into

Christian service. Through their ministry, she still touches count-less lives today. She was a woman of vision, and although she faced many obstacles and difficulties, she was determined to trust God through them all.

Dr. Mears established Gospel Light, Forest Home and Gospel Light International (GLINT), and she was instrumental in many organizations, such as Campus Crusade. Regal Books, the pub-lisher of *I Believe in Healing*, is a division of Gospel Light. But before any of this took place, young Henrietta experienced God's healing power in her own life.

When Henrietta was 12, she noticed a strange pain in her joints. The pain became constant and she was unable to walk. She be-came almost immobile and had to be carried from place to place. She also had heavy nosebleeds. When doctors were called, Henri-etta was diagnosed with muscular rheumatism, a potentially crip-pling and life-threatening disease. Other cases were reported in the region that year, and one of her friends contracted the disease and died from it.

For two years Henrietta lay sick. Various treatments were pur-sued, but nothing seemed to work. One day, when Henrietta's mother was reading Philippians 4:19—"But my God shall supply all your needs according to his riches in glory by Christ Jesus" (*KJV*)—she claimed that promise for her daughter and asked a fam-ily friend and devout believer, Mr. Ingersoll, to come and pray for Henrietta's healing.

"Henrietta, do you believe the Lord can heal you?" Mr. Inger-soll asked.

Henrietta's direct response was, "He created us. I see no rea-son why He cannot heal us."

Mr. Ingersoll prayed; the nosebleeds stopped immediately. But the rheumatism continued, even becoming more painful.

Mr. Ingersoll was called to the Mears home again. This time as he prayed, Henrietta was filled with a sudden and unmistakable confidence. She began to cry when she knew she was completely healed. The pain was gone—abruptly and miraculously gone! Out loud, while surrounding the bed where she lay, her family praised God and thanked Him for healing Henrietta. Her road to full recovery was swift and complete. She became more active, building up her muscles by working in the garden, swimming, and horseback riding. Within three months, her body was free of any trace of the illness, and she never had a recurrence of rheumatism.

Her eyesight, however, was another matter. Henrietta's eyes had never been strong. She was so nearsighted that she wore glasses from age 6. When she was 16, she accidentally jabbed a hat pin into the pupil of one eye. Her doctors could do nothing to heal it and predicted that she would be blind in that eye by age 30. Mr. Ingersoll came once more to pray for Henrietta's eye. She had no doubt that the God who had made her could also heal her. When specialists later examined her eye, they agreed there was indeed a hole in the pupil but shook their heads in amazement that Henrietta could still see. For more than two years they periodically examined her to see if her sight was declining; but even though they could find no change, they remained unconvinced that a miracle had taken place.

"You need to stop reading and studying," doctors warned her as high school graduation approached. "You will completely lose your sight even sooner."

Henrietta planned to attend university. With this grim prediction from her doctors, would she still be able to go? The decision was hers, her parents told her.

Her decision came without hesitation. "If I'm going to go blind by 30, then blind I shall be. But I want something in my head to think about. I'm going to study as hard as I can for as long as I can."

As a freshman at the University of Minnesota, Henrietta plunged into her studies and into Christian service, becoming Sunday School superintendent of the junior department at church. Always aware of her fragile eye condition, but desiring to continue in school and in her church ministry, she practiced her powers of concentration during lectures and made the most of her study times, resolving to study only during daylight hours. Immediately after every class she would prepare for the next day's lessons. She always finished each assignment while the subject was fresh in her mind. Her powers of concentration and her memory developed so strongly that she could fully grasp the content of a textbook in a single reading. She could remember and repeat almost verbatim nearly all that she heard in each lecture. Later, when asked about her lifelong struggle with her eyes, Henrietta said, "I believe my greatest spiritual asset throughout my entire life has been my failing sight, for it has kept me absolutely dependent upon God."[23]

Healing Stories from the International Order of St. Luke the Physician

Founded in 1932, the International Order of St. Luke the Physician is "an ecumenical organization dedicated to the Christian healing ministry." Members study stories of healing found in Scripture and other books, and they also engage in healing prayer on behalf of those in their communities who suffer from various ailments.[24]

Following are two of many accounts of how God has worked through this ministry to provide healing and restoration.

✣ Like Father, Like Son ✣
(Emily Parke Chase)

The news wasn't good. After weeks of coughing and wheezing, my grandfather, Hervey Parke, learned that he had tuberculosis. In today's world, the diagnosis wouldn't be devastating; however, in 1924, before treatments advanced and antibiotics were readily available, it was a death sentence. My grandfather had a wife and five young children to support.

"You have only three months to live," the doctor told him. "The only possible cure is to seek help at a sanatorium in Southern California, which is 3,000 miles away."

Grandfather left and lived in a small cabin at the sanatorium. He rested in the warm sun and dry air. Each day, he opened his Bible and read the gospel stories of Jesus healing the sick, the lame and the blind. Couldn't Jesus do for him what He had done for these others?

My grandfather also studied the writings of Dr. John Gaynor Banks. He had first met Dr. Banks in England decades earlier during his honeymoon; years later, during a visit to Boston, he had heard him speak of his healing ministry.

While at the sanatorium, my grandfather learned that Dr. Banks had become the rector at a parish in San Diego, only a few miles away. Someone drove my grandfather there for a worship service. At the end of the meeting, Dr. Banks anointed him with oil and prayed for his healing.

Several days later, a medical doctor examined my grandfather's lungs. "I find no trace of the TB," he reported.

Confused, the physician sent his patient to a second sanatorium near Santa Barbara. More tests confirmed that the TB had disappeared without leaving a trace of scar tissue on my grandfather's lungs.

Instead of dying, my grandfather moved his family to California, went on to serve as a pastor for 27 years, and assisted Dr. Banks in establishing what today is the Order of St. Luke (OSL).

One of the five children my grandfather had left behind when he sought TB treatment was John, who was only 10 years old at the time. John grew up, graduated from college, and, like his father before him, attended seminary and became a pastor. World War II interrupted John's parish ministry. He left behind his wife and three small children. Along with thousands of other troops, my father landed on the beaches of LeHavre, France.

Christmas snow and freezing rains pelted the troops. They marched through icy slush. With only wet boots and canvas tents to protect them, many soldiers became ill. My father developed a raging fever and was carried to the field hospital in Dieppe. The doctors diagnosed his condition as pneumonia and stuffed him with sulfa pills.

"One night a bead of light entered through a crack in the door," he said later. "It rose toward the ceiling and headed toward me."

Scared, he wondered if that light was an angel of death. Was he to die in a hospital bed far from home? Quaking under the sheets, he recited Psalm 23 several times.

John, don't you trust Me? a voice asked.

"I will trust You, Lord. I will." And he dropped off to sleep.

The next morning, the nurses were astonished when they found that my father had completely recovered.

"Did one of you come into my room during the night with a flashlight?" he asked. When each nurse said no, my father realized that God had healed him.

After the war, John returned to his pastorate. Renewing contact with Dr. Banks, he remembered that God had healed his father of TB and restored his own life during the war. He chose to follow in his father's steps and serve under Banks's leadership.

John became a chaplain with OSL. After Dr. Banks died, Dr. Alfred Price took over leadership of the ministry. In the 1970s, when Dr. Price retired, my father, John H. Parke, stepped into the role of national warden for OSL—the fledgling ministry my grandfather had helped found years earlier.

During the next 10 years, my father led 3-day healing missions in all 48 contiguous states, wrote countless articles for *Sharing* magazine, and divided the country into regional organizations to facilitate the ministry. He carried the message of God's healing power as far as Australia.

Two men, father and son, were each struck down by serious illness early in their careers. Both experienced their heavenly Father's healing touch. Both lived to humbly serve God's only Son. Like Father, like son.[25]

Emily Parke Chase worked with Wycliffe Bible Translators and taught Bible at Messiah College. She is the author of six books and speaks at conferences and retreats all across the country. emilychase.com.

✣ Freddie's Healing ✣

(Carol-Anne Foty)

Freddie showed up at our church on an April Sunday morning. He was from Iraq and spoke Arabic.

Freddie was a believer and a member of the Syrian Orthodox Church. He had been a teacher, but after Saddam Hussein came into power, Freddie's father was murdered by the regime, and Freddie fled Iraq.

With the help of a Greek Orthodox priest, Freddie stayed a year in the Canadian Embassy in Athens, Greece. Just before he was scheduled to leave for Canada as a government-sponsored refugee, he learned that Hussein's police had killed his wife and two sons.

Although deeply grieved, he came to Toronto in 1984. As a pharmacist, I began to work with Freddie when I learned that he was a heart-attack survivor and a diabetic. About a year after we met him, his right foot developed gangrene, and his leg had to be amputated just below the knee.

I invited Freddie to attend the High Park Chapter of the Order of St. Luke (OSL) to seek healing for the phantom leg pain that hurt him daily.

At the OSL chapter meeting, we prayed for Freddie—and he was healed. Later he asked me, "What was that electricity going through my body and down my leg when they prayed for me?"

I told him it was the Lord healing him. He has never had recurring phantom pain.[26]

Carol-Anne Foty is the Convener of the Order of St. Luke's High Park Chapter, and a member of the OSL Region 8 Council.

The Miracle Walker

(DEBBIE OLIVER)

"We are sorry to tell you the injuries you sustained in the car accident were severe," the physician said. "You'll never walk again. Even with extensive therapy, the very best prognosis would be shuffling with a severe limp. The surgery went well, and we anticipate your internal organs will heal completely."

My mind raced through a series of jumbled thoughts. I was 18 years old and had recently graduated from high school. I planned to begin college in September, obtain a degree, get married, and have a family.

Wasn't it enough to lose my father in the accident? My mom was only 38. She now faced a life as a widow, with a son who was healing from injuries and a daughter who would require constant care.

I refused to believe I would never walk again. I prayed for a miracle.

In the darkness of my hospital room, I promised God that if He allowed me to walk, I would serve Him for the rest of my life. Some might call that bargaining, but I grasped for anything that would help me cope.

Just then, I was startled when a burst of bright light shone through my window. I thought someone must be looking at me in my flimsy nightgown.

I needed to cover myself with the sheet at the foot of the bed, but I didn't know how to get it. For a month, I hadn't been able to move from being flat on my back. Above my head was a triangular bar. I grabbed it and was surprised to discover that I had enough strength to pull myself into a sitting position. My head spun as my body adjusted to being in a different position.

As soon as I was sitting up, the light went out. Everything was dark once again. I lay back down, placed my head on the pillow, and wondered if I had hurt myself further by sitting up. Mixed feelings of fear and jubilation swirled inside my head.

I pressed the call button to summon the nurse. When she came into my room, I asked who would have been outside the window. "There was a bright light shining through my window."

She shook her head. "You are on the third floor. There's no ledge outside your window. There is no way light could have shone through your window." She probably believed I was hallucinating from the medication.

After she left the room, I lay in the dark, smiling. I *knew*. I knew I would walk out of the hospital.

Two weeks later, the same doctors who had initially given me the grim prognosis came into my room and showed me two sets of X-rays. The first set showed a complex picture of shattered bones. Next came a series of images that looked like a perfectly formed pelvis, sacrum and hip sockets, with small cracks all over the X-rays.

One of the doctors said, "We didn't do this. None of us can take credit for this miracle."

"We are still trying to figure out if we had the wrong X-rays," another doctor said. "We don't yet have an explanation."

"In your case, it was as if God put Humpty Dumpty back together again."

The week before college started, I walked out of the hospital on crutches. I never missed any part of college life. It was difficult to believe that so much had happened within a month and a half. I was listed in the book of unexplained medical miracles that occurred in Charleston Memorial Hospital in Charleston, West Virginia.

Debbie Oliver has inspired others through her poetry, writings and storytelling to live a life of faith. God restored her physical and spiritual brokenness into a story of hope (debbieoliver55@yahoo.com).

Healings IN THE MINISTRY OF

David Nunn

(1921–2003)

As a child, David Nunn experienced healing for his foot. Although he drifted from the church, his parents prayed for him. In 1946, at services led by Anna B. Locke, Nunn returned to God and shortly afterward he became a minister.

✣ Facial Paralysis Healed ✣

In 1949, Nunn preached at Little Bethel Assembly of God Church in Dallas, Texas. During the meeting, a girl named Carolyn May, who suffered from facial paralysis, came forward. She could close one eye, but not the other.

Feeling deep compassion, Nunn prayed for her—but nothing happened. He told her, "Come back Friday night." In the meantime, he promised to fast and pray for God to heal her.

Unable to understand why God didn't heal Carolyn May, Nunn prayed earnestly for her and for himself. He was new at the healing ministry and asked God to heal Carolyn May "to confirm my ministry." If God healed her, Nunn would know that he had heard the call to preach correctly.

As Nunn promised, he fasted and prayed. By Friday night, he was weak from lack of food and the weariness of extended prayer. After he spoke that evening, Carolyn May was one of those who came forward. He laid his hands on her and prayed for her again.

Nothing happened.

He prayed again. There was still no change. "I prayed five or six times," Nunn said, "When I finished, I told her to go home and believe the Lord."

A dejected Nunn didn't see the healing, and he didn't have the confirmation he had sought.

The following Wednesday, Carolyn May was playing outside. Just then, her eye closed. She ran to her father and cried out, "Look, Daddy, what Jesus has done for me!"

Later that day, Carolyn May's mother called Nunn and told him the good news. But she added that the paralysis wasn't completely healed.

With holy boldness, Nunn promised that by Sunday every bit of paralysis would be gone.

On Sunday evening, he returned to Little Bethel to preach. Carolyn May came up behind him and tugged at his pants leg. He stared at her and saw that she had been completely healed.[27]

❖ Cancer on the Bottom of His Foot ❖

A cancer had grown on the bottom of one foot of Rufus Elbert Davidson of Columbus, Georgia. He suffered so much pain he could hardly walk. After hearing about David Nunn's meetings in Americus, Georgia, Davidson went on Sunday afternoon for prayer.

He went to the meeting, determined to have David Nunn pray for his healing. While standing in the prayer line, Davidson saw Nunn pray for a woman who suffered from varicose veins.

Davidson watched as the swollen knots in the woman's legs disappeared. He was sure God would heal him, but Nunn prayed for him and nothing happened.

Two days later, when Davidson was home, he put his hand on his foot, and the cancer fell into his hand. The man has been well ever since.[28]

Arteries Unblocked

In May 2011, a bilateral renal Doppler test confirmed that Dee Calvert had renal artery stenosis. The blockage was more than 60 percent in both renal arteries. An angiogram was scheduled so a doctor from the Vascular Intervention Center could stent both arteries.

Calvert went to Bethel's Healing Rooms twice before the procedure. Nothing happened the first time, but on her second visit, she "could feel something happening with warmth in the kidney area."

On May 24, Calvert arrived at the hospital at 6:30 in the morning. The procedure was scheduled to take place 90 minutes later. In pre-op, they drew blood to test her kidney functions.

In the operating room, the doctor and nurses were amazed at the test results: Calvert's kidney functions were normal; however, the doctor decided to go ahead with the angiogram.

The arteries were open and healthy. The doctor told Dee's husband and sister that he had good news and bad news. "The good news is that the procedure went well. The arteries are healthy. I wish mine were that healthy. The bad news is we don't know why!"[29]

Taste and See
(MAROLYN FORD)

After I graduated from high school, my central vision left me. I could no longer read or write, recognize people, drive a car, or distinguish the finer details of life.

I thought it was an infection, but after my doctor examined me, he arranged for me to be seen by physicians at the Ann Arbor Eye Clinic and later at the Mayo Clinic. The maculas in both eyes had deteriorated, and the nerve endings had died.

"You are blind and there is nothing we can do," the doctors said.

My heart cried out in anguish as we made the long drive home. I had planned to go to college, but that now seemed impossible. *How would I study? How would I function without sight?*

The thought of missing out on higher education wasn't my only sorrow. When I was 12 years old, I felt the Lord tell me I would become a minister's wife. From that day onward, I had prayed for the boy I would marry. Now I asked myself, *Who would want to marry a blind girl?*

I sat in my dad's recliner and grieved over the life I was sure I had lost. I reached for the recorded music and listened to Ethel Waters as she sang "His Eye Is on the Sparrow." I was especially comforted by the line about God watching over me. I listened to the song repeatedly, trying to find something to give me hope.

You take care of the little birds, God, and if You care that much about those little birds, surely You're going to take care of me. I'm Your child.

I couldn't read a Bible or songbook, but while growing up, I had memorized a Bible verse every week. Now I quoted those verses to myself and tried to break through my sorrow by singing the old hymns of the faith. In the wee hours of the morning, I quoted verses such as 1 Peter 5:7, which tells us to cast our care on God.

That's why I'm here tonight—casting my burden on you. Then I thought of those words of the song: "Why should I be discouraged?" I sang the familiar line: "For His eye is on the sparrow, and I know He watches me."[30]

I knew I was free. I asked God to show me His will, and I felt He definitely made it clear that I should go to college. I received my letter of acceptance as a blind student and learned that I could record class lectures and take exams orally.

After I arrived on campus, I met the man for whom I had prayed since age 12. Acie Ford and I married in 1962. After he became a pastor, I directed the choir, taught the college and career class, helped with the church visitation, went with my husband on hospital calls, played the piano for funerals, and developed a speaking ministry.

Many times, Acie and I prayed together for God to restore my sight.

On August 26, 1972, Acie read verses to me for our devotions. He prayed, "Lord, I know You can do it. I know You can give sight to Marolyn's eyes."

When I opened my eyes, I yelled, "Acie, I can see! I can see!"

"What do you mean?"

"I can see your rosy cheeks, your green eyes, and brown hair. I can see everything! I can see!"

God had restored my sight after 13 years of darkness.

When I called my doctor, he told me to get to his office early the next morning. I sat in the chair and read every letter on the chart.

"You've read the chart, and it's obvious that you can see," the doctor said, "but medically speaking, your eyes are still blind. The macula is full of holes. I don't know how you're seeing."

News of my miracle traveled quickly. Numerous invitations came for me to tell my story in churches, at conferences and crusades, and on radio and TV nationally and internationally over the next 20 years.

Then tragedy struck again.

In 1991, I slipped while getting out of our Jacuzzi. Acie ran into the bathroom. I was shaking and trembling as he helped me to my feet and into the bed. The next morning, I couldn't move my legs.

I had back surgery, which went well, but my colon and bladder stopped functioning. I suffered from a paralyzed digestive system: I couldn't eat, drink or eliminate.

Over the next 12 years, I fought malnutrition and dehydration. Homecare nurses tended to my needs night and day. My body weakened, and every six weeks or so, I was admitted to the hospital with a sepsis infection.

Many times I cried in despair and asked God for healing. *Please, God, deliver me from this awful pain. Help me be able to eat again.*

I had been near death many times. I had the feeling more intensely than ever before on the night of July 21, 2003.

Hardly able to move my hand to touch my husband's, I said, "I'm going home. We need to pray one last time." He held me gently and prayed, and I went to sleep.

I awakened the following morning with my nurse at my side. She gave me a fresh blueberry to put in my mouth to stimulate my taste buds. If I didn't do that weekly, I'd lose my ability to taste. Each time, I tried to swallow, but nothing ever went down.

That time, while I was swishing the blueberry around, it went down. The nurse phoned the doctor.

He said, "She isn't able to eat!"

But I did.

God had answered my prayer and completely healed my digestive system. Today I can eat anything I desire, and I can see what I'm eating.

Marolyn Ford is a singer and speaker. See www.marolynford.com.

The Deaf Are Healed

Rich Larcombe of Global Legacy was one of the participants in a Bethel School of Supernatural Ministry (BSSM) mission trip to South Africa.[31]

Larcombe recalls that at a mall in Johannesburg, the mission team encountered a group of students from a school for the deaf. When Larcombe and the others offered to pray for the students, they agreed. After prayer, six of the students reported that they had been healed. More than one had been mute before healing; these students not only received the ability to hear but also were enabled to speak.

That evening, one of the former mutes texted Larcombe to express gratitude and to tell of the shock her mother received when she came home able to speak and hear.

A few days later, Larcombe received a second text message from the same girl. She told him that she and another friend from the school for the deaf talked often on the telephone. It was the first time either had spoken on the phone.

After Larcombe returned to Redding, he shared the healing story at Bethel's Friday night service. A week later, he received a text message. It said that a deaf man had come to the service with an interpreter. When Larcombe told the story of the healing in South Africa, the deaf man in the meeting had his hearing restored as well.[32]

My Battle with Lyme Disease
(Lisa Buffaloe)

I sat under four blankets as a heating pad swaddled my head. My body was freezing, and my head felt like it was about to explode. For the past three days, I had been afflicted with an ice-pick-to-the-skull migraine.

My experience with Lyme disease had begun 11 years earlier, in 2000. My husband had carried me to the emergency room. My eyes had moved up and down at a rapid speed—much like a television horizontal control gone haywire. For 18 months, my illness came and went, often leaving me unable to do anything except sit or crawl.

Over the next few years, my body went into self-destruct mode: I suffered with kidney infections, kidney stones, hearing loss, tumors, cysts on my kidneys and liver, a softball-sized uterine tumor, numbness and nerve damage in my face and legs, migraines, bleeding issues, eye problems, severe cramps that lasted for hours, arthritis joint pains, dizzy spells and horrible fatigue.

Twenty-three doctors searched for reasons, and each one had a different opinion. Their diagnoses included multiple sclerosis, lupus, rheumatoid arthritis, autoimmune disease and many others. Six surgeries repaired areas where my body had attacked itself. Numerous hospitalizations, procedures, scans, X-rays, blood tests and nerve tests finally led to an official diagnosis of Lyme disease in January 2006.

Once I had been diagnosed, treatment began with IV antibiotics for 30 days. After that, I assumed I would be well—so I ignored ongoing symptoms. Then a friend referred me to a Lyme disease specialist. For the next year, he prescribed antibiotics and supplements—switching from drug to drug to combat the persistent symptoms.

My white blood cell count plummeted and my blood thickened, which necessitated the use of Heparin blood-thinner shots. When my health continued to decline, 24/7 IV antibiotics were used for 137 days. A blood infection forced the removal of the IV line, and a temporary line was used to fight that infection for the next month.

Doctors switched my medications to oral antibiotics and an anti-malaria drug. Another bleeding problem surfaced in March 2010, and an ultrasound and mammogram revealed the need for my seventh surgery.

I begged for healing. On that night in October 2011, at around 10:45, I lay in bed praying. God whispered in my soul, *Be healed;*

you are healed, little one. Heat enveloped my body from head to toe. My migraine was gone. But more than that, I knew God had healed the Lyme disease.

The healing is a faith walk—a call to "pick up your mat" and walk in the healing. A moment-by-moment trust. I don't want to pick up my mat and be too guarded to go the distance. I don't want to plop back down because I'm afraid. I am walking in faith and trusting God. I am believing, praising and walking.

And I remain symptom-free.

Lisa Buffaloe is a writer and host for Living Joyfully Free Radio. She is the author of *Nadia's Hope, Prodigal Nights* and *Grace for the Char-Baked*, and is a contributing author to *One Year Devotional of Joy and Laughter*. See www.lisabuffaloe.com.

Healings IN THE MINISTRY OF
John Wimber
(1934–1997)

John Wimber was converted in a Bible study by the Society of Friends. In 1977, he established a church. Shortly afterward, he began to teach and preach on healing. The following year he witnessed his first healing in the congregation.[33]

❖ Healed from Neck Pains ❖

Alan Davies suffered from neck pain that was so severe he gave up playing golf. He went with a busload of people to a John Wimber conference. The first night of the conference, Wimber came on stage in front of about 5,000 people and asked everyone who was having neck problems to stand. Many did, including Davies.

After Wimber prayed, Davies said, "I felt the pain squeeze out of the top of my head, like two hands squeezing my head, and I was free of it!" Davies reported that of the 20 people who stood, 7 or 8 were healed.[34]

✤ Signs, Wonders, and Cancer ✤

While speaking at a large conference in South Africa, Wimber, along with his friend, John McClure, went to visit a woman from a local church. This woman's body was filled with cancer. Believing her situation to be hopeless, her doctor sent her home to die. Her only hope was divine intervention.

Both men prayed for her. Later, Wimber—who was also suffering from cancer at the time—admitted that although McClure was certain God would heal her, he felt nothing. Later, the woman awakened with tingling all through her body. For four hours, intense heat filled her body.

Frightened, she crawled into the bathroom, certain that she was dying and her body was coming apart. Without her realizing it, her body was eliminating large tumors. Exhausted, she finally went back to bed, wondering if she would ever wake up again.

About 30 minutes later, she awakened feeling refreshed. God had healed her.

Two days after that, doctors confirmed that she was healthy. They could find no trace of cancer in her body.

In a *Christianity Today* article in which he recounted this story, Wimber went on to acknowledge that not everyone is healed after prayer. He cited the example of a woman named Margie Morton, who died of cancer despite prayers by Wimber and others.[35]

More Than I Asked
(T.L.C. NIELSEN)

I found myself in overwhelming pain after sitting on the floor incorrectly with my first grandchild. After two years of visits to specialists and physical therapy to rebuild muscles from an impinged nerve, I still walked with pain.

Desperate, I decided to attend an Elders Prayer Night at church. After praying for guidance, I felt God tell me to ask for what I needed, even though I didn't feel worthy to ask for healing. I really needed help with the spiritual discouragement that accompanied my chronic pain. After anointing my head with oil, the church elders prayed for both spiritual and physical healing.

As they laid hands on me, I felt tingling at the points of contact, and warmth rushed into my heart. I walked out of church without pain. God gave me far more than I asked for or even expected.

> T. L. C. Nielsen has followed God since 1985. She plays jazz trombone and enjoys working with kids at the local library. A Trinity International University alumnus (B.A. Cum Laude), former teacher and avid reader, Nielsen also writes poetry. See www.lookandbe.blogspot.com (soulfixer13@yahoo.com).

A Couple's Faith for a Baby
(ELAINE WRIGHT COLVIN)

At Calvary Baptist Church in Secunderabad, India, it's traditional to form either a prayer circle or a line-up of people seeking prayer after the morning worship service when there is a visiting speaker. This particular Sunday in February 2009 was no different.

Pastor Pasula Paul called me aside and asked me to pray for a young married couple, Jacob and Amulu, who desperately wanted to have a child.

I learned that a physician the couple had consulted had declared them to be sterile. But I also knew that I had the faith to believe for the miracle they sought. Their situation was so similar to my own daughter's story some 15 years earlier. At that time, God had asked me to pray that I might be able to see my own grandchildren some day.

Only God knows the faith, tears, emotions and words that went into our prayers that Sunday morning. But I knew that this young Indian couple and I believed in a God who both hears and heals.

I returned to Calvary Baptist Church one year later. I was caught off-guard when Pastor Paul turned to me, as we sat behind the pulpit, and whispered, "Remember Jacob and Amulu for whom you prayed on your last visit? They are just walking in the door with their new son, Babu. He is now three months old."

Astounded and joyful, I walked down into the midst of the group of women now sitting on the left-hand side of the church. I had to see for myself the wondrous and amazing gift of God, who had answered a simple prayer of faith that He would bless this family with the desire of their hearts—a child.

Elaine Wright Colvin, founder/director of WIN-India, has made seven trips to Hyderabad, India, since 2006. She is also founder/director of Writers Information Network and WIN Communications, helping others tell their stories.

An Inoperable Tumor
(JANETTE BUTTON)

As an infant, my son, Ryan, was diagnosed with neurofibromatosis type 1 (NF1). A neurologist followed him until he was five years old and then released him from care because the condition hadn't manifested any negative effects.

Ryan started having problems with his bones several months before he turned fifteen in February of 2009. His arms were different lengths. The muscles on the left side of his face were weak, and his left eye didn't fully close. The condition also impacted his speech because of the seventh-nerve palsy.

An MRI scan revealed hydrocephalus, caused by a blockage that kept Ryan's cerebrospinal fluid (CSF) from draining properly, as well as a tumor deep in the center of his brain. The neurologist referred us to a neurosurgeon for surgical consultation. The surgeon told us the tumor was inoperable and sent us to an oncologist.

The specialist discussed chemotherapy and other treatments for the tumor, but he believed the immediate problem was the hydrocephalus and wanted to address that issue first. The surgeon scheduled a third ventriculostomy for the beginning of July, which would open a hole inside the brain to reestablish effective flow of the CSF.

In June, a week before Ryan's procedure, Elim Gospel Church in Lima, New York, hosted a spiritual emphasis weekend with Dr. Michael Brown as the guest preacher.

Dr. Brown invited anyone with a need to come forward for prayer. Ryan went to the front, along with many others.

Our lead pastor, Joshua Finley, moved through the crowd at the altar, praying for the people who had come forward. He put his hand on Ryan as he moved past and simply said, "Touch him, Lord."

Ryan fell to the floor with his arms raised and stayed in that position. As I stared, I knew God must be involved, because Ryan has ADHD. For him to lie still without fidgeting was definitely a Holy Spirit thing.

More than an hour later, long after the others had left the altar, Ryan finally sat up. He knew something significant had happened.

Ryan's surgical procedure took place as scheduled. On July 27, he had a follow-up MRI scan to ensure that the procedure had worked and so the doctors could make treatment plans for the tumor. We returned to the oncologist a few days later to get the results and discuss our options.

The doctor came into the examining room after studying the images. He seemed confused and excited. "I've looked at the scans and compared the new ones with the old ones. The new canal appears to be working well, but there's something strange going on." He hesitated for a few seconds, and a broad smile came to his face. "I can't find the tumor. It's gone. I don't understand what happened, but it's fabulous news."

"I know what happened," Ryan said. "God healed me." He told the doctor about his experience at church in June. "We knew God was at work, and now we have proof."

Janette Button's blog, *Life as a Teacup* (lifeasateacup.com), includes stories of God's unfailing grace. She and her family are active members of Elim Gospel Church in Lima, New York. Ryan recently graduated from high school and continues to be tumor-free.

Healed of Tumors

(Dr. Charles Cullis)

For several years my mind had been exercised before God as to whether it was not His will that the work of faith in which He had placed me should extend to the cure of disease, as well as the alleviation of the miseries of the afflicted. I often read the instructions and promise contained in the fourteenth and fifteenth verses of the fifth chapter of the epistle of James.

They seemed so very plain, that I often asked of my own heart, "Why, if I can rely on God's Word, 'Whatsoever ye shall ask in my name, that will I do,' and every day verify its truth in the supply of the daily needs of the various work committed to my care—why can not I also trust Him to fulfill His promises as to the healing of the body, *The prayer of faith shall save the sick, and the Lord shall raise him up?*'" I could not see why with such explicit and unmistakable promises, I should limit the present exercise of God's power. I began to inquire of earnest Christians whether they knew of any instances of answer to prayer for the healing of the body. Soon afterwards *The Life of Dorothea Trudel* fell into my hands, which strengthened my convictions, and raised the inquiry, "If God can perform such wonders in Mannedorf, why not in Boston?"

At this time I had under my professional care a Christian lady, with a tumor which confined her almost continuously to her bed in severe suffering. All remedies were unavailing, and the only human hope was the knife; but feeling in my heart the power of the promise, I one morning sat down by her bedside, and taking up the Bible, I read aloud God's promise to His believing children: "*And the prayer of faith shall save the sick, and the Lord shall raise him up; and if he have committed sins, they shall be forgiven him.*"

I then asked her if she would trust the Lord to remove this tumor and restore her to health, and to her missionary work. She replied, "I have no particular faith about it, but am willing to trust the Lord for it."

I then knelt and anointed her with oil in the name of the Lord, asking Him to fulfill His own word. Soon after I left, she got up and walked three miles. From that time the tumor rapidly lessened, until all trace of it at length disappeared.[36]

In 1870, Charles Cullis went from Boston to a rural area to pray for physical healing. He prayed for Lucy Drake who had a large tumor that kept her bedridden. She was healed after prayer and walked three miles that same day.[37]

Healings IN THE MINISTRY OF
Dorothea Trudel
(1813–1862)

Dorothea Trudel grew up in poverty in Mannedorf, Switzerland. When she was an adult, a few of the workers in her floral business became sick. Trudel prayed for their healing. They recovered, and she became convinced that God heals through prayer.[38]

❖ Remarkable (and Documented) ❖
Cures by Dorothea Trudel

Doctors had given up on an elderly man who couldn't walk. After Trudel prayed for him, he was able to walk without any problems.

Another man with a burned foot was told that he would die unless he allowed doctors to amputate. He went to Trudel and was healed.

A leading physician at Wurtemberg confirmed that Trudel's prayers had cured one of his hopeless patients. He insisted that he had witnessed various sicknesses healed, including cancers, epilepsy and insanity.

One man went to Trudel because he had been suffering for six months from a bone disease. He had spent a long time in a Swiss hospital, but was apparently no better. After Trudel prayed for him, he was healed.

There were reports that Pastor Blumenhart of Wurtemberg had his home crowded for years with patients, and cures occurred constantly. One woman fell and injured her knee. For weeks, she suffered with agonizing pain. The doctors were unable to do anything for her. But Trudel prayed for her and within one day the swelling had vanished and she was set free from pain.

Some maintained that Trudel's work was one of hypnosis. One time Trudel prayed earnestly aloud so others could hear. She asked God *not* to heal the invalid through her means if she used hypnosis. She also did not visit the home so there would be no opportunity to place herself in a "mesmeric relation to this patient."[39]

Raising My Hands

(MARLENA DAMMÉ)

I struggled to lift my arms above my head, so I went to the doctor for a variety of tests. He took several vials of blood and a number of X-rays to rule out lupus and other diseases, and to determine the exact cause of the intense pain.

That evening, while I was driving home, a verse came to my mind. Tears flowed as I quoted it the way I remembered it (which wasn't literally correct): "You are healed by the blood of the Lamb and the word of your testimony for you love not your life unto death."

I sensed the Holy Spirit tell me to confess that 12 times, making it personal. So 12 times I said out loud, "I am healed by the blood of the Lamb and the word of my testimony for I love not my life unto death."

After I got home, I found the verse, Revelation 12:11, that says, "And they have defeated [Satan] by the blood of the Lamb and by their testimony. And they did not love their lives so much that they were afraid to die."

A week later, my doctor diagnosed the problem as degenerative arthritis. I wondered how that was possible. I was so young that it didn't seem right. Yet again, the Lord impressed on me to quote Revelation 12:11. I consistently did that for the next two years.

One night at church, a guest speaker invited those who needed healing to come forward. I went to the front, as I had many times before. A deaconess prayed for me, and my hands shot straight up in the air without pain. The previous day, I could barely raise my hands enough to shampoo my hair. Yet that Sunday night I praised the Lord with my hands in the air.

It has now been more than 20 years, and I'm still able to raise my hands and arms in praise to God—pain-free.

Marlena Dammé served in the military, where she met and married her husband (barney@gvtc.com).

The Faith of a Child

(ELAINE WRIGHT COLVIN)

"Aunty, Aunty," called the young boy loudly as he ran to our car just as we arrived at Grace Community Baptist Church in Secunderabad, India, for a baptismal service on Sunday, August 26, 2012.

I recognized the cute nine-year-old Prakash immediately from my visit to inaugurate his new church, Gethsemane House of Prayer, during my January 2012 trip to India.

"Aunty, remember me? You prayed for me and God healed me!"

I had only arrived in India the previous day. Even though I had prayed fervently that God would let me see many miracles, I was totally unprepared for how quickly I would receive His answers.

"Prakash, please remind me about what we prayed for you," I asked the beaming little boy.

"When we were leaving our new church in January, I stopped you on the sidewalk and asked you to pray for me because I was having fits and high fever, and I was unable to attend school. When I did try to go, I could not concentrate and do my work."

Oh, yes, it all came back to me. At the time I hadn't known what the term "fits" meant when used in India. It referred to uncontrollable shaking.

"So, what happened?" I asked.

"God healed me right after you prayed, and I have not had fits since, and I have not had to miss any more school," he said. He grabbed my hand and smiled. "Jesus heard our prayers."

The Healing Season
(VERONICA LEIGH)

"I constantly feel tired and dizzy," I told the doctor.

"And she isn't eating right," Mom said.

The doctor nodded, checking over my chart.

Mom was right. My appetite wasn't what it used to be. When the nurse weighed me, the scale showed that I had lost a total of eight pounds.

For the last eight months, I had battled against my nerves—and they were winning. My problems had begun in January, and everything from eating to sleeping to going places was affected. The summer months had been better, but as autumn settled in, I started to have strange spacey feelings.

One day in late September, I mowed the lawn, and after I completed the chore, I collapsed on the living room couch. The next morning I awoke to palpitations, dizziness, hot flashes, exhaustion and extreme moodiness.

Mom heard a report about anxiety attacks on the news and noticed that many of my symptoms coincided with those described in the news segment. Doing further research, she discovered that anxiety attacks were often caused by hyperthyroidism.

Despite putting a positive face on my problem, it only got worse. Not a day went by that I didn't have hysterics or trouble stepping out the front door. Only my faith in Christ and the support of my family carried me through.

My parents decided that it was time for me to see the family doctor.

"It's not uncommon for adolescents to suffer from depression or for them to have anxiety attacks," the doctor said.

"What about my thyroid?" I asked, "Could that be the problem?"

He shrugged. "It might, but you're awfully young to be having thyroid problems. Were I in Vegas and a betting man, I'd wager all my money that it's depression."

The doctor sent me down to have blood taken, so he could rule out thyroid, diabetes and anemia.

A few days later, the results came in. As it turned out, my thyroid was hyperactive—which was the cause of my mental and emotional issues.

"It's a good thing the doctor isn't in Vegas," Dad quipped.

That happened in mid-December, and we made an appointment to have my thyroid scanned after the holidays. People all over the country—many of whom I didn't know—prayed for me.

I had the scan, and the doctor promised to call within a few days. When he called, he said, "There is nothing wrong with your thyroid."

I still had many of the symptoms, but several months passed before I felt like my old self again.

The doctor gave me more tests, but everything looked normal.

He and the other medical professionals were baffled. There had to be an explanation, but no one could give me any.

Except Mom.

"God healed you," she said. "Many people were praying for you, and the Lord answered."

I had always believed in God's healing power and had witnessed it with others. It took me a long time to accept that He had healed me. When science could offer me no explanations, God did.

Veronica Leigh aspires to be a novelist and currently writes a blog, *Confessions of an Authoress*. See http://veronicaleigh.blogspot.com.

Healings IN THE MINISTRY OF
Agnes Sandford
(1897–1982)

Agnes Sanford suffered from severe depression for many years. In her autobiography, *Sealed Orders,* she reported that the depression began to leave her after a preacher laid his hands on her and prayed for her. Eventually she was totally free.

Sanford began her healing ministry in the 1940s. With her husband, John, she taught all over the country about the power of prayer. The Sanfords were primary agents for spiritual renewal in clergy of the mainline denominations. Sanford died in 1982 after 35 years of ministry.

✤ The Miracle on Ward 17 ✤

Frederick lay in a private cell, which meant that his death was imminent. He looked terrible, and Sanford "threw him a swift prayer" as she walked past. Yet she felt that wasn't enough. Filled with compassion, she went into Frederick's room. She spoke with him and asked what was wrong.

He told her, "Blood clots."

When she told him of God's power, he had no interest. She said she would like to pray for him anyway. He agreed.

He pulled back the sheet, and his abdomen looked like a pool of blood covered only by a thin membrane. He had been kept alive by intravenous feeding, drugs and stimulants.

Sanford laid her hands on him and prayed. Afterward, at home, she called her Christian friends to pray for a miracle for Frederick.

The following week, she passed his room, but he was asleep, so she didn't go inside. Two weeks later, the room was empty. His belongings were there and it was obvious he had slept in the bed.

Sanford went into the common room and saw a handsome young man. "You can't be Frederick, can you?" she asked.

He said he was and commented that his feet were still swollen, but that was the only remaining symptom of his illness. She assured him that was because he wasn't used to standing on them, and that they would soon be well.

When she returned a week later, he had been sent home.

One day she talked with the chaplain and mentioned Frederick. She told him the story of his healing.

The surprised man said that God had also healed Frederick's soul. He came daily to see the chaplain. He wanted a Bible and wanted to know about Jesus.

Three months later, Sanford again visited Ward 17 and saw a healthy Frederick standing there. He had returned for his three-month checkup. He was well and healed.[40]

Healed Eyes

(Cecil Murphey)

My wife, Shirley, was born and grew up in Zion, Illinois, the city founded by John Alexander Dowie with an emphasis on healing for the body. Her father worked for one of the industries started by the city.

Edith, Shirley's older sister, had to wear thick glasses. When she was 15 years old, she went to the church to ask an elder to pray for her. One wall of the Christian Catholic Apostolic Church was filled with braces, canes, wheelchairs, and other items no longer needed after people were healed.

Edith hesitated because the elder who prayed with her wore glasses, but she still asked for prayer.

The elder prayed, and God healed Edith's eyes. She never wore glasses again until she needed reading glasses—when she was in her seventies.

We Were Desperate
(PEGGY GAMBA)

My father had his first heart attack before I was born. He went from a hard-working farmer to a mostly disabled stay-at-home dad. He was grateful to be alive, yet burdened with a new kind of stress. How would he keep his farm? Who would do the work? The bank was already repossessing things. His dismal attitude and fragile health created a turbulent atmosphere.

My mother and siblings took over working the farm. I was too young to work, but I knew what they were doing. They farmed from Friday until Sunday evening. On Monday morning, my siblings were off to school, and Mom went back to her other job. It was a difficult and exhausting time for all of them.

Mom was barely over five feet tall, but she was a hard worker. I never heard her complain about the difficulties she faced each day. She'd do anything to keep us afloat. That's the reason she had taken a day job as a cleaning woman. My family was poor. With the farm's meager earnings and my mother's wages combined, we barely had enough money to keep nine people fed. Power, running water and heat became luxuries.

Everything depended on Mom's health. Then she started having problems with her hands. They cracked and bled. My father took her to the state-run health clinic where she could receive free treatment.

The doctors diagnosed her with a latex allergy. They told her to wear cotton gloves underneath her work gloves and provided ointment to heal her festering wounds. That helped for a time, but she had to keep working, and no one had a non-latex alternative back then. Mom's symptoms worsened, her wounds stopped healing, and the pain was severe.

Mom's illness spread to her feet. They too cracked and bled. She could no longer get out of bed. My strong little mother had become frail and crippled. While she stayed in bed and tried to heal, I watched Dad keep strict inventory over the few items left in our cupboards. We had to stretch what remained.

Mom's health wasn't improving, and we didn't know what to do. A devoted Christian, she told Dad, "I want to call the elders of the church to pray for my healing."

I was surprised when my father agreed to her request, because he wasn't a spiritual man. Her churchgoing had often led to major fighting. Dad made the call, and two members of the church came to our house.

They knelt beside Mom's bed and placed their hands on her head. While their words flowed, I watched intently. The men continued praying over my mom for what seemed like 10 minutes.

Her recovery was immediate. She never had pain again. The wounds healed rapidly, and her body stopped reacting to latex.

She worked at the same job the rest of her life.

Peggy Gamba works in the semiconductor industry and writes in her spare time. She is currently finishing her first novel (throughangelseyes@gmail.com).

God's Surgery

(VIRGINIA RUSH)

I had a sore throat for years. Several sinus surgeries provided no relief. The ENT doctor told me my tonsils were horrible. I fought it for years, not wanting to endure a surgery that involved a painful recovery. While visiting in Houston, I went to a new doctor to get relief.

Without asking, he set up immediate surgery.

In shock, I said, "I need to think about it."

"All right, but your tonsils are horrible."

A short time later, I went to church with my brother. They had a visiting evangelist, whom I knew. After the service, I asked if he would pray for my tonsil condition.

He did, and the next day, my throat looked different, and I had no problems with my sinuses.

What does this mean? I asked myself. I kept an eye on things for several days, and the next time I was in a doctor's office, I asked him to look at my tonsils.

"You don't have tonsils," he said. "You must have had them surgically removed when you were a child."

I left with a smile. God had performed the surgery I needed, and there had been no painful recovery.

Virginia Rush is an avid reader, reviews books, and loves to proofread (vrush 729@aol.com).

Healings IN THE MINISTRY OF
John Alexander Dowie
(1847–1907)

Born in Scotland and raised in Australia, John Alexander Dowie began preaching in Chicago in the 1890s. He published a weekly paper, *Leaves of Healing*, and operated 13 healing homes. Wanting to establish a community where church members could live and worship in a Christian environment, Dowie bought several thousand acres of land in Lake County, Illinois, and founded the City of Zion.[41]

❖ Severe Pains in Her Feet ❖

An illiterate woman who suffered from severe pain and used a crutch to walk asked Dowie to pray for her healing.

Dowie knelt at her feet and instructed her to put the diseased foot in his hand. She did so, and he removed her shoe and prayed that God would heal her. When he finished praying, he looked up and saw that the woman was crying.

"I think my attitude at her feet had deeply touched her; but she was looking upward lost in reverent prayer," Dowie writes. "I rose and said, 'In Jesus' name, rise and walk!' She looked for the crutch, which I had placed beyond her reach. I repeated the words,

'In Jesus' name, rise and walk!' She arose, and walked several times across the room. I said, 'You are healed!' "

As the woman prepared to leave, Dowie said, "You have left something which belongs to you." He pointed to the crutch.

"Oh," she said, "I don't need it anymore; I am healed."

"What do you intend to do with it then?"

She said, "O Doctor, if you would like to take it, I will leave it with you."[42]

✤ A Boy Born Blind ✤

A boy was born blind, and although a doctor operated on him three times, he remained sightless. Dowie laid hands on him and prayed. When the boy opened his eyes, he was able to see.

Later, the boy's mother, Mrs. Lula Ritchville of San Francisco, wrote a testimony about the healing:

> My little boy Georgie was afflicted from birth with blindness. Three years ago an operation was performed by Dr. Barcon of this city. . . . For ten years he has been unable to walk, until now, without being led by the hand, when outside the house. He never saw an object, so far as we know, during these ten years, not a single object to know what it was. Jesus has now, through Mr. Dowie's agency, restored his sight almost entirely; he can now walk alone, see houses, chimneys, and small objects very readily. . . . My little boy is bright and happy now, and gives God all the glory. Praise his name forever.[43]

It Might Go Away
(Barbara Wells)

When my husband, Jim, was pastor of Good Shepherd Church in Owensboro, Kentucky, he held a special service for those who needed healing. That Sunday evening, a mother brought her first-born son to the front for prayer.

A week after his birth, little Brad Dicēmo had developed a bluish-red raised bump that extended from the inside corner of his eye down onto his face. The bump was about the size of a three-carat diamond, and the doctor diagnosed it as a birthmark. "It could just go away," he said. "But if it doesn't, and it begins to grow, you might want to consider surgery, because it could affect his eyesight."

Baby Brad was nine months old when Pastor Jim anointed him with oil and prayed for him to be healed. Two days later, Brad's mother picked him up after a nap, and the entire bump and discoloration were completely gone.

Today, Brad is in his thirties and serves in the United States military. He's still healed.

Barbara Wells is a conference speaker and the author of *Cameos*. She serves as coordinator for the Kentucky Christian Writers Conference in Elizabethtown, Kentucky. See www.barbarawells.webs.com.

Healings by the Happy Hunters

Charles (1920–2010) and Frances Hunter (1916–2009) had a long-lasting ministry of praying for the sick in 49 countries as well as throughout the United States.

⊷══◦◦◦══⊶

A man known as Stoney Henry came to the Hunters with a malignant bladder tumor. Doctors had tried chemotherapy unsuccessfully. The tumor had gone from stage one to stage two with no evidence of remission.

After Henry read of others who had been healed of cancer, he attended a Full Gospel Businessmen's Fellowship International (FGBMFI) meeting. The Hunters were the speakers that day.

After Charles Hunter preached, he invited anyone who desired prayer to come forward. During their prayer for Henry, the Hunters "rebuked the cancer." Stoney Henry left, believing he had been healed.

During the next three months, Stoney Henry made two trips to the MD Anderson Hospital in Houston, Texas. There, doctors confirmed that he had been healed.[44]

The Hunters conducted a wedding ceremony in Anaheim, California. Afterward they spotted a teenage girl walking with a limp. One of the girl's legs was bent.

When Charles Hunter asked her what was wrong, she told him it was congenital. The tendons in her leg hadn't grown correctly. Because they were in a hurry, Charles laid hands on her and said, "Jesus, touch her." Then he and Frances rushed off to their meeting.

A short time later, at another meeting in California, Mike Esses, associate pastor of the church where the Hunters met the afflicted girl, came to the platform. He told the audience about God healing the girl and said, "I'm her Sunday School teacher. It was an instant and total healing and her leg is normal."[45]

Before the Hunters spoke at a FGBMFI meeting in Atlanta, Georgia, they read in Mark's Gospel about Jesus healing a deaf and mute boy. They felt God was preparing them for that meeting in Atlanta.

The third person who asked for healing was a deaf/mute engineer. The Hunters laid their hands on him and prayed for him. The man pointed at his ears. He then spoke the first words in his life: "praise" and "amen."

Three weeks later, the Hunters received a letter from the man's employer. He said the healed man was listening to the radio constantly and learning to talk.[46]

Healing from Rheumatoid Arthritis

Becky Neel, of The Mission Society's Global Resource Team,[47] was diagnosed with rheumatoid arthritis (RA) and a mild form of lupus in 1998. The disease came on her almost overnight, and she stayed in severe pain for the next 10 years.

During that time, a number of people prayed for Becky, but she didn't get any better. God did give her peace and strength to endure.

In July 2008, Becky and her husband, Doug, visited a friend who worked at the International House of Prayer, which is a 24/7 prayer and worship ministry in Kansas City, Missouri.

At the healing room, the Neels' friend and a man named Richard anointed Becky with oil and prayed for her healing. After several minutes, they stopped. She felt no relief.

Richard told Becky he had a message for her from the Lord. The message was for her to "stop trying to carry everyone's burdens and being everybody's fixer. You are trying to carry a burden that is not yours to carry."

Through Richard, the Lord told Becky it was time to allow Him to fix not only her, but also all the problems and hurts of those she was concerned about. God wanted her to rest in Him and delight in Him.

When Becky walked out of that room, she was completely pain-free and healed from RA—and also healed from thinking she was the great fixer.[48]

Unborn Baby Healed

Although she and her husband, Martin, had six children, Tracy Reeves had miscarried three times. When she and Martin learned they would have another baby, both were excited. However, after an ultrasound, they learned that the baby girl had a hole in her heart.

Tracy and Martin were missionaries in Peru,[49] and a week after receiving the news about his daughter, Martin left for Huancayo to train nationals. While there, he prayed with his training group and felt that God gave him a message. He was to go home and lay his hands on Tracy for the healing of the fetus.

After the prayer, and before Martin was able to tell the others what had happened, one of the nationals said he had a vision of Martin placing his hands on Tracy's stomach. When Martin got home, he laid his hands on Tracy's stomach, and they prayed for the healing of their baby.

A few days later, the doctor did a new ultrasound. Afterward he said, "I can't find the hole here; it's not there. That never happens in the womb. Sometimes after birth, the hole will close by itself, but I've never seen this happen in the womb."

Martin told the doctor of their faith in a powerful, loving God. The baby was born healthy.[50]

"I Can See Clearly"

Don Stewart's book *Only Believe* is subtitled *An Eyewitness Account of the Great Healing Revival of the 20th Century.* His insightful view of the last century reveals his intimate knowledge of the healing movement. His story began when he was 13 and was healed of a serious bone disease.

Stewart also tells the story of Cathy Williams, a high school majorette whom doctors diagnosed with "chronic retinal deterioration." Within months of the onset of this condition, Cathy was blind in one eye and had 80 percent use of the other. Her doctors expected her to lose all sight in the good eye by the end of the year.

The *Savannah Evening Press* published the story, and a plea went out for money to send Cathy to Johns Hopkins Hospital in Baltimore. At the time, there was no known cure for the disease she had, but the doctors at Johns Hopkins agreed to examine her.

The Williams family attended St. Michael's Catholic Church in Savannah Beach, Georgia. Cathy's mother knew of Don Stewart and his ministry. She prayed that he would visit the area. When he came for a crusade, she begged him to pray for her daughter.

Stewart wrote, "I prayed for her and then put a handkerchief over the one eye that still had partial vision. I asked her what she could see through that blind eye, and she screamed, 'I can see you! I'm healed! I can see you!'

"She grabbed me and hugged me. Her mother started sobbing like a little child. Her boyfriend ran up from the audience saying, 'Cathy, can you see me? Cathy, can you see me?'

" 'Yes,' she said. She was crying and screaming. 'I can see you clearly. I can see! I can see!' "[51]

Bone Displacement

George Jeffreys (1889–1962) was a Welsh healing evangelist. One of those touched by his ministry was James Gregson, an ironmaster who had suffered a work accident that "resulted in the displacement of many of the bones within his body." Medical doctors were unable to help him. To sit caused excruciating pain, so Gregson lay down much of the time. He was able to get around with crutches by dragging his legs behind him.

Gregson's wife learned that George Jeffreys was coming to Leeds, England, where they lived. Gregson was at the Saturday meeting on crutches. He had a conversion experience and returned the next day.

He reported that "when [Jeffreys] laid his hands upon me, I felt as if a dozen hands were placed all over my body, and I felt every bone going back into place. I was instantly released and I was completely healed."[52]

A Healing During the Great Awakening

In 1726, Mercy Wheeler had become unable to walk because of a "wasting fever." Sixteen years later, she walked only with crutches.

At her request, Pastor Hezekiah Lord of Preston, Connecticut, came to preach a special message at her home.

Only days before the service, Wheeler began to feel confident that God would heal her. At the meeting, Pastor Lord preached, and Wheeler believed the promise was meant for her. She started to tremble, and they placed her on a bed.

Pastor Lord spoke to her. She told him that God would heal her. Immediately after she said those words, Wheeler felt a strange shaking in her hands—and then it spread all over her body. She rose from her bed and, to the astonishment of herself and those about her, she walked.

The shocked minister told her that she was "in a frenzy" and instructed her to sit down, but she refused and walked across the room several times.

Wheeler's healing caused a minor sensation in New England in 1743, and generated a debate over the legitimacy of miracles after the apostolic period.[53]

Healings IN THE MINISTRY OF
Jack Coe
(1918–1956)

❖ Restoring Sight to the Blind ❖

Jack Coe's healing ministry began in Longview, Texas, in 1945—a year after God healed him of malaria when doctors could do nothing for him. He announced that at his healing meeting the blind would see, the deaf would hear, and the lame would walk. The next evening the church was full, and Coe was given an opportunity to deliver on what he had promised. After he finished preaching, people lined up for prayer—and among them was a blind woman who wanted healing.

Coe felt convicted about what he had said, as if he were the one who healed, so he repented before he anointed the blind woman with oil and prayed. Her sight began to return as "vague impressions." Coe prayed again, and the woman cried out that she could see.

That healing launched Jack Coe's healing ministry.[54]

❖ Cancer of the Hand ❖

Pauline Young of Texarkana, Texas, wrote that in January of 1950, a doctor removed a cancerous growth from her hand. After the surgery, she had radium treatments. Six months later, a growth showed up on her arm. In July, she decided to go to the Horsey Cancer Clinic in Dallas. The staff there told her that even if she took medicine, she had only about a 20 percent chance of full recovery. Young hesitated, but kept going back for treatment. Each time the growth was larger and more painful. Within three months, she could hardly get out of bed because of the pain.

Young learned that Jack Coe was coming to Dallas. She had heard of the wonderful healings under his ministry, so she got up from her bed, and her parents took her to the meetings where he was ministering. After they had attended several services, Coe prayed for Young. All pain left her body and she was healed.[55]

Prayer from Camps Farthest Out

(KRISTIE HEADINGTON)

"You have precancerous cells," the endocrinologist told me after performing a biopsy on my thyroid. "We need to schedule surgery."

We planned the procedure for Friday of the following week, and I immediately began praying for healing.

My neighbors and good friends, Cal and Ann Klopp, prayed faithfully for me as well. "This weekend we'll be at CFO," Ann said. CFO, or Camps Farthest Out, holds interdenominational Christ-centered retreats across the nation. "We'll pray for you as a group while we're there."

Ann's promise encouraged me. I knew that those who attend CFO camps are godly, praying people. "I'm counting on it."

On Sunday afternoon, while I was napping, a warm, blanket-like feeling flowed across my neck. It frightened me at first, but then I realized God had healed me. The next day I told my husband, "I've been healed. I need to call the doctor."

"That's good," he said, "but I think we'd better continue as planned."

I listened to him and respected what he said, but the next day I thought, *This is God working in my life. I can't ignore what happened.* So I called my surgeon and explained that I didn't need surgery. "I'm healed," I said.

The doctor's voice didn't display the same confidence I felt. "Okay, but we don't want to fool around with this. I still want to see you on Friday."

I promised to come in as scheduled and told the doctor I'd be prepared for the surgery. "But I want you to check my neck. Would you just feel it to see?"

At the urging of my husband and my doctor, I went through with the procedure. Two days later, the doctor called with the details. "I don't know what's going on, but there are no cancerous cells. It's completely clear."

When I returned to the surgeon's office for my follow-up appointment, he showed me the results. My thoughts went back to the warm feeling I had experienced. "Do you believe in miracles?" I asked.

"Yes, I do," he said, "because I can't explain it. You have no cancer. There's no need for treatment of any kind."

"Then all I can say is, 'Thank you, Lord!'"

I reported the news to Ann and told her about my experience. "When did the healing occur?" she asked.

"On Sunday afternoon while I was napping."

"That's when we prayed for you at CFO."

Kristie Headington has taught for 40 years in elementary, secondary and college classrooms.

Marriage, a Miracle and Ministry
(Dr. James B. Keiller)

"No, don't get married," the members of the Gospel Tabernacle in Beloit, Wisconsin, urged my father. He had announced his intentions to wed. "You're our pastor, and the Lord is going to come soon."

Back in the early 1930s, many Pentecostals believed that pastors should give themselves fully to the ministry and remain celibate.

My father married my mother when he was 30; she was 5 years older.

My parents desired to start a family, but they were unable to conceive. Because they made it a practice always to trust God for their healing, regardless of the physical problem, they didn't seek medical attention.

After a few years, they adopted a baby boy who had been born outside of wedlock. Yet they continued to long for a biological child. Finally they gave in and consulted a doctor.

The doctor examined my mother. "You have a large tumor on your uterus," he told her. "We need to schedule surgery to remove it."

"No, we'll wait and pray," Mother said, convinced that God would take care of her.

My parents asked God for His healing touch. One day my mother felt different and knew she'd been healed. She was certain of God's divine intervention, so she returned to the doctor, who verified that the tumor was gone.

My parents conceived me when their adopted baby was only five months old. God worked a miracle in their lives.

I'm grateful my father resisted the pleas of his church members to refrain from marriage. God used him for many years as a preacher, and he went on to become president of Beulah Heights Bible College (now Beulah Heights University) in 1956.

Following my mother's healing, I was born, and I became a preacher in my teenage years. I've been the vice president and dean of academic affairs of Beulah Heights University since 1964.

Because of marriage and a miracle, my father's ministry goes on through me, and the ripple effect reaches around the world.

Dr. James B. Keiller was senior pastor of Maranatha Temple in Boston and Midland Full Gospel Church in Midland, Michigan. He is vice president and dean for academic affairs at Beulah Heights University in Atlanta, serving in that position since August 1964 (James.Keiller@beulah.org).

Healings IN THE MINISTRY OF
John G. Lake
(1870–1935)

From 1915 (some sources say 1914) to 1920, John G. Lake ran the Healing Rooms, a healing center in Spokane, Washington. For those five years, the center claimed more than 100,000 medically confirmed healings. According to newspaper reports at the time, this ministry caused quite a sensation: "Rev. Lake through divine healing has made Spokane the healthiest city in the world, according to United States statistics."[56]

The Healing Rooms ministry was the climax of Lake's life's work. As a result of his ministry during that time, Spokane came to be known as "America's healthiest city," similar to Zion City, Illinois, where John Alexander Dowie had ministered a few years earlier.

❖ Afflicted with Catalepsy ❖

In a letter dated May 20, 1918, Louise Reinbold of Davenport, Washington, wrote that three years earlier their physician had stated that both she and her sister had appendicitis and must be operated on at once. The girls were rushed to the hospital, and her sister's surgery took place on December 10, 1915, followed by a second surgery on January 2, 1916. The sister died immediately after the second surgery.

Louise was operated on and for three years could only whisper in an indistinct manner. In her letter, she also said she had been "afflicted with catalepsy and would fall under its power and become unconscious." As time went on, the bouts became more frequent. She suffered "constantly with a violent pain in my side until life became unbearable. Doctors could give me no relief and gradually I sank in despair until I was persuaded to visit Rev. Lake at his Healing Rooms in Spokane."

After one month of daily prayer and laying on of hands at the Healing Rooms, Louise was completely healed on May 16, 1918.[57]

✢ John G. Lake's Sister ✢

"No words of mine can convey to another soul the cry that was in my heart and the flame of hatred for death and sickness that the Spirit of God had stirred within me. The very wrath of God seemed to possess my soul!"[58]

John G. Lake spoke those words in reference to the intensity of emotion he felt as his 34-year-old sister lay dying. Eight of his 15 siblings had already died from illness. He himself had been healed of childhood rheumatoid arthritis. He had seen his sister delivered from cancer and his brother's blood disease healed under the ministry of John Alexander Dowie.

Lake telegraphed Dowie with a desperate plea for prayer. The reply came back: "Hold on to God. I am praying. She will live."

Within the hour Lake's sister was completely healed.

On April 28, 1898, Lake's wife, Jennie, was very near death. Lake prayed earnestly, and Jennie rose up healed, praising the Lord in a loud voice. News of Jennie's miraculous healing spread, and from that time on, John Lake was sought after for his healing powers.

✢ Inflammatory Rheumatism ✢

A woman who had suffered from inflammatory rheumatism for 10 years asked Lake to pray for her. He sat on the opposite side of the room and prayed. He said he felt as if he passed under a warm tropical rain that fell not only on him, but also through him.

He got up and laid his hand on the woman's head. Just then, her clenched hands opened and her joints began to work. She arose from her wheelchair and was perfectly healed.[59]

A Little Discomfort

(CAROLYN POINDEXTER)

I had listened to Kenneth Hagin on the radio for years, so I was excited when he came to Minneapolis to hold a weeklong conference in 1982. His was primarily a healing ministry, and I initially attended because I sought healing for my son, who went to most of the services with me.

During one of the morning sessions, which my son did not attend, Kenneth Hagin's colleague, Mark Brazee, taught about healing. Toward the end of the service, he called for anyone who needed healing to come forward. Sick and crippled people, some with casts on their limbs and others in wheelchairs, moved forward.

I sensed God speak to me: *Go down to be healed.*

For the first few moments, I remained in my seat, trying to figure out why I needed healing. I wasn't sick like some who were already moving toward the minister, so I was confused.

Again I sensed God instruct me: *Go down to be healed.*

The only thing that came to mind was an issue in my lower back that I had nursed for 12 years. I received a spinal tap when my first child was born, and every night at bedtime and every morning on waking since then I'd had to wait several minutes until the pain eased its way out of my back. When I bent over, I had to do it slowly or the pain would appear.

After so many years, I didn't think anything about it, and I didn't pray about it. The pain was as natural to me as making coffee in the mornings. I just accepted it as something that was there and would be there until the day I died.

Finally convinced that God was referring to my back issue, I went to the altar and stood with the others awaiting their healings.

When the man of God approached, he laid his hand on me and said, "Be healed in the name of Jesus." The ushers behind helped steady me, and I went back to my seat. No lightning. No thunderclaps. No visible signs of angels ascending or descending in the auditorium. It was just business as usual.

When I prepared for bed that night, I washed my face, brushed my teeth, put on my nightgown, turned off the light, and lay down to pray. A minute or two into my prayers, I realized that I hadn't needed to shuffle into a comfortable position as I normally did. For the first time in 12 years, I had absolutely no pain.

The next morning I got up with no pain. To this day, 30 years later, the pain has never returned.

Carolyn Poindexter enjoys freelance writing and amateur photography. A church administrator by day, her nighttime passion is working on her first manuscript, *When It's Time to Say Goodbye,* a story of emotional healing after losing her only son to cancer.

Miracle Twins

Doctors told Wes and Kimberly Funk they could never have children. After years of praying, Kimberly became pregnant. On July 17, 1994, she gave birth to twin sons, Kyle and Corey.

Days later, however, she developed severe abdominal pain and became delirious. CT scans showed the presence of gallstones and inflammation in her gallbladder. She had immediate surgery to remove her gallbladder.

About three hours later, doctors informed Wes that Kimberly had a five percent chance of surviving. While performing the surgery, they had discovered that she suffered from acute pancreatitis and a blood clot in her lungs. Her kidneys and liver were failing. She was in a coma and put on a respirator.

Wes grabbed his wife's Bible and went into the chapel to plead for God to spare her life. He reminded God that the birth of the twins was a miracle. "Now I need another miracle."

Friends and family members started prayer chains that went all over the world. Wes said that even Kimberly's physician, Dr. Mullen, prayed for her. Although Mullen felt powerless, he and his wife said they were going to ask for a specific intervention from the Lord.

The next day, Kimberly's condition had worsened. Dr. Mullen decided to do a high-risk surgery, which was his final option. Just before 11:00 that morning, Kimberly was wheeled back into the operating room.

As soon as Dr. Mullen cut into the abdominal wall, a flood of fluid gushed out—a sign of decompression of the abdomen. Dr. Mullen later said, "When you release that, the pressure goes down and you never get these people back." Three other doctors were in the OR with him, and all believed that Kimberly was going to die.

But Kimberly survived the surgery. Within a short time, she was off the ventilator, her liver functioned normally, and her kidneys were also normal. In fact, everything in her body was normal. A few days later, Kimberly was able to take her twin sons home.

Sixteen years later, Wes and Kimberly appeared on the *700 Club*. She reported that she is healthy and so are the twins.[60]

A Cup of Cold Water

(BARBARA SNYDER)

Sunday, June 7, 1981, began like every other day: I was confined to bed and connected to tubes to keep me alive.

I loved God, but because of my illness, I hadn't been to church for several years. The only time I left home was by ambulance, and the last time I had been at the hospital, the medical staff didn't expect me to return. I received in-home hospice care, and a nurse stayed constantly with me.

Sixteen years earlier, at the age of 15, I had developed multiple sclerosis (MS). This incurable neurological disease affects people in different ways. As my MS progressed, it attacked my arms, legs and vision, and paralyzed my internal organs. I felt trapped inside my own body.

Although I couldn't attend services, my church family at Wheaton Wesleyan Church in Wheaton, Illinois, didn't forget me. Two friends, Joyce and Angela, came to see me after the morning worship service. They joined my aunt, who sat at my side reading aloud stacks of cards and letters. They brought a bundle of mail that had been delivered to the church's address.

Someone had nominated me for *Cup of Cold Water*—a special Moody Bible Institute radio program that shares prayer requests over the air and asks listeners to pray—and I was that week's recipient. I received hundreds of messages from people I'd never met, all saying they were praying for me.

One card read: "Things don't just happen to those of us who love God. They're planned."

Just then, I heard what seemed to be an audible, authoritative voice over my shoulder say, "My child, get up and walk." I knew it was the voice of God.

I had a tracheostomy tube in my neck because of horrible lung disease. My hands were curled up, and my fingers touched the insides of my wrists. If I wanted to talk, someone else would have to take the tube from my neck and plug the hole so I could take a breath and speak.

My visitors knew I wanted to say something because I appeared agitated. One of them came over to me and plugged the hole. I pushed out the words, "I don't know what you're going to think about this, but God told me to get up and walk."

They said nothing.

"God just told me to get up and walk. Get the rest of my family. I want them to be here." My visitors told the others to come quickly.

The normal procedure for getting me out of bed involved two nurses, a lapboard, and 10 minutes. This time, I pulled the oxygen tube from my neck and leaped from my bed, *without help*. I couldn't wait for the others to come into my room.

I stood with my feet flat on the floor. My toes had been curled so I couldn't wear slippers. I stared at my feet. *I'm standing!* My hands were fully open. I also realized that God had restored my sight.

I turned around and stared at my visitors, who were quiet again. Then praise burst forth from all of us.

As soon as my mother walked into the room, I ran to her. She dropped to the floor near my feet. She lifted the hem of my nightgown and squeezed my legs. "You have calves again!"

I walked to the family room. My father was just coming in. He swept me into his arms and waltzed me around the room.

That evening, after an afternoon of celebration, we went to church as a family. I climbed the stairs by myself in high-heeled sandals, entered the sanctuary, and walked down the center aisle.

The next day I went to Wheaton Medical Clinic. For more than three hours, my internist examined me—and it seemed every other doctor at the clinic wanted to take a look at me as well.

No signs of the disease were present. My lungs were whole and working properly, with the diaphragm pumping normally. My trachea tube was pulled out, the catheter removed, the pain unit taken off, and all medication discontinued.

The medical personnel declared that they had witnessed a miracle and gave God credit.

On Thursday, I was a special guest on the Moody radio station. I had the opportunity to tell the listeners who had prayed and sent cards and letters to me about the wonder-working power of our amazing God.

The best words to describe the reactions of those who knew me during the previous 16 years are "shock" and "awe." People who encounter me today, and who didn't know me then, have no reason to believe I was ever in that condition.

Barbara Snyder is a pastor's wife currently living in Fredericksburg, Virginia. She works full-time in real estate and lives a life rich in God's blessings (buyfrom barb@msn.com).

Healing Across the Airwaves

Mike Fisher, a hockey player with the Nashville Predators, was interviewed on the *700 Club*. He told of once having an earache that lasted for about a month. At the time, he was still playing with the Ottawa Senators.

While watching TV, Fisher heard hosts Pat Robertson and Terry Meeuwsen say during a prayer that someone was suffering from an ear infection in the left, inner ear. That sounded like his condition, so he joined in their prayer. By the time they had finished praying, Fisher's ear was healed.

He also said the pain never returned.[61]

"God Just Healed Me"
(VERN BOGARDUS WITH CAROLYN BOLZ)

I had been sick for a month with pneumonia and couldn't seem to recover, so I finally went to the emergency room. Within 48 hours, the doctors diagnosed me with acute leukemia, a cancer that weakens the immune system.

After two oncologists gave me only a 25 to 40 percent chance of survival, I thought of 1 Thessalonians 5:17, which tells us to pray without ceasing. I began to pray often.

Soon after my diagnosis, I began chemotherapy. My doctors had prescribed three rounds of a weeklong 24-hour-a-day intravenous treatment with a two-week rest period between each round. Two days after starting chemo in the hospital, I was praying when I felt a hand on my shoulder. I thought a nurse had come to wake me, but as I touched my shoulder, there was no hand.

I knew it had been the Lord.

Shortly after that experience, my pastor, Reverend Tim Klinkenberg, came to my hospital room.

"I know that God just healed me!" I told him.

The results of the next set of medical tests were nothing short of miraculous. After only a single chemo treatment, no cancer cells remained. I had the second treatment, but my oncologist waived the final round. Even he said, "That is impossible!"

Nine years have passed since I heard the grim diagnosis of leukemia, and I'm still cancer free.

Vern Bogardus grew up in Cleveland, Ohio. After graduating from high school, he joined the U.S. Navy and went through Officers' Training. He worked in finance for many years. Carolyn Bolz is a graduate of the University of California, Riverside. After working as a bilingual elementary school teacher for 25 years, she now enjoys public speaking as well as writing poetry and short stories.

Azusa Street Healings (1906)

Many historians view the Azusa Street Revival, which began on April 14, 1906, and lasted until 1915, as the primary catalyst for the growth of the Pentecostal movement in the twentieth century. A number of books and articles have been published about the events of that revival, including *They Told Me Their Stories: The Youth and Children of Azusa Street Tell Their Stories,* by Tom Welchel. The book is filled with rich, personal stories.

Dr. Yoakum had been struck by metal that extended from a buggy driven by a drunk. The impact broke several of his ribs and caused internal hemorrhaging. The injury was so severe he could have died from it. After several months, he still hadn't recovered.

The following year, Dr. Yoakum, almost in desperation, visited the Christian Alliance Church on Figueroa Street in Highland Park. Pastor W. C. Stevens prayed for him, and he was instantly healed.[62]

A woman whom Welchel refers to only as Sister Carney was used by God to heal many who suffered from physical ailments. One of those was Brother Aubrey, who wore heavy braces and hadn't walked in years. He came to her in his wheelchair.

Sister Carney didn't speak, but pulled up the footrests and put Brother Aubrey's feet on the floor. She told him to get up and walk. He protested that he couldn't because of the heavy braces. She told others to take off the braces. They did, and the lame man got up and walked—instantly healed.[63]

✦━❈❀❈━✦

When Brother Anderson was just 15 years old, God started using him to heal the sick. On one occasion, another teenage boy, who had a clubfoot, came to Anderson, who assured him that he could be healed.

> The young man finally believed a miracle was possible, and Brother Anderson began to pray for him. To their astonishment, shortly after the prayer, the foot didn't just pop out, but rather it . . . started to slowly move outward. In a matter of minutes, the young man was jumping, running, and shouting. The foot had been deformed since he was a young child, and it had just gotten worse as he had gotten older. Yet, [within, sic] a few minutes, the foot was healed and perfectly formed.[64]

✦━❈❀❈━✦

When Welchel was asked about the most unusual healing, he mentioned Diana, the mother of two young children. She had a growth on the side of her head "about half the size of a basketball."[65]

After Anderson and others laid hands on her, the tumor started shrinking before their eyes, and it didn't stop until she was healed.

Healings IN THE MINISTRY OF
Hilarion
(c. 291–371)

At the age of 15, Hilarion spent two months with Saint Anthony, who had a ministry to those suffering from disease or demonic affliction. As an adult, he lived a sparse, sometimes nomadic, life in the wilderness and eventually was sought after for his own healing ministry.

A woman from Eleutheropolis had been married for 15 years and had been unable to bear children. She felt that her husband despised her because of her sterility. When she came to Hilarion, she fell at his knees and begged, "Forgive my boldness; forgive my importunity. Why do you turn away your eyes? Why do you shun my pleas? Do not look upon me as a woman, but as a creature to be pitied, as one of the sex that brought forth the Redeemer, for 'they that are whole need not the physician: but they that are sick.'"

He asked her why she had come and why she was weeping. When he learned the cause of her grief, he prayed for her and told her to believe and to go home. A year later, Hilarion met the woman again, and she showed him her son.

From the Egyptian village of Facidia, a woman who had been blind for 10 years was brought to Hilarion for a blessing. She told the holy man that she had spent all her money on physicians and was still unable to see.

"If what you lost on physicians you had given to the poor, Jesus the true Physician would have healed you."

She begged him to have mercy on her. He rubbed spittle on her eyes and she was immediately cured.

A charioteer from Gaza was struck by a demon while in his chariot. His entire body was so completely stiffened that he couldn't move his hands or bend his neck. He was carried on a stretcher to Hilarion. The godly man said the soldier couldn't be healed unless he believed in Jesus and renounced his former occupation. The man believed and promised to leave the army. Just then he was healed, but he rejoiced more in the salvation of his soul than in the cure of his body.[66]

Multiple Tumors

(TIM ENGSTROM WITH FLORENCE BENNETT ROBB)

"Is there anything else we need to talk about?" Dr. Tom Flaming asked on January 16, 2008, as he ended our review of a medical test taken six months earlier.

"I have a persistent cough, usually when I talk or I'm in the cold air," I said.

I pulled up my shirt. After listening to my lungs, Dr. Flaming said, "I want you to go over to the hospital right now. I'm ordering an X-ray on your chest."

That Friday afternoon, he ordered a CT scan for Monday morning.

Two days later, he called me with the results. "I've reviewed the CT scan with the radiologist. We're looking at multiple tumors. Three are very large." Before I could reply, he said, "I've arranged for you to see a pulmonologist."

Both my son, with whom I had been visiting, and I were stunned, but we decided not to call my wife, Diane, at work. When I gave her the news that evening, she was also shocked.

The next day, we met with Dr. Shultz, the pulmonologist, who placed the X-rays in the light box and went to retrieve the CT scan report. Diane and I looked at the X-rays, noting 22 circles and arrows. Several circles were large; one in the lower left lung looked as large as an organ. I assumed it was my heart.

Dr. Shultz explained the X-rays. "The circles are tumors identified by the radiologist." He sent me to see an oncologist.

When we met with Dr. Flaming again, he said, "I believe we are looking at non-Hodgkin's lymphoma. Cancer. This is as bad as it gets. I'm so sorry."

We left the clinic shortly afterward and sat in my pickup for a while. That's when the news really hit me. I started to weep. "I'm not going to live much longer."

Later, our daughters, Annalisa and Allison, and our son-in-law, Nathan, came to our house. We also invited a few friends over for prayer. Nothing spectacular happened. The next day, our pastor, Robert Flores, came to pray with us.

I went back to the hospital and underwent a series of tests and surgical biopsies. The findings baffled the doctors.

"There are tumors but no cancer cells," Dr. Shultz said. He ordered a CT scan on March 14. Diane requested that the results be sent to our friend, Dr. John Currie, a dermatologist.

On March 18, I was at home when Dr. Currie called after reading the radiologist's report, in which they reported the current measurements of the tumors and compared them with the January X-rays. He read the measurements of the large tumor in the bottom of the left lung (the one that was the size of a grapefruit) and the radiologist's note: "The mass has resolved."

"What does that mean?"

"That means it's gone," Dr. Currie said.

"How can that be?"

"Divine intervention," he replied calmly. "It's a miracle."

Five other tumors were also gone, and the large tumor in the upper left lung had *decreased in size.*

Additional X-rays followed on April 24, at West Valley Hospital in Dallas. After reading those X-rays, Dr. Currie called again.

"More of the tumors are gone," he said. "Only 12 remain."

Two of the masses in my right lung had grown considerably larger, but I was still elated as I trusted the Lord's healing power.

The next CT scan was scheduled for June 3. After a visit with Dr. Shultz and still more tests, the radiologist said, "Your doctor will call you tonight with the results."

He didn't call. Not on Wednesday and not on Thursday.

On Friday, Diane called the clinic four times. The receptionist finally told her that Dr. Shultz needed to consult with the radiologist again before he spoke with her.

At 5:45 that evening, he called. "I have the report from the radiologist from your June 3 CT scan. It is a comparison report of the scan in March. All of your tumors are resolved."

"Resolved? All of them? You mean they're completely gone?"

"Yes. A small remnant of the large tumor in the upper left lung remains, as is expected," he said as he continued his report. "Two small tumors remain in the upper right lung where the two large ones were. They have decreased in size—too tiny to biopsy, and they will probably resolve."

"Is there any scarring from surgery?" I asked. "And the tumor is still in the upper left?"

"Yes. But the phenomenon here is that we're not seeing significant scarring."

"How do you explain that?"

"You're getting better. Congratulations!"

"I mean, how do you explain the absence of cancer, pain, and all the tumors and scars in so short a time—in only six months?"

"There is no explanation."

"I truly believe God healed me."

"That's the explanation then."

"Would you say, Doctor, this is a verifiable healing?"

"Yes, I would have to."

After I hung up, a flood of emotion flowed over me. Rather than feeling elation and joy, I wept with deep sobs of relief and gratitude.

The report for a follow-up X-ray in March 2009 was written to Dr. Flaming and was four pages long.

Under "Findings" were these words: "Multiple masses scattered throughout the chest all appear to have resolved. There are no visible stigmata of surgical intervention."

Even the scarring—the so-called permanent damage—was gone. Under "Impressions" were these words: "No visible recurrence of lung masses; chest essentially normal."

Reverend Tim Engstrom grew up in a ministry family. Tim and his wife, Diane, met at Briercrest Bible College in Canada and married in 1976. They served in Christian camps and churches in Nebraska, Wyoming, Montana, and Oregon. Tim has served with the Salvation Army for the past 15 years (timanddiane@live.com). Florence Bennett Robb was born and raised in the Salvation Army. Now retired from full-time service, she is still a member of the Salvation Army (fbennettrobb2008@hotmail.com).

Dare to Believe
(FRANKLIN BLODGETT)

In October 1978, Herb Mjorud, an evangelist and author of a book titled *Dare to Believe,* came to speak at our church in Ketchikan, Alaska. On the first night of his meetings, many people came forward to receive Christ as their Savior, and also to get prayer for physical needs.

Herb prayed for a woman with back problems. After a while, he stopped praying for her and said, "I don't think your back is the problem. Do you have a short leg?" She told him she did. "That's your problem," Herb said. "You're putting stress on your back because you're out of alignment with the short leg."

Herb prayed for her again—and her leg grew an inch and a half. I'd never seen anything like that.

My wife, Bonnie, and I were hosting Herb in our home during his time at our church. The next day, as we sat in our living room by the fireplace, I pointed to my built-up shoe and told him how in January of 1968, while flying on my five-hundred and twentieth combat mission in Vietnam, I was shot with an armor-piercing bullet from an AK-47. The bullet went through my right femur, my kneeboard, and across my right wrist. I stayed in the Great Lakes Naval Hospital for almost eight months recovering.

As a result of the combat wound, my leg was an inch shorter, and I couldn't move it more than 90 degrees. After three different physicals, I was told I had 50 percent disability for life.

"I have a short leg, but I don't want you to pray for it because I get tax-free money," I said. "It doesn't affect my work in a negative manner." Herb understood because his brother had a disability from World War II.

During the same series of meetings, our pastor, Arne Halvorson, said, "I think the Lord wants to heal you more than He wants your money." He and others prayed for my healing. As they prayed, my leg grew—I could see and feel it.

"Don't forget to pray for the missing movement," Bonnie said. As they prayed, I started swinging my leg until I could bend it the same as the one that had not been shot.

I bought new shoes, threw away the built-up ones, and went to the doctor.

My job as a pilot in the Department of Public Safety required me to have a physical every year. Dr. Wilson in Ketchikan examined me and said, "The legs are the same size now. You didn't fall on the other leg, did you?"

I assured him I didn't. He wrote in my file, "Leg the same size now," and followed the statement with multiple exclamation points.

I reported my healing to the VA because of the money I received. "Jesus healed me," I said.

They set me up with Dr. Shields, a former flight surgeon and an orthopedist, who took X-rays, made dots on my legs, and measured between them. He showed me the results.

On the X-ray, I could see where the armor-piercing bullet had broken my femur. It was darker and thicker. "With this type of injury, your leg should be shorter, and you shouldn't have the movement you do," Dr. Shields said. "How do you explain it?"

"We prayed that Jesus would lengthen my leg, and apparently He's done that. We prayed that the Lord would restore my movement, and He's done that as well."

I asked to see the deposits on my knee. "That's why I was put in for disability in the first place."

The doctor pointed to that area. "The deposits are gone, except for one the size of a pinhead."

God did a wonderful work in my life when He grew out my leg. But that's not all He did.

Bonnie and I had been married many years, but had not had children. One day, while waiting at the airport for my flight to take off, I took out the New Testament with Psalms that I carried in my uniform pocket. I turned to Psalm 113, and when I got to verse nine I read, "He gives the childless woman a family, making her a happy mother."

Nine months after I was healed of my combat wounds, Bonnie gave birth to our firstborn, Rachel Joy. Two years later, our son, Daniel Joel, was born.

Chaplain Franklin Blodgett has been a USMCR pilot, a Fish and Wildlife Officer, a pastor, a CAP chaplain, and a prison chaplain for Alaska Correctional Ministries (revfnb@msn.com).

A Hindu Has Faith for Healing
(ELAINE WRIGHT COLVIN)

On September 2, 2012, at the end of a worship service, Pastor Irwin Chebrole of Gethsemane House of Prayer in Kompally, India, came to me. "A Hindu woman from the village just walked into our church to ask for prayer. Would you pray for her?"

Immediately my traveling companion, Theresia, and I followed Pastor Irwin over to a quiet corner of the sanctuary. The woman was trembling and crying. A wide-eyed nine-year-old daughter stood by her side.

"What would you like me to pray for?" I asked as Pastor Irwin interpreted.

"My husband is very ill at the hospital, and the doctors say he must have gallbladder surgery in the morning."

I told her I would pray for him and his healing in the name of Jesus, the great Physician. "Will that be okay?"

She mumbled yes and nodded through her tears.

I held her hands and prayed for her husband and for the peace of the family, while Pastor Irwin and Theresia laid hands on her head and shoulder, praying along in agreement.

I gave her a long hug before Pastor Irwin and two women led her to the front yard of the church for the "love feast" meal they were serving.

Soon her mobile phone rang. It was her husband calling from the hospital.

Her tears turned to tears of joy, as she'd never expected to be able talk to him again. She left, saying she had never experienced such compassion and interest in her and her husband.

When Pastor Irwin and a church elder, Mani, visited the hospital the next day, the doctors told the men to wait a minute while they went to read the reports of their patient's latest tests.

The doctors returned and told the husband, "There is no need for surgery. You appear to be well and can go home now."

The woman was so happy, she told everyone in the Indian government hospital emergency room that we had prayed and God had healed her husband.

The people lined up immediately, asking the men to pray for their healing for a wide variety of diseases. Pastor Irwin and Mani were there for well over three hours, praying for many sick Hindu and Muslim patients and their families.

"She Won't Survive"

(MICHELLE AVERY KUBIAK WITH SUSAN D. AVERY)

I was eight years old, alone in a hospital room. My body had been ravaged by a bone marrow transplant and chemotherapy—treatments for aplastic anemia. A nurse came in to cheer me up, but I was exhausted after several bouts of vomiting. She laid a cool washcloth on my bald head—all my lovely little blond curls were gone. Then she left me alone again.

I thought of the words of my doctor: "We have attempted this transplant several times over the past four years, and no one has survived."

Although I was too young to understand all of this at the time, the doctor gave me only three months to live without the transplant. Yet they didn't want to do the transplant, because no one who had gone through the procedure had survived. With or without the transplant, I was not expected to live.

I wasn't only sick and in pain, but I also felt alone and afraid. Earlier I had overheard the doctor tell my parents that I wasn't doing well. He had also said something about liver problems and my kidneys shutting down—again, I didn't understand everything he said. I lay as quietly as I could, closed my eyes, and prayed. My parents believed in God and taught me that God loves me.

Someone came into the room. At first I thought my parents had returned, scrubbed up, and were gowned. But I looked up and saw a man—someone I hadn't seen before. He wore no gown or mask and didn't have on gloves. He looked at me, and—as strange as it may sound—I felt that he looked at me with love. He sat on the bed next to me.

I knew the man was Jesus, although I couldn't explain it. As he looked at me, I thought he had come to take me to heaven.

He smiled and said, "I have not come to take you home. You have work to do here. Be brave and strong and know that I am always with you."

"I'm scared."

"It's all right. Everything is going to be all right. You'll get through this." He bent down and kissed me lightly on the forehead, turned, and left the room.

Almost immediately, my parents came in through the other door to my hospital room.

"Did you see him? See that man?"

"We didn't see anyone," Mom said.

Less than an hour after that event, my organs began shutting down, and my blood pressure was at stroke level. The doctor brought in other professionals, and they agreed I wouldn't make it through the night.

My parents watched and prayed. I had told them about Jesus coming into my room, and they believed me. They prayed for Jesus to touch me again.

Around six o'clock in the morning, the nurse checked my blood pressure, which had dropped significantly. That meant I was better. The doctors ordered more tests. My parents later told me that I stirred a little—my first movement since the medical emergency.

When my parents decided to get breakfast, Mom leaned over, kissed me, and whispered, "We'll be back in half an hour. Hang on to Jesus."

My overjoyed parents stood outside the window of my room, talking to the doctors. They were crying and hugging each other. The doctors told them what I already knew: I had been healed of my aplastic anemia.

That made me the first patient to have a successful transplant for aplastic anemia at Egleston Children's Hospital in Atlanta. Even today, my doctor calls me a miracle and says that he was "a hammer in the Carpenter's hand."

Michelle Avery Kubiak holds a BGS in Marine Biology and an MAT in Elementary Education. She is co-owner of Oh Sew Fabulous Monogramming and Specialty Gifts. See http://www.ohsewfabulous.net. Susan D. Avery, a freelance writer with a BS in Religion and Education, is the co-founder of Bluesun Ministries with her husband, Bill. See http://www.bluesunministries.com/Susan-Avery.html.

A Yearlong Journey
(JAN VIPPERMAN)

Early in 2007, I began a yearlong journey of multiple episodes of diverticulitis. That journey included emergency room visits, hospitalizations, IV antibiotics, oral antibiotics, and visits to Mayo Clinic. I struggled with fear, knowing that if I had surgery, it could be complicated. When my brother had surgery for diverticulitis, he nearly died.

I prayed for healing, and as I prayed, I visualized God's hands knitting each pouch of diverticulitis back to wholeness. I shared my situation with my small groups, and the members of each group laid hands on me and prayed for me.

During many sleepless nights, I got up and read my Bible. One morning at about four o'clock, I felt impressed to go to Exodus 15:26, where God says, "If you will listen carefully to the voice of the Lord your God and do what is right in his sight, obeying his commands and keeping all his decrees, then I will not make you suffer any of the diseases I sent on the Egyptians; for I am the Lord who heals you."

I considered that a message directly from God. At first I thought it meant that He was going to heal me exactly the way I wanted Him to, and I was excited. But time passed and nothing changed. The episodes continued. My frustrations returned. I talked about that experience with my small groups.

One Tuesday at the meeting, our small-group leader, Diane, said, "I have something I feel I need to share with you. It's a tough teaching." She read the passage, beginning in 2 Corinthians 12:7, that talks about the thorn in Paul's side—some type of affliction he suffered with. She reminded us that Paul asked God three times to heal him, and each time God responded with: "My grace is all you need. My power works best in weakness" (v. 9).

Diane encouraged me not to think I was being punished, or that I wasn't praying well enough, long enough or often enough. "Maybe you're not trusting God to work in His own way. Maybe He has a different plan than yours."

My prayer life changed after that. I began to thank God for the healing that was coming. I asked Him for clear discernment about what to do. I praised Him with a grateful heart. Early one morning, when I couldn't sleep, I got up to read God's Word, and I noticed that for once I felt peaceful. I wasn't afraid.

I went back to my doctor to discuss surgery, thinking that's what God wanted me to do. My doctor looked at my charts and said, "You're not a good candidate for surgery. It would require removal of your entire colon."

He hadn't mentioned that to me during previous visits. My fear came back, anxiety and doubt returned, and I knew surgery wasn't the answer.

I searched for a surgeon who was a specialist in gastrointestinal surgery and who knew how to treat diverticulitis. I wanted someone who used less invasive procedures. When I discovered the head of GI surgery at Duke University Hospital, well-meaning people told me that I probably wouldn't be able to get an appointment with him for months. Yet within 10 days I had my first appointment, saw the doctor, scheduled and completed a Barium X-ray to show him exactly where the diverticulitis was, and came back for the follow-up/pre-surgery visit.

During the X-ray, I could see my insides on a screen. I knew the way they had looked before, because I saw my internal organs on a movie-theater-type screen at the Mayo Clinic. *That doesn't look like me*, I thought.

Later, the radiologist met me in the hall and said, "You know, you really have a pretty colon." I didn't know if she was trying to be funny, cheer me up, or what. It didn't make much sense.

While I waited in the surgeon's office for the results, he reviewed my medical records spread on the table in front of him, crossed his arms, turned to look me in the eyes, and said, "You don't have diverticulitis."

He agreed with the diagnosis from the scans taken previously. "You *did* have diverticulitis, but you don't have it now and you don't need surgery. I can't explain it to you scientifically or medically."

"You don't need to explain it," I said. "I want to thank you, because you are part of God's plan that resulted in a miraculous healing. I'm grateful."

Jan Vipperman lives in Chapel Hill, North Carolina, where she and her husband, Tom, operate their own consulting business, ActSixHR (Jan.Vipperman@act sixhr.com).

Healings IN THE MINISTRY OF
Lester Sumrall
(1913–1996)

Diagnosed with tuberculosis when he was a teenager, Lester Sumrall said God gave him a choice between dying and preaching. Sumrall chose to preach. He and his wife, Louise, saw many healings take place through their work overseas as missionaries, as well as through the Lester Sumrall Evangelistic Association's radio and television ministry.

❖ Headhunters in Luzon ❖

Elva Vanderbout Soriano, a mission worker among the headhunters of the Mountain Province in Northern Luzon, Philippines, needed help in her work to evangelize the Igorot people. She sent pictures of tribe members to Sumrall and asked him to join her in spreading the gospel to the headhunters.

Sumrall came, and Soriano showed him a map of the vast mountain region and explained the hardships of travel and what he would face with the nationals. The fierce and violent headhunters lived in the upper mountain ranges and dwelt in thatched huts. Sumrall went to parts of the mountains that few Christians had seen.

Leonardo, one of Soriano's trusted Igorot students, volunteered as a guide and interpreter. They brought several boxes of food and clothes to give to the people. They traveled by jeep as far as they could, and then had to climb by foot and crawl the remaining distance deep into the jungles.

On the evening of their arrival, Leonardo called the people together, and the team distributed the gifts and food they had brought. Leonardo translated Sumrall's message to the people about Jesus the Savior.

The witch doctor angrily dispersed the people who had gathered. A sick young girl lay on a mat in the middle of the circle while the chieftain cried out to their pagan gods and to their ancestors. Several times, he unsuccessfully tried to raise her arms. Each time, when he released the arms, they fell limply back to the mat.

Sumrall knelt beside the girl. Through Leonardo, he told her that those gods couldn't heal her, and her ancestors had no power. He came to tell her about a new God—Jesus—who could heal her body and her soul. He promised that after he prayed for her, she would receive new life and strength.

Sumrall prayed for a witness to the people so that by God healing the sick girl, the tribe would convert to Christianity. To the girl, he said, "I command you to get up in Jesus' name."

He held onto her arms and helped her stand. Her eyes opened and she stood on her own. She was completely healed.

The chieftain stood by and watched, now disappointed with his dead gods. He made it obvious that he had no further use for them by burning pieces of ceremonial wood in front of the whole group.[67]

❖ Mother Healed of Breast Cancer ❖

When Sumrall was a boy, his mother, Betty, had breast cancer. She had an open sore about the size of a silver dollar. Because of the pain, many nights she cried herself to sleep.

In those days, shortly after World War I, surgeons didn't have the techniques or medications that modern doctors use. Her doctor said that if he attempted to remove the cancer, she would die. He dressed the sore and kept it clean.

One night, Betty walked the floor most of the night, crying to God for relief from her pain. Just before sunrise, she fell exhausted across her bed and went to sleep.

Sumrall's mother dreamed that Jesus walked into her bedroom and looked at her with compassion. He tenderly touched her chest. After she awakened, she told Sumrall's father, George, about the dream. He was skeptical.

A few days later, George asked about her pain. Betty said she had "almost forgotten about the cancer." She added, "The pain is gone."

Later, when Betty went into the bedroom, "the cancer . . . dropped off her body." Betty Sumrall lived more than 40 years after that healing. She died at the age of 87 from natural causes.[68]

✣ Grandfather's Stroke ✣

Sumrall's maternal grandfather, Chandler, lived in Hattiesburg, Mississippi. Chandler went downtown on business one day, and while he was walking along the street, he suffered a stroke and fell to the sidewalk.

The stroke was so severe that it paralyzed both legs, both arms, his speech, and his bowels. Betty wanted to call for church members to pray, but other family members overruled her and sent Chandler to the hospital.

Because of a train wreck, the hospital was filled with emergency patients. But the doctor did go out to the car with Betty. After examining Chandler, the doctor told Betty that her father was near death. She should take him home and make him comfortable.

After that, no one objected to Betty calling Christians to pray. Next door lived a young man named Campbell, who was not a believer. He scoffed when he learned that the church people were praying for Chandler.

The next morning, Chandler awakened completely healed. When his family showed their shock, he said, "Didn't you pray for me? Didn't you ask God to give me a miracle?"

According to Sumrall, Chandler got up, dressed himself, walked into the kitchen, ate a big breakfast, and later walked outside. The neighbor, Campbell, saw him and tearfully apologized to Betty for how he had spoken the day before. He said seeing the old man made him realize that God does answer prayer. He asked Betty to pray for him.

Sumrall's Grandpa Chandler "lived a strong and vigorous life for thirty-two years after that without ever having another stroke."[69]

❖ The Woman with a New Tongue ❖

Lester Sumrall met Mrs. Williams several times while he was living in England. She told him her story of healing and appeared in several of his meetings. (She had not been healed in Sumrall's meetings, but was there to give hope to others who needed prayer for their bodies.)

Mrs. Williams had had a sore on her tongue, which festered and grew steadily worse. A surgeon in Liverpool diagnosed it as cancer and prescribed surgery at the local hospital. Her tongue was cut off at the base. For 12 years, Mrs. Williams lived without a tongue and without the ability to speak. She communicated with her husband, children and neighbors by writing words on a pad of paper.

In the town of Walstow, where she lived, Mrs. Williams was well-known as "the woman without a tongue."

One night she attended a revival meeting. She had a bad cold that night and went up to have the evangelist pray for her. When the evangelist asked, "What do you want?" she suddenly realized that she had left her pad and pencil back at her seat and was unable to tell him. She pointed to her mouth.

This is the way Sumrall describes the event (even though he wasn't present): Laying his hands upon her head the evangelist prayed, "O God, give this lady the desire of her heart." As he prayed Mrs. Williams began to choke. Something began to move in the back of her throat. Right there on the platform, a new tongue formed in her mouth. She began to speak, to the delight and amazement of the local citizens who knew her.[70]

❖ The Healing of a Chinese Girl ❖

For several years, Sumrall and his family lived in Manila, Philippines. Dr. and Mrs. Go Puan Seng related the terrible sickness of their teenage daughter, Marcy. (Dr. Go was editor and publisher of the *Fookien Times,* the largest Chinese-language newspaper outside of China.)

Marcy's problem started when she began dieting to lose weight. As she dieted, her personality slowly began to change. Previously she had played the piano, but now she banged it violently with her fists. Her temper became such that she was extremely difficult to live with. On one occasion, while playing with her cat, she became so violent that she choked her pet to death.

Marcy's parents, being wealthy, called on the best doctors to treat her. Nothing helped. Marcy's diet seemed out of control, and she continued losing weight until she dropped to 64 pounds. To keep her alive, doctors fed her intravenously.

Mr. Go invited Sumrall to a party with about 200 employees of the newspaper plant present. Sumrall met Marcy, who was so emaciated she hardly looked human. She had not eaten solid food for three months. Marcy roamed around the house and garden, often raging like a maniac. Mr. Go asked Sumrall to pray for his daughter.

Sumrall sensed the need for *special* prayer, so he promised to fast and pray for two days—and then he would return to minister to her. To his own surprise, Sumrall added, "Prepare a special meal for her. When I am through praying, Marcy is going to eat."

Sumrall spent the next two days in fasting and prayer for Marcy's healing. Early on the third morning, he returned to the Go estate. The girl yelled that she wouldn't see him. She hid from him.

The Gos apologized and said Marcy refused to see him. Sumrall said he had fasted and prayed, and he was ready. He asked for permission to find Marcy and pray for her.

They gave Sumrall permission to find her, but they warned, "She is dangerous. . . . She may try to harm you."

He persuaded them to let him pray. Alone, he went through the house and found Marcy in the unlighted basement. Sumrall touched her back and said gently, "I have come to pray for you."

Marcy jumped up and tried to slash him with a butcher knife. Sumrall grabbed her tiny wrists "just as the knife touched the front of [his] shirt," and he held tightly enough to force her to drop the knife.

Sumrall rebuked the demon spirits that bound the poor girl and ordered them to come out in the name of Jesus. For about an hour, the spiritual struggle continued before he felt a divine release.

Marcy was set free, and Sumrall embraced the girl and talked to her about God's love. He stressed that Jesus had set her free. Marcy's personality changed dramatically, and she was like her former self. Before long, she was ready to eat.

The Gos had ordered a caterer to bring out an enormous banquet with a dozen courses of food. Marcy began to eat and then stopped. She said she was going to vomit everything.

Sumrall laid his hand on her and asked God to "open these intestines, create and multiply the digestive juices, and let this stomach settle." They continued the meal with no further problems. Marcy remained healed.[71]

❖ "Take Three Deep Breaths" ❖

Jean Kincaid was 25 years old and suffered from frequent chest pains that "radiated down [her] left arm." She was aware that the pain was connected to her heart.

One night at a meeting, Sumrall said there were three people in the audience who suffered with chest pain.

After Kincaid stood, Sumrall pointed to her. "You, lady in the blue suit—take three deep breaths. You will never again experience that pain."

She did as he instructed, and the pain disappeared. It never returned.[72]

The Doctor Is on Vacation

(LINDA K. RODANTE)

The gynecology exam room had a painted lizard on the ceiling, about two feet long. I had studied its form for the last couple of minutes. The doctor's hands continued to probe. He pressed my lower abdomen. His face told me nothing, but his hands activated a voice inside me.

I grunted as his fingers jabbed again. "Anything wrong, doctor?"

He turned, pulled off his gloves, tossed them into the red trash receptacle, and looked back at me. "You're not in any pain?"

"No."

"Your left ovary is the size of a grapefruit."

I stared mutely. An ovary is normally the size of a walnut.

I knew I should have some questions for the doctor. He seemed to expect me to speak, but I was too shocked to say anything.

"I'm scheduled to leave for vacation on Monday," he said, "but I want you in for an ultrasound on Monday. We'll see what this is before I go."

"Good. I have until Monday," I said. "I'll go for prayer before I come."

"You do that."

After I left the doctor's office, I reminded myself that God had done a miracle in my life when I gave birth to our first son. Justin had aspirated pneumonia, and the doctors told me for four days that he would probably die. "He won't make it through another night," they said. On the fifth day, they released him. I took him home. He's been fine ever since. God's grace and healing were part of our lives.

I told no one but my husband, and on Sunday, at the end of the church service, many of us went up for prayer. My church congregation believes that God still heals today. Elders pray for whoever comes forward.

I told one of the elders what the doctor had said. He grabbed a small vial of oil, rubbed a drop on my forehead, and began to pray—a short plea for God to give me comfort and to heal me.

Others from the congregation gathered around, put their hands on my back, and prayed. I felt peace—but no sense of being healed.

Monday morning I had the ultrasound. After the procedure, they sent me home and told me the doctor would be in touch. I waited all day Monday and Tuesday but heard nothing. Early

Wednesday, I called my doctor's office. After I explained the situation to the receptionist, she put me on hold.

When she came back to the phone, she sounded impatient and in a hurry. "The doctor's on vacation."

"But he said he wasn't going until they did my ultrasound."

"Yes, and they did that Monday."

"But what was the result? He said my ovary was as big as a grapefruit."

"The ultrasound showed that it wasn't."

"It wasn't? But he could feel it."

"Yes, but you're fine. That's why he left on vacation. Nothing to worry about. He'll see you in a year."

"A year?"

"Yes, for your annual checkup."

"But—"

"We'll send you a reminder."

After I set the phone down, I stood still for a moment. Warmth and joy and excitement swept through me. "Thank you, Jesus!" I grinned and laughed. "Now, Lord, whom should I tell?"

Linda Rodante worked as a center director with the Pregnancy Center of Pinellas County, Florida. Today, she works at Trinity College of Florida and speaks for Clearwater's "Community Campaign Against Human Trafficking." See linda rodante.wordpress.com.

A Serious Back Injury
(CINDY ADAMS)

"There's no other option." The doctor studied his clipboard then looked at Nelson. "You're on the largest dosage of pain pills I can give you. They're not working for you."

My husband bit his lower lip. "Is it guaranteed the surgery will work?"

"I can't promise 100 percent—there's always that slim chance it doesn't work or something goes wrong."

What if something goes wrong? Back surgery could leave him crippled. Panic came over me and I could hardly think of anything except what might go wrong. *God, you're our last option for a miracle. Please heal him so he won't need surgery.*

Two months earlier, a car accident had left Nelson with a debilitating back injury. Tests revealed a herniated disk that supported the physician's advice that medication would no longer work. Day after day, out of work and on disability, Nelson lay on the couch while his spirits sank lower.

The news we received left us with little hope. Neither of us said much that evening. Nelson retired early. I wasn't tired—just scared.

I turned on the TV as I settled myself on the couch, not really caring what was on. As I flipped through channels, I paused at Pat Robertson's show. He was praying.

As I listened to Pat's prayer—he was praying for the healing of someone's back injury—I joined in with fervent pleas of my own and continued to pray for two hours after the program ended.

The following morning, Nelson slowly made his way from the bedroom to the living room. He clicked on the remote and eased himself down on the couch.

"How are you feeling this morning?" I asked him.

"I don't feel as stiff as I usually do in the mornings," Nelson said. "But I still can't function like this much longer."

Any improvement is good. Thank You, God.

I determined to pray without ceasing—desperately calling on God for His healing power. I prayed that morning in the shower. During the day, I knelt by my bed. In the evening, I stayed up by myself for two more hours of prayer.

The next morning, I anxiously waited for any positive feedback. "How do you feel this morning?" I smiled at Nelson with hopeful anticipation as he walked into the kitchen.

"I'm feeling better than yesterday." Nelson made his own coffee and gave me a kiss on the lips. "The pressure seems to be letting up."

"I want you to know I've been praying—a lot—for your healing."

I continued to pray several times every day. Each morning, my husband felt a little better than he had the day before.

As the days and weeks passed, I persevered in daily heartfelt prayer and tried to be patient as I observed Nelson's slow recovery. After several months, he went back to the doctor.

"I'm releasing you to go back to work," the doctor said. "It's a miracle—you healed on your own."

I smiled at my husband and he took my hand, squeezed it, and winked at me.

Chills ran through my body. Both of us knew Nelson hadn't been healed on his own.

Cindy Adams resides in Duluth, Georgia. Widowed at age 34, she went to college and obtained a LMSW degree in social work. She writes a weekly blog, www.widowspursuits.blogspot.com, and has recently written a memoir about pursuing her faith, achieving her goals, and finding new purpose after loss.

"He'll Never Walk Again"
(MAX ELLIOT ANDERSON)

No one in the Baby Boom generation can easily forget the polio epidemic that ravaged the United States when we were kids. Almost everyone knew a friend, relative or neighbor who contracted the dreaded disease. Not even President Franklin D. Roosevelt was spared. For me, polio became personal when Anita, a girl in our neighborhood, came down with it.

Because no one knew how polio spread, parents were terrified. We weren't allowed to play with our friends, go swimming, or spend time around groups of people.

My oldest sister began experiencing some of the symptoms, which included fever, headache, stiffness and sore throat. My parents rushed her to a hospital where the diagnosis came back quickly.

Polio.

I grew up in a family of seven children, so the likelihood that more of us might also be infected remained high. Not long after my sister was hospitalized, my older brother began complaining of stiffness. Polio struck our family for the second time.

Most adults would have to search their memory banks to remember anything that happened when they turned three years old. But memories of the time around my third birthday couldn't be any clearer in my mind.

One morning, I found it difficult to swallow. It also hurt to turn my head from side to side. But I pretended nothing was wrong.

My mother saw it quite differently. "Are you okay?" she asked.

I moaned in response, "Uh-huh." Thoughts of my sister, brother and Anita raced through my mind. I, too, was hurried off to the hospital that would become my home for the next few months.

We were confined inside an isolation ward filled to overflowing. My four-year-old brother and I were allowed to stay close together in crib-like metal beds. Treatment each day included time in an iron lung to help our breathing, and baths in a metal tub of hot, swirling water. Our parents could visit us only two days a week. Each time they came, they brought my brother and me a new toy.

Of the three cases in our family, mine was the most severe. The doctor put his arm on my mother's shoulder and said, "I'm sorry to tell you, but Max will never walk again."

My mother wept.

From 1942 to 1955, polio infected hundreds of thousands of victims from all ages and walks of life. Many either died or became crippled for life. The area around Muskegon, Michigan, where we lived, was especially hard hit by that epidemic.

My father was involved in various ministry and writing activities that included working with Billy Graham. A Billy Graham Crusade took place in Los Angeles between September 25 and November 20, 1949. My birthday was on November 3. Dad sent a telegram to Graham telling him that three of his seven children had been infected with the terrible, crippling disease. The report came back by telegram that Graham had stopped his crusade meeting for a few moments and asked the entire crowd to join him in prayer for the Anderson children.

The healing of my sister, brother and me came soon after. The doctor who had given my mother such a devastating diagnosis was particularly surprised by my dramatic recovery.

Ever since those childhood experiences, when I see someone wearing leg braces, using crutches, or in a wheelchair, I offer a silent prayer of thanks because, not only can I walk, but I also have no other lasting effects that would indicate polio had ever entered my body.

Using his extensive experience in film, video and television commercial production, Max Elliot Anderson writes adventures and mysteries for readers aged 8-13. See http://booksandboys.blogspot.com.

Healings IN THE MINISTRY OF
Charles S. Price
(1887–1947)

After having been a pastor for more than 10 years, in 1921, Dr. Charles S. Price attended a meeting led by Aimee Semple McPherson in San Jose, California. Price returned to his home church and shared what he had experienced, and the news spread about healings under Dr. Price. He founded a new congregation, Lodi Bethel Temple, and traveled and preached in a number of foreign countries. Many were healed through his ministry.

❖ Price Confounds the Skeptics ❖

From April 8-29, 1923, Price held meetings in Victoria, British Columbia, Canada, in a newly constructed hockey rink that seated nearly 10,000 people. They estimated that more than a quarter-million people attended the services, and that Price prayed for at least 5,000 people.

On April 17, Price prayed for Reverend W. J. Knott, who was seated on the platform. Knott had a large goiter and had suffered with it for a decade. It was clearly visible for everyone to see. Knott also suffered from palpitations of the heart and intense headaches resulting from severe eye problems.

Price prayed for the afflicted man. While Knott sat on the platform, the people watched the goiter shrink until it totally disappeared. Knott also said that the heart palpitations stopped and his eye problems were cured.

A month later, Knott reported that he could eat any kind of food, slept like a baby, and could read fine print without glasses.[73]

❖ The Healing of Ruby Dimmick ❖

Ruby Dimmick was the 21-year-old daughter of J. F. Dimmick, pastor of the Wesley Methodist Church in Victoria, British Columbia, Canada. At the age of 13, Ruby's spine had begun to curve, until it drew up her right leg about an inch and a half. Surgeons in Toronto operated, but were unable to lengthen the leg.

For eight years, Ruby wore a built-up shoe with a three-inch heel and walked by using a cane.

Ruby was sitting beside her father in the pew, quite a distance from the pulpit from which Price preached. But as he spoke, she was touched by the healing power of God. Her right leg lengthened, and she ran excitedly down the aisle.[74]

❖ New Organs Created ❖

An Anglican clergyman and his wife attended one of Price's meetings in Saskatoon, Manitoba, Canada. The wife had had an operation "in which the organs in her body had been removed" (which was probably a euphemism for a hysterectomy, because she wasn't able to bear a child).

She had prayed for a baby, but doctors assured the woman she would never bear a child. After Price prayed for her, she became pregnant and bore a child. "The organs MUST have grown back. There can be no other explanation. This was the testimony given to us from the lips of that minister who now believed in and practiced divine healing with all his heart."[75]

A Message of Hope

(DON PIPER)

I believe that God is doing some of His best stuff now! I've stood in too many hospital hallways and heard doctors remark incredulously, "We've done this test several times. We can't find the tumor now! It's just gone!" I've seen too many broken relationships restored, personal and/or financial catastrophes overcome. I have spoken to hundreds of congregations and other groups.

At one such occasion, I met parents whose son clung to life in a nearby hospital. This was the first time they had left him. They came to hear a message of hope that night from a man who had experienced miracles. We prayed for their boy in the lobby of that church.

Two years later at another speaking engagement, the same couple, faces beaming with delight, moved aside as they approached me to reveal their son walking and smiling, just like the doctors said he never would. Yes, I believe in miracles. I am one, and so was their precious son.[76]

Don Piper is the author or co-author of four books, including the *New York Times* bestseller, *90 Minutes in Heaven*. See www.DonPiperMinistries.com.

"Deafness Be Gone"

(PATTI RICHTER)

A sneeze sent a burst of air through my left ear. Bothersome noises, like clanging, let me know something wasn't right. More worrisome, my hearing seemed diminished. I didn't go to my doctor about it, though. I assumed my ear would heal—like it did when I'd had ear infections as a child.

I'd outgrown the childhood infections, but my left ear still seemed prone to trouble. I'd been accidently kicked in that ear while swimming as a kid. That caused a ruptured eardrum.

I was a mother, and I could hear my young children. But when I watched television, I turned my right ear toward the screen. At church, I strained to hear the pastor's sermons.

One night I sat in bed, enjoying *Reader's Digest.* The magazine sometimes included a questionnaire related to health or marriage. I usually skimmed over those to get to the stories. However, that issue's questionnaire was on hearing loss, so I answered the questions, hoping to dispel my fear. Instead, the results strongly recommended further tests.

I didn't want to believe my problem could be serious. I could hear well enough—out of my right ear anyway.

At church, the bulletin announced a guest preacher coming that evening. Our casual Sunday night service usually included a family time of sharing testimonies or having Bible quiz games with the kids. A guest speaker would be something new.

The church was crowded. I settled our young son in the nursery and joined the rest of my family in a pew at the back of the sanctuary. We sang a few songs in worship before the visitor stood to give his testimony.

The man had come to know Christ after dying from a heart attack. He told his amazing back-to-life story with little emotion or extra details, as if he'd shared it a hundred times. He emphasized the message of Christ's power to save and to heal. When he finished, he invited those in need of prayer to come forward. I joined 10 or so others in a line in front of the altar. The preacher asked me what I needed.

I indicated my left ear.

"Deafness, be gone in Jesus' name."

As I returned to my pew, I felt a tingling in my left arm—as if lightning had struck nearby without harming me.

I could hear.

A few days later, I told our pastor and others about my ear. My healing became an opportunity to tell of Jesus' love and power.

Patti Richter is a freelance journalist in North Texas. Her nearly 300 published articles include news and feature stories, ministry and people profiles, and book reviews. She writes for several local and national publications. She is also a regular contributor of faith essays for a Dallas-area news site (richter_patti@msn.com).

Only an Ankle

(Tawanda Mills)

On August 26, 2008, I fell while I was at work and twisted my right ankle. I didn't think much of it. "It's minor—only an ankle," I said.

My co-workers made a big fuss over me. I ignored their comments about the swelling until later that morning, when my foot began to throb and became difficult to walk on.

"You should get that checked out," my supervisor said. "You might be making it worse by walking on it." At her insistence, I went to a clinic.

An X-ray revealed a fracture, and the doctor gave me an ugly boot to wear and a metal cane to stabilize my steps. A nurse showed me how to walk with my new devices. "You'll have limited use of your right foot for a few weeks," the doctor said, "and it'll probably be at least another eight weeks before it's completely healed."

I felt like crying. I'm an active person and had just started a kickboxing class. "How long before I can get back to kickboxing class?" I asked.

The doctor grinned and shook his head. "Let's schedule your next appointment. We'll talk about that later."

I didn't like the boot I had to wear. I didn't like the attention and pity people gave me because of it.

I especially didn't like people's negative comments. One person said, "I had to have surgery after a fracture like that, and it took me a whole year to heal."

Another said, "Don't do too much too soon. It'll probably take a lot longer to heal than what the doctor said."

I know people meant well, but whenever I heard remarks like that, my faith wavered.

My pastor, Creflo Dollar, teaches: "Whatever you believe from God's Word, hang on to it and don't let go." I value his wisdom, and I latched on to Isaiah 53:5 that foretold that Jesus was "beaten so we could be whole [and] whipped so we could be healed." I repeated the verse again and again.

I returned to the clinic for my check-up on September 5 and had more X-rays taken. The doctor, in comparing the images with the first ones, stared at them for a while and seemed confused. Finally he told me that I could remove the boot. "I don't know what was going on with the first X-ray, but according to this new one, there is no fracture." He showed me the films and pointed out the differences. I had a hard time distinguishing what was what, but I knew something had changed. I was healed.

When I left the clinic without that silly boot and cane, I practically bounced to the car. "I'm healed!" I praised God the entire trip home. I know God's Word is true. I'm glad I hung on and didn't let go, even though it was only an ankle.

Tawanda Mills is a senior writer/editor for World Changers Church International (WCCI), and she volunteers as a youth specialist for B.I.G. Student Ministries at WCCI. Her articles have appeared in publications such as *Change Magazine*, *Black Enterprise Magazine*, *Atlanta Journal-Constitution* and *The Max Newsletter*. See teefood4thought.blogspot.com.

The Pillow Fight
(HELENA SMRCEK)

In the spring of 1993, two years into our marriage, our life together was full of promise. After a year of dealing with immigration to Canada, my husband, Martin, who came from what is now the Czech Republic, finally received a work permit, and soon found a job. I was relieved; the financial responsibility no longer rested on my shoulders.

One Sunday, just as the pastor closed the service in prayer, Martin's breathing suddenly became heavy. He sat down and reached for my hand. I stared at him as his body shook and beads of sweat covered his forehead.

We hurried to the car and sat inside, waiting for the strange feeling to pass. The symptoms subsided and we drove home—concerned, but glad the incident was over.

It happened again that night, and fear entered my heart. The episodes continued over the next several months, each one lasting longer then the previous one.

Martin lost his appetite, couldn't sleep, and hated to be left alone. He lost his job and could hardly walk on his own. He went to see a doctor several times but received no help. The doctor insisted that there was nothing physically wrong with him. Nothing showed up on any of the many tests the doctor requested. Finally he wrote a prescription for antidepressants. Within a few days, Martin developed a psychological addiction to his medication.

The pills had to be in his pocket at all times. If he left them in the other room, the symptoms kicked in. What was worse, the drugs did nothing for his existing condition. That continued for several weeks, until Martin realized the depth of his addiction. He talked to his doctor and asked if he could decrease the dosage, and eventually stop taking the pills. He weaned himself off the medication, but the original symptoms continued.

Martin lost more than 20 pounds and couldn't complete the simplest task without being completely exhausted. My husband, always full of energy, had changed. He was vanishing before my eyes.

I worried that Martin was going to die. We had withdrawn from friends and stopped going to church because the half-hour drive was beyond his strength.

One afternoon, Hana, a friend from our church, called to ask how we were. She hadn't seen us for a while. Unsure how much to tell her, I explained that Martin was unwell. She listened and asked a few questions, genuinely concerned. She invited us over for dinner.

The dinner was delicious, but Martin couldn't eat much. As the coffeemaker gurgled, her husband, Paul, and their two children sat with us in the living room. When Hana came in from the kitchen with a plate of pastries, she sat down and asked if we knew that God had healed her.

She told us her story and asked, "Have you prayed for Martin's healing?"

"We just hadn't thought about it." (We were new Christians, and praying for healing wasn't something we'd heard about in our church.)

"May we pray for you? Right here?"

Although unsure if prayer would actually help, since even the doctor couldn't, I looked at Martin. Seeing him pale and hunched over, I knew we had nothing to lose; God was our last hope. We knelt in their living room and prayed. As each person took a turn petitioning God for Martin's healing, my heart swelled with hope. For the first time in my life, I actually felt the presence of God.

I might have decided later that the strange feeling was only a result of my rattled emotions, but I couldn't deny the instant change I saw in my husband. A few minutes after we got off our knees, Martin picked up a couple of throw cushions from our friends' sofa and started an old-fashioned pillow fight with their son. They laughed and rolled around the living room floor; all I could do was cry.

My husband came back to life. I hadn't seen him smile for months. The joy of life that had left him weeks ago suddenly returned, and I knew I owed God a prayer of gratitude and thanks.

I can't explain what happened—and it doesn't matter. Our friends prayed, and Martin was healed. That mattered.

Helena Smrcek, a former refugee, has written more than 100 articles since 1999, graduated from Jerry B. Jenkins's Craftsman Program, and published her first book, *Kingdom Beyond Borders*. She is currently working on a screenplay and two fiction projects (helena_smrcek@yahoo.ca).

Healings IN THE MINISTRY OF
F. F. Bosworth
(1877–1958)

After being healed of severe lung problems that nearly took his life, Fred Francis Bosworth moved with his family to Zion, Illinois.

While there, he witnessed many healings through the ministry of John Alexander Dowie.

As an adult, Bosworth served as a local pastor for a decade before he became a traveling evangelist. Bosworth wrote and taught on the subject, and many people were healed, particularly of deafness, in his meetings.

✤ Deaf Students Are Healed ✤

David Du Plessis reported being in a Bosworth meeting to which numerous students from a school for the deaf were brought.

Du Plessis watched as Bosworth prayed for each deaf child, and he rejoiced as all of them were healed and began hearing perfectly.

Afterward the school for the deaf was forced to close: they had no students.[77]

✤ Deaf for Six Years ✤

When Ruth Peiper was 11 years old, she contracted diphtheria and scarlet fever and lost hearing in both ears. She also had to wear a body cast and walked with a noticeable limp because of scoliosis (severe curvature of the spine). Doctors hadn't been able to help her. Six years after she first fell ill, someone took Ruth to an F. F. Bosworth healing meeting at the Chicago Gospel Tabernacle.

That night, March 2, 1928, Ruth was healed. Riding home on the bus afterward, she couldn't believe how loud everything sounded. Whenever someone paid the bus fare and the bell rang, she jumped. The sounds were loud, but they were also wonderful.[78]

✤ Sarcoma Cancer ✤

On a cold winter morning in 1925, in a schoolyard in Scranton, Pennsylvania, nine-year-old Raffaela Serio was in a swing. She fell to the ground, crying and clutching her chest, but had no visible injury, so the teachers did not think much of it.

But Raffaela's pain didn't go away. Her concerned parents took her from one doctor to another, but she didn't get better. She had bruised the area near her left breast; as the pain increased, a small lump formed and grew until it was about the size of an orange.

Doctors at Johns Hopkins University Hospital in Baltimore, Maryland, performed tests and diagnosed Raffalea with sarcoma cancer of the left breast.

Her condition worsened, but the doctors said the cancer was too deep for surgery and they could do little for her. She also developed an open, seeping sore. The medical profession knew little about cancer in those days, so Raffaela's doctor prescribed a salve to apply to the affected area each day and bandaged her. There seemed little chance for a recovery.

After months of ineffective treatment and worry, Raffaela's doctor told the Serios about a healing evangelist named F. F. Bosworth, who was holding special services in Scranton. "He prays, and people get well," the doctor said.

Raffaela's parents were skeptical, so the doctor told them about one of his patients who had been healed of a large goiter after Bosworth prayed for her.

Despite their doubts, the Serios drove their daughter to Scranton. They also bought a copy of Bosworth's book, *Christ the Healer*, which became a Christian classic on the power of Christ to heal. For the next week, her parents read portions of the book aloud to Raffaela.

At the meeting, Bosworth prayed for Raffaela. That evening at home, Mrs. Serio got the salve ready for Raffaela's daily treatment; however, her daughter refused and insisted God had healed her. Although the lump and the open sore were still present, Raffaela insisted she had been healed.

Mrs. Serio later said she worried most of the night. The next morning, she examined Raffaela. Swelling from the collarbone and from under the arm were gone, and there was no open sore. Five days later, the lump was the size of a hickory nut; shortly after that, it disappeared completely.[79]

❖ A Woman Without Hope ❖

In the summer of 1920, Bosworth preached in Lima, Ohio. A woman named Alice Baker attended one of the early meetings. A cancer on Baker's face had eaten away part of her upper lip. She kept her face covered so others couldn't see her diseased face. The doctors gave her small doses of ether.

After prayer, Baker said, "It seemed a rubber cap was drawn over my face, and it gradually slipped off, and I knew I was healed."[80]

❖ "John Sproul Can Talk!" ❖

John Sproul inhaled mustard gas, which the Germans used against the Allies in World War I. Sproul barely survived and endured a total of 14 surgeries, 6 on his throat and 8 on his lungs. He couldn't speak and had trouble holding his head erect.

After the war, Sproul lived in constant pain. He traveled to many places in an attempt to get medical help, but he found no relief. Doctors called his case incurable, and he received a disability pension from the federal government.

Not because he believed in divine healing, but because he felt he had tried everything else, Sproul went to a meeting Bosworth conducted in Pittsburgh. When the evangelist called for those who wanted to be healed to come forward, Sproul went.

After prayer, someone told him to praise the Lord, which seemed ridiculous to a man who couldn't talk. But Sproul opened his mouth—and, to his amazement, "a strange power" seemed to fill his body. In an instant, Sproul knew he was healed. At the top of his voice, he shouted praises to God.

Word spread everywhere, and a Pittsburgh newspaper ran the headline:

"John Sproul Can Talk!"

The Veterans Bureau tested Sproul and declared him well. They stopped his disability payments because Sproul was now able to work.[81]

SIX ABLE TO SPEAK AND HEAR THROUGH FAITH AND PRAYER

CHICAGO, May 5. (Exclusive)— Six normally intelligent young people in the little town of Rochelle, Ill., sat in a special class in the basement of the Baptist Church there this morning and repeated over and over the simplest words. Miss Gertrude Virgin, their teacher, encouraged them. Soon they will know the whole alphabet, she told them, and will be able to talk.

Nothing is wrong with the minds or bodies of the two girls and four young men in the class. But a month ago they could not speak and could not hear.

They had been deaf from birth, four in one family. Elvira Houston, 23 years of age; Samuel, 21; Russell, 16, and Margaret, 15; and the two others in the class, Gather Bellows, 11, and Miles Peckham, 15.

Last month a woman, an old church member in the town, went to the Houston home and said that God would cure the four deaf children if they had faith. In Chicago, she said, is Rev. F. F. Bosworth preaching in the Gospel Tabernacle. Thousands of sick have been made whole after this man had prayed over them, she added. Why not send the children to Chicago?

The four Houston children and the two others were sent to Chicago. At the service in the Tabernacle one night they went to the platform when Pastor Bosworth asked if any sick or infirm wished to be prayed for.

Healing was instantaneous for all six that night, they testify. The next day their class in the church basement in Rochelle was continued, but teacher and pupils faced an educational revolution.

Excerpt from the *Los Angeles Times*, May 6, 1928
by Healing and Revival Press (2006).

In 1950, William Branham was challenged to a debate on divine healing by W. E. Best, the pastor of a large Baptist church in Houston, Texas. Best believed that miracles and divine healing had ceased, and that the healing evangelists were frauds. Branham declined the challenge, but 73-year-old F. F. Bosworth accepted it enthusiastically. Bosworth was an adept apologist and welcomed the opportunity to spread the truth about God's healing promises in the atonement.

The local newspapers covered the event. During the debate, Bosworth presented the scriptural evidence he had outlined years earlier in his book, *Christ the Healer*. Among other things, he spoke about healing in Christ's atonement and the redemptive name of God, Jehovah-Rapha ("The Lord That Heals").

Bosworth paused and appealed to the "living witnesses" who were present, asking them to stand if they had been healed by God.

The *Houston Press* reported: "When the Rev. Best made a point, the Rev. Bosworth would rush to the microphone on stage and dramatically ask those in the audience who had been cured through faith to stand. Each time hundreds would rise. 'How many of you are Baptists?' the Rev. Bosworth shouted. At least 100 stood up." Bosworth was confident in the Word of God and the proof that God was still ministering healing power to His people.[82]

Anointing with Cooking Oil
(CECIL MURPHEY)

Although I'd believed in healing for years, and occasionally prayed for the sick, one experience stands out clearly. I preached a series of messages on the book of James, ending with James 5. "God heals today," I said, "even though we don't see a lot of evidence of it."

Three days later, Donna called me. "My doctor did a biopsy and I have skin cancer."

After we talked, she invited me to her home that evening.

"I called you," she said, "because you showed us where the Bible says to call the elders of the church—and you're an elder. I want you to anoint me with oil and pray for me."

I was a little nervous and pointed out that I couldn't guarantee healing.

"I want to do what the Bible says," she insisted.

I had no oil, and Mazola for cooking was the only oil in her kitchen. It wasn't olive oil, but I reminded myself that even though that was probably what the Early Church elders used, James said simply *oil*.

I laid hands on her, and I asked God to heal her. Nothing changed, as far as we could tell, but we knew we had done what the Bible commanded.

A week later, Donna called me. "God healed me!" she screamed. "I was at the doctor's office today. All evidence of skin cancer is gone."

After that experience, I prayed for sick people and anointed them with oil. We had a few dramatic experiences, and several members believed. After that, we kept a small bottle of oil inside the pulpit to use when requested.

Miracle Man

(DIANE BRAUN)

On November 15, 2005, my father suffered a cardiac arrest. The doctor told us that if he survived, he'd be severely brain damaged because of the length of time his brain was without oxygen before he was revived. My father was non-responsive and on a respirator. After several days in an induced coma, his condition showed no change.

I arrived at the hospital early one morning, before the rest of my family, to visit my dad. The doctor was making his rounds and was in Dad's room, so I sat in the waiting room and read the book I had brought: *Too Busy Not to Pray*. I got to a section about praying specifically, and one sentence stood out to me: "If you need a miracle, ask for it without shrinking back."[83]

As that thought sank in, I closed the book and turned my attention to God. "Restore my father's health," I pleaded. "Completely. Make him whole again."

My husband, Michael, arrived shortly after that. I didn't tell him what I had read or about my prayer.

The doctor walked into the waiting room a few minutes later. "Where's the rest of your family?" he asked.

"They're not here yet," I said.

"The two of you are the only ones who get to see your father awake."

The three of us walked to Dad's room, and he was alert and sitting up in bed. He couldn't speak because he was still connected to the respirator, so he responded to the doctor's questions by nodding his head.

"Why don't you return to the waiting room while we get rid of this tube?" the doctor said. "We'll let you know when we're finished."

As soon as we got back to the waiting room, I grabbed my book, opened it, and pointed to the sentence I had read earlier. "Look at these words." I could barely contain my excitement as I talked to my husband. "I read them before you came in this morning and decided that I should pray boldly for Dad to get better, so I did. God didn't waste any time!"

In between my bursts of praising God and joyous babbling, Michael called the rest of the family to tell them the good news. "Dad is awake."

As promised, the doctor returned to the waiting room and asked us to rejoin him in my father's room. Michael and I stood beside the hospital bed. I put my hand over my father's and gently stroked it.

This time the doctor asked, "Joe, do you know who this is?" My father nodded.

"Tell me who this is. I want you to say her name."

"Diane," he said. Although rough and gravelly, my father's voice sounded beautiful to me. My eyes watered. God had truly done an amazing thing.

My father made a total recovery, and the hospital medical staff gave him the nickname of Miracle Man. They were in awe that he survived, and even more that he still had full brain function.

Diane Braun has a passion for women's ministry and enjoys serving at two Christian nonprofit organizations (dbraun28@gmail.com).

A Skeptic Prays
(Marcia Zimmermann)

I began YWAM's (Youth With A Mission) Discipleship Training School in September of 1980, and in January 1981, our group of 40 students and 10 staff members spent two months in Monterey, Mexico, for an outreach project. Our ministry there included performing dramas and sharing the gospel with people in various villages.

During a visit to a village in a remote desert area, one of the girls in our group helped Charlotte, another team member, by holding her 10-month-old daughter. As Dawn walked, she stumbled and dropped the infant. Baby Christian hit her head and suffered a concussion. Our leaders took a large bus, the only vehicle we had, to the hospital and left the rest of us stranded.

The intense heat of the sun and our thirst, coupled with our concern about little Christian (who was released the same day with no complications), caused the time to pass slowly. While we waited, we performed our drama and interacted with the villagers as best we could.

After we'd been there about two hours, a boy tapped on my elbow. He seemed desperate as he tugged my arm and tried to pull me forward.

"*Señorita, venga conmigo.*" I had a limited vocabulary in Spanish, but I knew he wanted me to go with him. He talked about his mother who was very sick.

His words and his dark eyes pleaded with me to follow. He motioned that he wanted me to pray for his mama. My heart melted as the child looked at me. How could I say no to him? I asked how far away he lived.

"Very close," he said. And I believed him.

I left our group without telling anybody and walked with the boy toward his *casa*. We walked at least a mile. I became concerned that I wouldn't find my way back, and no one knew where I was.

Finally we arrived at his home, which was more like a little shack. A mother, father and two smaller children greeted us. "She came to pray!" the boy announced in Spanish.

I learned that the mother had no feeling in her hands, wrists or forearms, as well as other places in her body. The lack of sensation made it impossible for her to change diapers, cook, or perform the other normal daily tasks a wife and mother needs to do.

The family wanted me to pray.

I felt so inadequate. How could I expect God to answer my prayers for healing? I was a skeptic because of a bad experience I'd had a few months earlier, when our group attended a service at Angelus Temple, where everything seemed showy and phony. I didn't believe that any of the healings that night were legitimate.

My friend and fellow student, Larry Art, had struggled, too. Afterward we told our director about our doubts, and he gave us resources to read. Larry and I poured over the books about prayer and healing. We wanted truth.

Now I was in front of a Mexican family. They wanted me—a skeptic—to pray for healing for the precious woman sitting beside me.

I swallowed hard and haltingly told them that I was going to pray in English because my Spanish wasn't good. I grabbed the mother's hands and held them up to the Lord. "Oh God, You know how weak my faith is, and I'm thankful that You're not limited by my puny faith. I don't deserve an answer to my prayers. You know how I've struggled, and You know my skepticism. But God, if it's Your will—"

The woman's screaming interrupted my prayer. She could feel!

Sensation had returned to all her limbs. The family danced around the tiny house. It was a hysterical time of rejoicing.

While they celebrated, I spoke again with the Lord—this time privately. *God, You are so awesome. I didn't deserve for You to answer my prayer. Please forgive me for doubting. Thank You for showing me the truth of Your miraculous healing power.*

God changed the hearts of two big skeptics during that outreach trip. My friend, Larry, went on to work with Steve Hill, an evangelist with a healing ministry. I'm still involved in YWAM ministry with my husband, Andy. Larry and I have seen God do numerous healings in the years following our trip to Monterey. I no longer doubt what God can do.

Marcia Zimmermann joined Youth With A Mission in 1980. Marcia is an intercessor with a heart for young people and Jewish/Gentile reconciliation (marciaz2030@gmail.com).

Healings IN THE MINISTRY OF
William Branham
(1909–1965)

William Branham, a former pastor in Indiana, became the most famous of the healing evangelists during what is called the Latter Rain Movement. Branham and his associates started the *Voice of Healing* magazine, which contributed greatly to the healing revival of the 1950s.

✣ Poor Man's Ministry ✣

During a worship service early in his healing ministry, Branham received a telegram begging him to go to St. Louis to pray for a sick girl. Branham didn't have the money, but the congregation collected enough for him to go by train, and he borrowed a suit of clothes.

The girl was dying from an undiagnosed sickness. The record says, "She was weak and wasting away, hoarse from crying out in pain."[84]

Branham prayed for the girl and she was healed. The story spread, and in June of 1946, Branham returned to St. Louis for a "twelve-day healing revival there where tremendous manifestations took place. The lame walked, the blind saw, the deaf heard, and the dead were raised. A woman who stood mocking outside dropped dead from a heart attack. Branham went out to pray for her and she revived praising God. The healings that took place were beyond count as Branham often stayed until 2:00 A.M. to pray for the sick."[85]

✣ Congressman William Upshaw ✣

Congressman William Upshaw's story is the most famous healing account in the ministry of William Branham, probably because of the prominence of the outspoken Christian senator from Georgia.[86]

On February 8, 1951, Upshaw attended a meeting conducted by William Branham at Calvary Temple in Los Angeles. Branham was praying for the sick, and he stopped and turned to the audience.

The evangelist said he had a vision of a young man falling from a haystack and breaking his back. After that, the young man was unable to walk. Branham described the doctor who worked on the young man, with no improvement. "The youngster grows to become a famous person who writes books. People are applauding him."

The Senator was able to get a microphone passed to him. The 83-year-old Upshaw asked Branham, "How did you know that I fell and hurt myself when I was a boy?"

"I can't tell you, sir. I can only say what I see."

Upshaw joined the prayer line. Because he was on crutches and unable to walk, he sat in the first row, waiting for his turn for prayer. A weary Branham stopped and asked the sick people to lay hands on each other and pray for healing.

After he said those words, ushers carried the exhausted preacher off the platform. Just before they reached the exit, Branham had a further vision and described what he saw to the church's pastor, LeRoy Kopp. The pastor raced to the platform and told the congregation what Branham said, adding, "Brother Branham says, 'The congressman is healed.'"

When Upshaw heard those words, he stood. Even though he hadn't walked in 66 years, he began to walk. After that, Upshaw traveled across the country, telling others of his healing.

The final paragraph in the Wikipedia account of Upshaw's life reads: "In February 1951 at the age of 84 Upshaw claimed he was supernaturally and miraculously healed after being crippled for 66 years in a William Branham Healing Service. He died on November 21, 1952."[87]

❖ Healings in South Africa ❖

In 1951, Branham held meetings in Johannesburg, South Africa. A reporter from the *Durban Sunday Tribune* reported the story in an article on November 11, 1951:

A faith cure, described by his mother as a "miracle" has enabled 16 year old Ernest Blom, of Eastview Road, Red Hill, Durban, formerly a cripple, to walk normally for the first time in his life.

Last Sunday Evening, Ernest astounded a packed congregation of more than 500 people, by rising from his seat and walking without the slightest difficulty to the pulpit to testify that "A miracle happened and I am completely cured."

Excited groups of people gathered outside the church later to see Ernest walking and to congratulate him on his recovery. His mother said, "Ernest is the youngest of my family of 10. When he started to walk I noticed that his left leg was shorter than his right. He could only walk on the tips of his toes, and had to drag his left foot.

"From the age of four until a month ago, he was under the care of a specialist. For two years he wore a leg iron without any noticeable improvement. The specialist suggested an operation, but he could not guarantee that it would be a success, so I gave up on the idea.

"I heard of Pastor William Branham's remarkable faith healing success in the United States. When my daughter and a friend heard he was to visit Johannesburg they motored from Durban three weeks ago and took Ernest along. They attended his opening meeting at which 15,000 people were present."

Ernest himself tells the rest of the story. He said, "I was right at the back of the hall. Pastor Branham asked all the people wanting to be cured to lay their hands on each other. I laid my hands on a man sitting beside me. Pastor Branham said, 'I will pray for you.'

"I experienced a weird sensation. It was just like cold water running through my body. I began to cry. My sister said, 'Are you healed?' I replied that I was sure that I was healed. But because of the huge crowd I could not move. As I was being helped from the back of the hall I kept repeating, 'I am sure I am healed.'

"Pastor Branham asked all who were healed to come forward. I was assisted to the sick bay by others. He asked me to walk up and down the platform on which he was standing. I broke into a sweat, but something urged me on and I managed to walk normally across the platform and back.

"When I got back to Durban and my school friends saw me walking into the classroom, they were flabbergasted. My left leg is getting stronger everyday. I can now play cricket and other games.[88]

On another evening in Johannesburg, while Branham was talking to someone in the prayer line, he turned to the audience and pointed out a young woman lying on a cot. "Lady, your back has been broken in three different places as a result of a fall," he said. "Jesus Christ has made you whole. Stand up and accept your healing." The woman was startled, but in faith she stood up and then praised God for the healing she had received. The following evening, she spoke publically about her healing.[89]

"I'm About to Be Healed"

(Colleen Capes Jackson)

My husband, Dwayne, took Heath, our seven-year-old son, to practice an hour early for a Little League baseball game.

Our three-year-old daughter, Whitney, and I were en route to the game when a drunk driver in a stolen Impala hit us head-on, sending our Honda Accord into someone's front yard. Seconds later, a woman ran out of her house with a towel to wrap my bleeding head and called 911. In a moment of consciousness, I glimpsed my daughter's bloody face. Fading in and out, I was somewhat aware of sirens and the sound of tearing metal as workers pulled us from the wreckage.

The officer took names and phone numbers from me and promised to break the news to my husband and son. My pastor's wife arrived and took charge of Whitney, who had only a bloody nose.

As I lay in the hospital bed, my husband and our pastor whispered about my condition: severe damage to my right leg and ankle, and other undetermined injuries.

The following day, I awakened to what felt like a ton of bricks on top of my leg. The surgeon had put pins in my right ankle and set my leg in a cast. Six weeks later, I had to learn to walk again. The following year, I had two additional surgeries to remove the pins. The injury left me with a noticeable limp, and I often relied on crutches. The cartilage in my ankle wore thin over the years, and I began walking bone-against-bone.

About that time, I learned of a healing service in Atlanta and asked my husband to take me. We had been in church all our lives, but had never attended a service dedicated to healing. The energy was incredible. People were praying and praising God. We had agreed to accept whatever God chose to do that night. Although I wasn't healed, I left with an amazing peace.

Months later, the simplest of tasks took me twice as long. I was exhausted from dragging my crutches while caring for my family and working a full-time job.

Around 7:00 one night, I welcomed some needed rest and settled into the recliner. I was dreading my appointment with the orthopedic surgeon the following day. We were going to be discussing additional surgery on my ankle.

I turned on the television and was surprised to hear the same minister who had preached the healing service we had attended in Atlanta. He called out the Scripture as my husband walked into the room. I reached for the Bible on the end table and was amazed when it fell open to the verse: "Then Peter took the lame man by the right hand and helped him up. And as he did, the man's feet and ankles were instantly healed and strengthened" (Acts 3:7).

"Did you hear that?" I yelled. "I'm about to be healed!" I don't remember if my husband responded. I know I listened closely until the conclusion of the broadcast. I was at peace and went to bed.

The next morning, I stood without pain and without crutches. I couldn't wait for 2:00 P.M. to come so I could tell my doctor what had happened. He confirmed that I didn't need surgery. Jesus had taken me by the right hand and healed me.

Colleen Capes Jackson is founder/director of the East Metro Atlanta Christian Writers. An award-winning freelance writer and photographer, motivational speaker, and songwriter, Jackson has 188 published credits in newspapers and magazines; she has also released two inspirational CDs. Awards: 2008, Writer of the Year, American Christian Writers; 2009, First Place—Religion, Georgia Press Association. See www.colleencapesjackson.com.

No Amputation

Leroy Jenkins, like many of the American healing evangelists, came from an impoverished background and received little education.

In an accident, his arm was almost severed by a broken large plate glass window. Despite medical help, there was no circulation in his arm. He couldn't move his hand or fingers. Doctors said his arm wouldn't heal properly. They suggested amputation.

Jenkins begged them not to amputate. They agreed not to operate immediately, but warned that the arm wasn't going to heal, and that they would eventually have to remove it.

Jenkins went to a meeting held by healing evangelist A. A. Allen.

Allen heard the story and called Jenkins out of the audience. Even before Allen prayed, Jenkins began moving his hand and fingers.

He raised his hands heavenward and cried with joy.

Allen handed Jenkins the microphone, and Jenkins told the story of his accident and testified to his obvious miracle of healing. That was the beginning of Leroy Jenkins's ministry.[90]

Don Stewart was an eyewitness to this event; he was the one who escorted Jenkins to the front. You can read the full story in Stewart's book, Don Stewart, *Only Believe: An Eyewitness Account of the Great Healing Revival of the 20th Century* (Shippensburg, PA: Treasure House, 1999), p. 122.

Just Ask

(KELLY J. STIGLIANO)

By the age of 18, I had formed a pattern of bad choices that had left me with stomach ulcers, colitis, and excessive acid in my gallbladder. A visit to the emergency room, ensuing tests, and shocking diagnoses ended with the doctor pausing at the door, looking over his shoulder, and saying, "Oh, and you *do* know you're pregnant, don't you?"

I had no idea. My wild lifestyle had finally caught up with me and promised to whip me around for years to come.

What followed were a quick wedding, a violent marriage, a second baby, and (at last) the courage to flee. At age 23, I worked two jobs, and partying left little room for positive parenting. My excessive drinking exacerbated my intestinal issues. After the doctor would no longer prescribe Tagamet, insisting instead on a lifestyle change, Maalox became my best friend. I kept a large bottle in my desk at work and one at home. I guzzled it like water.

About that time, Mark came into my life. While he wasn't living the life he had grown up with, Mark still had the path to God in his peripheral vision. We started going out, and he invited me to go to church with him. Through his family, my two toddlers and I became faithful church attendees.

The kids and I went to church and Sunday School. We read the Bible and prayed together. I learned patience, respect and kindness, becoming an attentive and loving mother to my children.

As I grew in my Christian walk, the desire to put my daughter in Christian school kindergarten became overwhelming. Although I was poor, in my newfound faith, I enrolled her in a small Christian school in the country. That's where I met the unmarried principal, Jerry Stigliano.

After a while, Jerry asked me out. My children loved him; he was so caring and patient with them. His interest in me and concern for our well-being warmed my heart.

One evening, after we had been dating for a couple months, Jerry asked my kids and me over for dinner. He had made spaghetti.

It was delicious, and we all ate our fill. I still suffered from colitis, and it wasn't long before I knew I had to get home. As I hurriedly carried my sleeping children out to the car, Jerry said, "Have you ever asked God to heal your colitis?"

"I never thought about it."

"You should ask Him," he said. "It's a problem from your old life. You're now a new creation in Christ."

I looked up at him and tilted my head sideways, thinking about what he'd said. As I drove home, the children were sleeping in the back seat. I prayed out loud, "My colitis *is* from my old life. I *am* a new creation. God, please take away my colitis."

Almost instantly I felt warmth deep within my lower hips. By the time I arrived home, my symptoms were gone. I've not suffered from colitis since.

Kelly J. Stigliano has been a speaker and writer for more than 20 years. See www.kellystigliano.com.

Dylan's Story
(NICOLE GANT)

The week before we were scheduled to relocate to another city, our eight-month-old son, Dylan, was diagnosed with kidney disease. The best prognosis was that he might reach adulthood before needing a kidney transplant. I felt devastated at the thought that he would suffer throughout his life with this condition.

I prayed, and other family members did the same.

God blessed us with strength so we were able to keep up with the demands of our toddler and the move. That last week was chaotic with packing boxes, and I was also trying to manage Dylan's new dietary and medication requirements. I didn't think I had the energy to attend our church playgroup, but Dylan seemed excited about going, so I took him.

At that playgroup, a friend suggested that I call a retired priest who had been miraculously healed of lung cancer while on his deathbed. She said he had a special gift for healing prayer.

I called. He said that if we stopped by his home, he would pray over Dylan. While the movers loaded our things into the truck, we visited the priest, and he prayed for us.

During the following months, I gave Dylan his medication and watched his dietary requirements, but after receiving the healing prayer, I believed he was going to be fully healed. My emotions so quickly shifted from fear to faith that I believe there is no other explanation than divine intervention.

I also had new experiences while praying. I actually felt a divine energy flow through me. During the children's naptimes and after they went to bed, I prayed until my own bedtime. Instead of focusing on Dylan's prognosis, I read healing stories on the Internet and in the Bible.

For more than a month, I prayed—and my faith grew stronger. One night while praying I had a strong sense that Dylan had been healed.

I was so convinced of his healing that I called the doctor's office to make sure he wouldn't be harmed by taking his medication in the absence of kidney disease. I explained to her about his healing, but I followed the nurse's advice to continue giving Dylan the prescribed medication until the doctor saw him again.

On our next visit, the doctor examined him and ran tests. The results showed that Dylan had perfectly functioning kidneys. A few weeks later, more comprehensive tests confirmed the earlier results so conclusively that his nephrologist said that "just to be safe," he wanted to see him only once a year.

Dylan's doctor didn't have an explanation for his healing, but I wasn't shy about telling him mine.

Nicole Gant plans to set up her own blog soon (n.gant.@mchsi.com).

Ruth Carter Stapleton's First Healing

Ruth Carter Stapleton (1929–1983), a sister of former president Jimmy Carter, was a healing evangelist. In her book, *In His*

Footsteps: The Healing Ministry of Jesus—Then and Now, she tells of several healings.

Her first recorded story took place when she was asked to pray for a deaf woman. She was unsure about healing, but:

> I walked to the deaf woman and placed my hands over her ears, having once seen a faith healer . . . do that on television. I prayed.
>
> "Lord," I prayed. "I know you can heal this woman. Heal her now."
>
> That was all, but that was enough. When I removed my hands the woman could hear—perfectly![91]

In 1974, Stapleton went to Solo, Java, Indonesia, as part of a healing team. At one service, the leaders invited people to come for prayer. People led a blind woman to the altar.

> As we all prayed, she began to speak excitedly.
>
> "She says she can see!" said our interpreter, with equal excitement.
>
> I put two fingers before her once sightless eyes and asked her, through the interpreter, how many fingers she could see.
>
> "Two," she responded without hesitation.[92]

Stapleton then stood more than 100 feet away and held up all 10 fingers—and the woman could see them.

A Song Born of Obedience

(JEANNE GOWEN DENNIS)

The music director motioned to me. As if in a dream, I stood up and approached the platform, my heart racing. I didn't know how I would get through the next 10 minutes, but I had to obey what God was urging me to do.

My thoughts drifted back a few months to the severe coughing that had accompanied my summer bout with bronchitis—coughing so violent that I felt as if my esophagus were turning inside out. I felt a constant pain in my throat for two months, especially when I talked. While sitting on the floor with my two-year-old granddaughter trying to sing, "Jesus Loves Me," I couldn't hit the notes. This was heartrending for me, because music has always been an important part of our family life.

For days, I felt God urging me to have the elders pray over me. I was new in that congregation, and I didn't want to be prayed over in public by people I barely knew. I begged the Lord not to make me do it, but I knew I had to obey.

It had been so hard walking down that aisle alone, even though the pastor was expecting me. He had me sit in a chair facing the people. The elders surrounded me, and they prayed and anointed my head with oil. But the pain was still with me when I got home.

Even though I had washed my face, for the next three days, I could still feel the spot of oil on my forehead. *God must have been doing something*, I reasoned. After all, the elders had obeyed the Scriptures.

Three days after the elders prayed for me, I felt an urge to go to choir practice. It didn't make sense. I still had pain and couldn't sing, but I obeyed.

As I tried to sing, I felt my voice coming back. By the end of the rehearsal, I knew I could sing again.

Now, two months later, I stood on the platform and turned toward the congregation. The music director reminded them of the Sunday evening a few weeks back when the elders had prayed for me.

I stared at faces, most of which were unfamiliar. It had been 17 years since the last time I had stood at the front of a congregation like this ready to sing a solo.

This time, in obedience, I had volunteered to do special music, even though I wondered if my voice would hold out. Would this healing I claimed prove to be real?

When I opened my mouth, a powerful voice I didn't quite recognize emanated from the depths of my soul and body. The voice I heard was like mine, but it sounded much better than it ever had before. God had done something even more wonderful than I had imagined. He not only healed my physical voice, but also gave me a richer tone.

Jeanne Dennis is an author, singer, songwriter, BreakPoint Centurion, and host of *Heritage of Truth* TV. See http://heritageoftruth.com.

"Do You Believe I Can Heal You?"
(SARA SCHAFFER)

"This is for you," Josh said as he tossed a slip of paper on the bed and headed to the closet to dress for work.

I read aloud, "Do you believe I can heal you?"

"It's from my daily calendar," Josh said. He usually pulled off each day's saying and kept it in his pocket to remind him throughout the day to pray. "I think this one is for you."

I glanced at the medicine bottles on my nightstand. "Do you think I could get rid of these someday?"

"Yes, I do."

My medications eased the muscle pain of my fibromyalgia, but they made getting up each morning a challenge. Groggily, I stumbled into the bathroom and put the slip of paper on the mirror. "Yes, Lord, I believe You can, but will You?"

A few days later, Josh got up early to go to Keystone Ski Resort on opening weekend. Before he left, he gently shook my shoulder. I gained enough consciousness to say goodbye to my smiling husband before succumbing to more sleep.

The next morning, I needed to be up early to catch a ride to church. As I opened my front door to wait on the porch steps, I saw a note from the local police. A phone call and several minutes later, Officer Dowling stood in my living room.

"I have bad news," he said soberly. "Joshua was killed in a ski accident yesterday."

I called the friends who were scheduled to bring me to church. They agreed to share the news with our small congregation. I phoned family and told them Josh was gone. After church, friends started arriving to offer comfort and condolences.

I went into the bathroom and read the note on my mirror: *Do you believe I can heal you?*

"Yes, Lord, You can heal even this shattered heart."

For the next few months, I grieved. My intense sorrow overshadowed the chronic pain of my fibromyalgia until May, when I felt God asking again, *Do you believe I can heal you?*

I called my pastor friend, Richard. He and his family came over, anointed me with oil, and prayed for me. No dramatic episode occurred during our prayer, but God's peaceful presence enveloped me.

A few days later, I told my grief counselor about the prayer time with my friends and my confidence that I was going to be healed. I sat back in the therapist's leather armchair and realized that I experienced no pain in my body.

God had healed me.

The next month I met with my doctor. After a thorough examination, she declared that I didn't have fibromyalgia.

Sara Schaffer is the author of *Up to Know Good Daily Inspirations* and co-creator of the album *There Is Hope*. See www.uptoknowgood.com.

The Voice of Healing

Most healing evangelists in the past 100 years started their own magazines. For at least a decade, beginning in 1948, *The Voice of Healing* was probably the most significant for people who were interested in the healing movement.

The February 1952 issue of *The Voice of Healing* is typical of the contents during that period. The title of the issue was "Historic Convention of [Voice of Healing] Fellowship Great Success."[93]

The magazine included numerous reports and personal testimonies of healings.

Reverend M. E. Collins, president of Southwestern Bible Institute in Waxahachie, Texas, described five recent healings connected with his school.

A salesman had come to see Collins, but was interrupted by a female student who was sick. Collins and other staff members prayed for her and for four other students. All were healed. The salesman said he had been on the road for more than 20 years, "but never before have I ever seen anything like this taking place."

A female student had been injured in an automobile accident and was paralyzed on her right side. Collins and his wife prayed for her, and she was healed. The woman finished college and became a missionary to Alaska.

The Advanced Choir visited Grapevine, Texas, and while there they prayed for a boy with polio who wore a brace on one leg and walked with crutches. The boy was healed. "That same night he walked without his crutches, and the following day he removed the brace from his leg."[94]

Elsewhere in the magazine are testimonies of healings signed by those who were healed and by witnesses to healing events.

For example, W. W. Movehead of Knob Creek, Arkansas, said that he had a growing tumor on his right cheek. He went to a meeting held by A. A. Allen and received prayer for healing. He wrote: "Three days later . . . I realized that something was taking place as the *cancer began to tingle. . . . I ran to my wife and asked her to look. THERE WAS NO SIGN OF THE CANCER! Even the skin where the cancer had been was smooth and no discoloration was left.*"

Movehead wrote his story three months after the healing and reported that "*no soreness or pain has ever returned.*" He included with his statement before-and-after pictures.

Below that are two signed documents affirming that Movehead attended the meeting on October 26, 1951, and that he remained cancer free.[95]

In "Letters to the Editor," Mary Thompson of Detroit said Jesus had healed her while she read *The Voice of Healing* magazine.

Below Thompson's letter is a note that says the assistant editor of *Voice of Healing* visited the Thompsons and verified her story. He pointed out that the magazine had published her testimony, in May 1950, of "how this woman, an alcoholic, dope fiend, and cripple was miraculously delivered through reading *The Voice of Healing.*"[96]

It Really Works
(CHARLES EARL HARREL)

The phone rang early Monday morning with an urgent call from Melvin, the director of His Place, an outreach ministry to the homeless sponsored by our church in Reno, Nevada. Melvin asked me to go to the outreach center. Paul, who had come to our center two weeks earlier to get help with his substance abuse, had become suddenly ill. As I drove toward the center, I tried to remember the address of an urgent care clinic on the west side of town.

When I went inside, I found Paul lying in his bed with a high fever. His body shook with chills. His face was flushed, and his eyes had a pained look to them.

"Have you taken any drugs or anything else that might have given you an adverse reaction?"

He shook his head. "I've been clean since I moved in." He paused and then said, "I think I might have the flu. I've been vomiting all night, and my head hurts."

One of the residents, standing outside in the hallway, asked, "So, what are you going to do? Pray for him?"

Pray for him? No one had ever asked me to pray over a sick person before. I believed that God had healed people and performed miracles that were recorded in the Bible, but that was a long time ago. *Does God still use people to do such things today?*

I wasn't sure. I tried to think of a situation where I had actually seen someone healed. Sadly, all I could remember was a man from our church who suffered with a pinched nerve in his lower back; he recovered after personal prayer and a visit to his chiropractor—not exactly the best validation for divine healing. I needed a better example—something to build up my faith—but nothing came to mind.

"Are you going to pray for him or not?" the man chided.

By then, others had gathered in the hall.

I closed my eyes and tried to form a prayer, but the words stuck in my mouth. I seldom prayed aloud—and never before an audience. I wouldn't really call my next words a prayer. I simply said, "Fever, go away!"

Not waiting for the outcome, I hurried down the stairs to call Melvin. I told him that Paul probably had a bad viral infection and needed to see a doctor.

Just as I hung up, Paul walked into the office. He was smiling.

"The fever is gone and so are the chills. The headache and sick feeling in my stomach left the moment you prayed."

I stared in amazement.

"I wanted to thank you before I take a shower and get ready for work."

Paul's instantaneous recovery was the first true healing I had ever witnessed.

Charles Earl Harrel was a pastor for 30 years before pursuing a writing ministry. He has 421 published works. His teachings, stories and devotionals have appeared in various magazines and in 27 anthologies. Charles enjoys photography, playing guitar and family camping trips (harrelce@aol.com).

The Power of Faith

(MARYANN DIORIO, PhD)

"She looks pale," the pediatrician said as he examined my two-month-old daughter, Gina. "I want to run some blood work on her."

I don't know what's happening, Lord, but whatever it is, I will trust You.

When I told my husband about the doctor's words, we called a friend who was a priest. All three of us laid hands on Gina and prayed.

Then we waited for the test results.

One test showed indications of intestinal bleeding. After ruling out the most common possible causes, our pediatrician sent us for further tests to St. Christopher's Children's Hospital in Philadelphia.

One of the tests required that my baby fast. When I heard the instructions, my heart sank. Gina nursed every two hours.

Hearing my baby scream in hunger all night is more than I can bear. Please help me.

As my maternal heart fought fear and worry, I prayed. For the first time in her young life, Gina slept through the night. Not only did she sleep through the night, but she also slept through the hour-long ride to the hospital and the entire medical procedure. When she finally awoke, it was nine o'clock in the morning, and I had a hungry baby on my hands.

After a series of tests and physical examinations, we learned that Gina had an incurable lymph gland disorder. While the news rocked my soul, it didn't rock my spirit. I continued to cling to God's promise of healing.

One afternoon, Gina was sleeping in her cradle in the family room. Sitting beside her, I turned on the television to *The 700 Club*. As I tuned in, Dr. Pat Robertson was praying. The next words out of his mouth were: "There's a baby in the TV audience with a lymph gland disorder, and God is healing her now."

I jumped out of my chair. "That's my Gina! That's my Gina!" Just then, warmth cascaded down the entire length of my body. I knew a major turn-around had taken place.

And Gina was healed.

A few days later, I took her back to the pediatrician. He could find no signs of bleeding, and her blood count had returned to normal.

Today, our Gina is a beautiful, 35-year-old woman who is a living testimony of God's power to heal.

Dr. MaryAnn Diorio writes fiction about the deep issues of the human heart. MaryAnn is also a Certified Life Coach whose passion is to help people find freedom in Jesus Christ. See www.maryanndiorio.com.

Healings IN THE MINISTRY OF
Aimee Semple McPherson
(1890–1944)

Aimee Semple McPherson, whose extensive and well-documented healing ministry was officially approved by the American Medical Association, said she started her ministry with no experience in praying for the sick. When she began, "few people talked about healing."[97]

✤ Sister Aimee Begins Her Healing Ministry ✤

McPherson's first healing occurred when a young woman named Louise came forward at the end of the service. Louise's fingers were gnarled and twisted, and she wasn't able to comb her hair or feed herself. Her joints were swollen, and her chin pulled forward until it lay on her breast.

As she made her way toward the front, McPherson cried out, *Oh, Lord, You are able to heal her, though I admit she seems to be a hopeless case!*

Louise was helped to the platform to surrender her life to Jesus Christ. Earnestly, she prayed and gave her life to Jesus.

Then McPherson prayed for her healing and told her to lift her hands and praise the Lord. As Louise obeyed, her gnarled joints began to straighten out. She lifted her hands as high as her chin, then her eyes, then the top of her head.

"Oh!" she exclaimed. "This is the first time I've been able to lift my hands to the top of my head in so long! Praise the Lord!" She was totally healed.

Louise began to walk as her limbs straightened. After she arrived home, her mother praised God for the healing. One of Louise's companions handed her the crutches, and she threw them away.

Two years later, McPherson returned to the same church. She told of the lively young woman who came up to her. "Looking at

the sparkling eyes, the clear complexion and the trim little figure," it took a moment for McPherson to realize it was Louise.
She was still healed, and she reported that her entire family had
come to faith.[98]

✤ Doubters Believe When Sister Aimee Is Healed ✤

McPherson tells this story about her own healing in Durant,
Florida. While preparing for the night service, she decided that
kerosene and gasoline lamps weren't bright enough. She brought
in a calcium carbide lighting outfit. While she was making adjust-
ments, the thing blew up. Searing flames enveloped her.

McPherson's face was blackened, and her eyebrows and eyelashes were gone. Her pain was violent. Others put soda on the
blisters. She walked outside under the trees, while the crowds were
gathering in the tabernacle. In the meantime, someone repaired
the lighting system.

A man had insisted that miracles ceased at the end of the
apostolic era and that no healings would take place that night.
As she suffered, McPherson kept wondering, *What will that brother
say who told the people that the Lord no longer answers prayer on the behalf of the afflicted?*

Still in agony 10 minutes after the announced starting time,
McPherson, who until then had a never-late-to-service record, hurt
too much to go inside.

Just then, the man stood and began making a speech, assuring
the people that there would be no meeting because the woman
who preached salvation and divine healing was ill, having burned
her face. McPherson heard most of what he said and was "shaken
with righteous indignation."

She washed the soda off her face, and with her starched collar
spattered with water, her eyebrows and eyelashes gone, and her
hair singed, she went on to the platform. As she announced the
first hymn, she hurt so badly she could hardly talk. At the end of
the first stanza, McPherson raised her hands and cried out, "I
praise the Lord that He heals me and takes all my pain away!"

As she spoke, her pain vanished. "Right before the eyes of the audience the red burn faded from my face, the white blisters disappeared, and at the end of the service, the flesh had resumed its natural appearance."

That healing turned the tide of the battle in favor of the present-day acceptance of the power of God, and the doubter was put to shame and silence.[99]

✣ Aimee Semple McPherson's Revival in Denver ✣

McPherson ministered frequently in Denver, Colorado. During her first campaign there, in 1921, Mr. O. A. Priest was one of the first people for whom she prayed. Priest had suffered three strokes that paralyzed one side of his body. When McPherson asked him if he had faith to be healed, he said he did.

McPherson proclaimed, "Then, in the name of Jesus, this side is restored to life and strength."

Priest began swinging his arms and said he was healed. "Mr. Priest first walked with vigor then commenced running up and down the steps of the platform. Reporters collared him when he finally left the stage to interview him about his recovery."

Hattie White, the mother of a policeman assigned to crowd control, was healed of paralysis during the same campaign. After prayer, the woman skipped down the platform and hurried home. Her son, who was off-duty that evening, heard about the healing, but he was skeptical. When he reached home, his mother was walking around and singing. He was shocked, but he had to believe her when she insisted that she was healed and her paralysis was completely gone.

Officer White rushed back to the auditorium with his mother and was able to stand on the platform and talk to the crowd. He told of his mother's condition and the healing she received. From then on, mother and son both became workers in the meetings.

A year later, Hattie White published her testimony in McPherson's magazine, *The Bridal Call*.

Alma Lafferty, a former state senator and one of Denver's most prominent club women, was healed of deafness caused 20 years earlier by an accident.

Mrs. George Dunklee declared that her sight had cleared and a slight paralysis had disappeared.

The Denver newspapers reported the healing of a widely known attorney, Horace Benson, who said, "I have not been able to hear since I was twelve years old, but Saturday evening when Mrs. McPherson prayed with me I heard and have continued to hear since. I know my ear has been healed."[100]

John's Heart
(Jennifer Maxwell)

We lived in three thatched-roof rooms in Thika, Kenya. Our front yard reached beyond the horizon. Our children, Trevor, Jason and two-year-old Tanya, took safaris into the coffee plantations and Birds of Paradise flower fields.

Shattering that idyllic place, at 2:30 A.M. on January 9, 1979, my husband, John, developed recurring left-arm pains and shortness of breath. I counted the diminishing beats on his wrist with alarm.

Running off into the bush in bare feet, with thorns and grass cutting my legs and feet, I banged on the door of my neighbor, Moria, pleading with her to care for our children while I took John to Nairobi Hospital, about 30 miles away.

I got John into our beat-up Peugeot station wagon, with its exhaust pipe dangling into the mud, and barreled down the drive. Jason ran after the car shouting, "Please don't die, Dad."

They hurried John from the emergency room into the ICU. While I waited, the money question blitzed my mind. We lived on so little and had no medical coverage.

When the doctor finally appeared, he said, "Your husband has a 50-50 possibility of survival." He explained that there was massive damage to his lower heart area.

Thus began 10 days of tests, trips by ambulance to various hospitals in Nairobi, and John's being hooked up to machines in ICU.

Missionaries, Kenyan pastors, and supporters joined in prayer for John.

On the tenth day, a cardiologist came to John's room. "Stop limping about. Get out of here, walk and live," he said. "There is no evidence of heart damage."

All evidence of a destroyed heart was gone.

When I went to pay the hospital bill, the cashier handed me back half of the amount I paid, saying, "Someone has paid the rest."

We left the hospital with cash in hand and a healed heart. John has never had trouble with his heart since.

Jennifer Maxwell's parents came from Europe to Nairobi, Kenya, where Jennifer was born. She and her husband, John, served with Elim Missionary Fellowship in Staten Island, New York, and Tauranga, New Zealand, before being called to serve in Kenya in 1971.

Deliverance

(DELILAH MOORE LEACH)

Pain. Debilitating pain. Stabbing from my shoulder to my fingertips every time I tried to move my left arm. The knife-like pain kept me awake most of the night.

I was used to pain. When I was seven, I contracted polio and woke to find myself incarcerated in the iron lung. I learned pain's meaning while struggling to breathe without a mechanical assistant.

After that I suffered from incapacitating headaches, which sent lightning bolts of pain behind my eyes, into my temples, and down the back of my neck. This pain was my partner for years, because painkillers couldn't dispel the tom-toms throbbing inside my head with each heartbeat. They only dulled the agony enough that I could continue teaching while popping pills.

Once again, I was suffering with severe pain that conventional remedies didn't alleviate. I couldn't lift my arm to fix my hair, put on my clothes, or put in my contacts without having to rest my elbow on the windowsill in my bathroom.

Despite the pain, I went to church on Sunday morning and decided that I'd go to the doctor the next day. During the service, I couldn't sit comfortably in the pew. I kept trying to find a less painful position. There wasn't one.

By Sunday night, I was so miserable I decided I wouldn't go to church. But my husband, Jeff, said, "You'll be miserable whether at home or at church, so why not go with me?"

I sat in the back row, leaning forward, scooting back, holding my arm, and squirming back and forth as I tried to get relief. That night a special speaker from Romania preached. My fiery pain and his heavy accent made it almost impossible to stay focused on his message.

"The Lord told me he's going to heal someone tonight." I understood those words.

Jeff leaned toward me and whispered, "It's going to be you."

Why would God single me out? Other people attending the service are suffering from critical illnesses and need healing, and all I have is an excruciating pain.

Even as I thought those words, I knew I wanted to be healed.

The speaker invited anyone who had physical problems to come forward for prayer. I walked forward, holding my arm, and joined 10 others who lined the altar area. Jeff and a few friends placed their hands on my shoulders and prayed for me while the speaker prayed for all of us.

I felt no change.

After the service, Jeff helped me get into our car and buckled my seat belt. We drove to a restaurant.

When we parked, I automatically undid my seat belt, jolted my left arm, and realized that I had no pain. I moved the arm up and down and sideways. It was fine. *No pain.*

Tears flooded my eyes as I realized that the Lord had healed me. I've never had trouble with that arm since.

Delilah Moore Leach taught high school English for many years before she had to quit because of complications caused by Post Polio Syndrome. Delilah spends her time writing, reading, and keeping up with her husband, Jeff (snapshot delilah@comcast.net).

Healings IN THE MINISTRY OF
A. A. Allen
(1911–1970)

Asa Alonzo Allen ran away from home at the age of 14. Nine years later, he attended a meeting at the Onward Methodist Church in Miller, Missouri. He returned the following evening and committed his life to serve Jesus Christ. After two years, Allen began serving as a pastor and later as an independent singing, healing evangelist.

✤ Blind Coal Miner ✤

A blind coal miner came forward for healing in one of Allen's meetings. Before he prayed, Allen said he sensed unbelief in the room and announced it to the congregation.

Almost immediately one man got up and left the church.

Allen then prayed, and "the blind man could name the color on Allen's tie."[101]

✤ Replaced Lung and Ribs ✤

Surgeons had removed G. E. Mullenax's right lung and three ribs and left a large hole in his back for a drainage tube. In May 1958, Mullenax attended a meeting Allen conducted in Little Rock, Arkansas.

When Allen laid his hands on Mullenax, the man felt he had been healed. He felt where the hole had been and was positive he had his right lung and three ribs replaced.

A year later, Mullenax came to another meeting in Dallas, Texas, where A. A. Allen was preaching. Mullenax stood on the platform and quoted his surgeon as saying, "Of all the X-rays I have ever made . . . you have two of the healthiest lungs I have ever seen in my life! You also have three ribs in place, where they were removed!"[102]

Healing for Four Generations

(REVEREND ANNALEE DAVIS)

Four generations of us sat at the breakfast table. My mother and I had traveled to Massachusetts from New Jersey to visit my son, his wife, and their daughter—my mother's first great-grandchild.

As we held hands and prayed, I realized what a privilege it was to be sitting together—these four generations—and remembered that a series of miracles had brought us together. The first miracle began with my grandmother.

My mother was three years old when her mother became ill. She and my grandfather had emigrated from Italy to the United States and settled in Elizabeth, New Jersey. My mother was the youngest of five girls. At the age of 28, my grandmother became ill. My grandparents visited doctor after doctor seeking a cure. At their last stop in New York City, the doctors told my grandfather to take his wife home and prepare for her funeral.

My grandparents remembered hearing about a small storefront church where people prayed for the sick. Together they walked the two miles to a service where my grandmother was anointed with oil and prayed for—and she recovered immediately. Grandmother lived to be 74 years old.

My mother was 29 when she went to the doctor because of an allergic reaction to detergent. The doctor gave her a sulfa drug, unaware that she was allergic to sulfa. Her flesh began to burn from the inside out.

Within weeks, she was bedridden, and the skin fell off her body. She screamed when Father picked her up off their bed and gently placed her in a bathtub full of a purplish-colored solution that was supposed to bring relief and comfort. It didn't help.

The doctor came to the house, stood at the bedroom door (he didn't enter because of the odor), and pronounced that she would be dead within two weeks.

On Friday night, people at our church prayed for her. About the time they prayed, my father again lowered my mother into the tub of liquid. This time, when he raised her out, she had new skin on her body—like that of a newborn baby.

Mine was the third miracle. In 1999, my last year of seminary, I awoke with chills, abdominal discomfort, and a fever of 102.4° F. I thought I had the flu. A week later, the sickness lingered. I missed my last week of classes and feared I wouldn't be able to attend graduation ceremonies. I was terribly weak and couldn't take care of myself.

I desperately wanted to walk down the aisle with my classmates, so I forced myself to finish my last two papers.

Three doctors were unable to determine what was wrong with me. I gained a measure of strength and was able to go to the baccalaureate and graduation ceremonies. Afterward, I returned to bed absolutely worn out and in pain.

An ultrasound and other medical examinations revealed a growth on my left ovary. Before I could receive treatment, I was in the emergency room with severe pain and admitted for tests. My abdomen was swollen, and I was having difficulty breathing.

The doctors came to my room, not having met me before, and said they would perform surgery on me the following Monday.

After surgery, the doctors spoke to my mother and son. "It's as if she were filled with cancer," the doctor said. "She was filled with infection with peritonitis setting in and had an abscess the size of a cantaloupe on her left ovary. We give her a 50-50 chance of survival. If she survives, she will be in intensive care for two weeks, and rehabilitation for four weeks. If you have faith, pray for a miracle."

My mother and son went home and called the prayer chains, the churches, family and friends. My classmates offered prayer in their churches. My brother vowed to fast and pray until I came out of intensive care.

I stayed in the ICU for only two days and was out of the hospital in three weeks. God had shown Himself merciful to yet another generation.[103]

Annalee Davis is an ordained minister, conference and retreat speaker, author, harpist, and adjunct professor (reverendannalee@comcast.net).

A Burned Face
(LOUISE LANKFORD-DUNLAP)

While I was washing my husband's gasoline-soaked clothes, the fumes filled the laundry room. When the washing machine changed cycles, an electric spark ignited the fumes and caused a loud explosion.

Both washer and dryer were blown apart, the window above them shattered, and curtains set afire.

Because I was standing near the washer, I caught the full force of the blast as a ball of fire burst into my face. My face and right arm were severely burned, and so were my eyelashes, my eyebrows, and my hair all the way to the scalp.

I cried out from the excruciating pain.

Hershel, my husband, rushed into the room and began praying for me. The pain subsided somewhat, but blisters formed over my burned, swollen face. Still in pain, I feared permanent scarring and disfigurement, and I agonized in prayer throughout the night and the next day.

We were pastoring the Assemblies of God Church in Smith River, California. That Sunday, I attended church with a painful, unsightly face.

Many in our congregation cried at the sight of my burned face. With love and compassion, they joined in fervent prayer for my healing.

By the time of the evening service, the pain and swelling were gone. Everyone witnessed the remarkable improvement. Three days later, the burned skin peeled off—leaving a smooth, scar-free face. My eyelashes, eyebrows and hair soon grew back, and neither my face nor arm shows any signs of ever having been burned. God still works miracles.[104]

Louise Lankford-Dunlap was credentialed as a minister in 1957. With her husband, Hershel, she saw many miraculous healings over more than 50 years of ministry. Now a widow, at age 81, her ministry has transitioned from the pulpit to the page (loudnherd@aol.com).

The Auntie in Fiji
(JANICE RICE)

The story I like to tell most often is from my mission trip to the island nation of Fiji in August 2009.

We woke up to our first day of ministry still suffering from jet lag. One of my youth group kids and I joined a Fijian sister and knocked on a door in Lautoka around nine o'clock that morning.

I didn't feel ready for ministry. But our mission team had sought the Lord with fasting and prayer for six months before coming to Fiji. I trusted that God would prepare the way for us.

The door opened and a tall native Fijian man invited us in to sit on his grass mat with him. We slipped off our flip-flops and stepped inside. The man's wife and daughters stood behind a makeshift kitchen counter, watching us closely. They were friendly but didn't seem open.

I thanked them for welcoming us into their home. Then I noticed a Bible on a shelf and asked if they were believers. They said they attended the local Assembly of God Church in Lautoka.

I told them we had come to Fiji to share the love of Christ with them. "Could we pray for you in any way? Do you need a job? Is anyone sick or in need of healing?"

Fiji, like many unindustrialized nations, has little medical help available for the poor. A hospital stay is only for life-or-death situations. People won't go to the doctor unless they are desperate or in horrible pain. Infections, nagging-but-manageable pain and disabilities are simply accepted as a way of life.

Just as I asked if anyone needed healing, "Auntie" entered the room. She couldn't walk, but pulled herself in on her hands, dragging her legs behind her. Words stuck in my throat at the realization that only a miracle would heal this dear woman.

Oh, Lord, I prayed silently. *What have we gotten ourselves into?*

The man of the house invited us to pray for his sister, who was obviously lame. Auntie leaned against the wall and pulled her legs under her long skirt with her hands. I turned to the youth group member who was with me and asked, "You ready?"

He smiled and said, "Let's do it."

We crossed the grass mat, aware that every eye in the family was on us. We knelt on either side of Auntie and started to pray. Suddenly, the power of God fell on her, and Auntie began to shake. I can describe it only as something like lightning filling her whole body. Her arms shot straight out in front of her.

"Lord, we can do nothing for this woman," I cried out, "but You can do anything. We ask You to touch her now with Your power. Heal her in Jesus' name."

Auntie planted her hands on the floor in front of her and pushed herself up to her feet. Strength filled her legs, and she started dancing and shouting, "Hallelujah! Hallelujah!"

I remained silently amazed.

Auntie's family watched in shock at what was happening.

I regained my voice, turned to her niece, and asked, "Can your Auntie walk?" I thought I was mistaken thinking she had been lame.

Without taking her eyes off her aunt, the niece answered, "My Auntie hasn't walked in five years."

I looked around the room. Auntie's family was in tears. I grabbed my youth group kid, amazed at what we had just seen. We started praising God and laughing in awe of this miracle.

"We've just seen the lame walk!"

A few days into the mission trip, I began to doubt whether Auntie's healing would last. Could she still walk? Her niece stopped us in the marketplace that same day, smiled warmly, and said, "Auntie is still walking. Thank you so much for praying for her."

Janice Rice is a pastor, speaker and writer. She has led numerous mission trips to Mexico and Fiji. She is the author of *Acsah* and a contributing author in *Heavenly Company* (janice.riverside@hotmail.com).

Pregnant with Appendicitis
(EDNA M. ELLISON)

When I was seven months pregnant with our second child, my husband had to take a business trip two states away. That night, as I sat on my four-year-old son's bedroom floor to play a game before bedtime, I felt a throb in my right side. During the night, the bursts of discomfort didn't subside but became more frequent. At dawn, I knew I needed help. My dad, who lived a few miles away, took me to the hospital.

Immediately upon our arrival, a nurse shouted, "Pregnant woman with appendicitis. Make way!" She wheeled me into an examination room, and an attending doctor diagnosed acute appendicitis. I almost passed out as he pushed and thumped my side.

Coming in and out of consciousness, I was aware that my father was calling my husband to tell him to return home immediately. My mother made arrangements for someone to take care of our son the next day.

I was admitted to the hospital and settled in a room with instructions to let the nurse know every time I had a pain. She assured me that if a pregnant woman had to have emergency surgery, the seventh month was a good time to have it. I didn't believe a word she said. For a pregnant patient, no time is a good time to have abdominal surgery.

Worried about my four-year-old and my poor husband, whose fanatical driving would probably result in a fatal wreck on the trip home, I drifted in and out of sleep. In a twilight state, I prayed throughout the night that God would heal me so I could escape surgery. I told Him I feared having a baby six weeks later with stitches still fresh from the surgery. I couldn't imagine how that would work successfully, and it sounded painful.

As I prayed, God reminded me of the prophecy in Isaiah 53:5 that says we are healed by His stripes.

Before dawn, the surgeon came in to begin the pre-op process. "Show me where it hurts," he said.

I thought for a few seconds. "Uh . . . I'm not hurting now."

He blinked. "You gotta be—"

I waited to feel the pain. "It's gone!"

I spent the next day in the hospital, but the pain never returned. Blood tests showed no infection or appendicitis.

Two months later, I delivered a beautiful baby girl, and I still have my appendix.

America's Christian mentoring guru, Edna Ellison, has trained and served as keynote speaker in diverse places such as London; Frankfurt; and Panama City, Florida. She has published 26 books and more than 400 articles (ednae9@aol.com).

Blind Eye Healed

James Hammonds wrote to *The Voice of Healing* magazine (and his testimony was also signed by a witness who knew the story). Hammonds said that arsenic lead had caused pus pockets to form behind his eyeballs. He underwent surgery in Memphis, Tennessee, for his right eye; however, the sight was completely gone, and they could do nothing to help him. For eight years, Hammonds remained completely blind in that eye.

Then W. V. Grant prayed for him during the Grant Campaign in Flint, Michigan. Afterward, Hammonds wrote, "I can see to read with my right eye and do not need glasses."[105]

Grossly Abnormal
(HELEN HEAVIRLAND)

"The results of your blood tests are slightly abnormal," my doctor said. "They indicate a tumor on your pituitary gland. There's really nothing to do right now, but come back in six months and we'll repeat these tests."

Maybe it was a fluke, I consoled myself when I started to worry. After all, I'd taken thyroid medication for 30 years—the tests were routine and had always been normal. *Lord, You've watched over me all these years*, I prayed. *Please handle this too. Help me not to worry but to keep trusting You.*

Six months later, we repeated the tests. Several days after that, my doctor telephoned. "This time the results are grossly abnormal," he said. "They definitely show the profile of a tumor on the pituitary gland. I want to run an MRI right away."

While I waited for the appointment, my mind raced. *Grossly abnormal ... tumor on the pituitary ... grossly abnormal ...* What I had heard of the doctor's report replayed in my mind.

Sunday, after I'd fasted and prayed, an impression so strong it sounded like a voice said, "Ask the doctor to recheck the lab work."

Monday, I called the doctor's office. Tuesday morning, 13 days after the previous blood was drawn, a lab technician drew more. Several days later, the office nurse called. "The doctor said to tell you, whatever you're doing, keep doing it," she said. "Your lab results look perfect. But be sure to repeat the tests in a month."

A month later, the results were normal again. Five months after that, the lab work was repeated again, and again it came back normal. This time I had a doctor's appointment.

"What happened?" I asked the doctor.

He had no answer. He paged through the lab reports in my chart. "Are you having any of the symptoms you had when the tests were abnormal?"

When I said no, he looked through his earlier notes, the question on his face growing. He finally looked back to me. "I don't know what happened."

"After you gave me the 'grossly abnormal' news, I fasted and prayed. I think God did a miracle, but I don't want to say that if there's a medical explanation."

"There's no medical explanation," he said. "Your words make more sense than anything I can come up with."

The next time I had routine lab work, I expected to hear that the results were normal, but now a different problem arose—my thyroid level was too high. Over the next few months, my doctor recommended dosage changes and repeated tests, and he referred me to an endocrinologist.

The endocrinologist looked over my records and asked numerous questions. Finally he said, "I rarely tell anyone who's been on thyroid medication to stop taking it, but I want you to stop.

You may feel tired and sluggish. Call if you have problems. If you do okay, have blood drawn after 30 days and make an appointment for a week later."

I didn't feel much different. Thirty days later, the lab drew blood. The next week, I saw the doctor.

"Normal," the endocrinologist reported.

"Your thyroid has started working again," he said. "I don't know how and I don't know why. Looks like you don't need to take the thyroid medication—at least for now."

God decided to repair the pituitary and did a good job—in the ensuing 15 years, both my pituitary and thyroid glands have functioned perfectly.

Helen Heavirland is a speaker, teacher and author. Her stories, articles, devotions and poems have appeared in a variety of compilations and magazines. She has published three books. "Grossly Abnormal" is condensed from a book in progress.

Afflictions and Fevers

Charles and Sarah Parham traveled and ministered across the plains of Kansas. Soon after the birth of their first son, Charles was afflicted with heart disease. As he battled physical weakness, their tiny son was stricken with a mysterious fever.

Nothing helped—not doctors and not medication. In his weakened state, Parham went to pray for a sick man. As he prayed, he heard the words in his heart, "Physician, heal thyself." He realized that was a word for him—and God healed him instantly.

When Charles came home, he told Sarah about his healing. He threw out his medication and vowed never to trust in anything but the Word of God. The fever miraculously left his son, who grew to be a healthy child.

The Parhams later moved to Ottawa, Kansas, where Charles held his first healing meeting. He preached and then prayed for the sick. One woman, given three days to live, was instantly healed, and a blind woman received her sight.[106]

A Lost Voice

The morning of January 14, 1990, Pastor Duane Miller awakened with flu-like symptoms and an extremely sore throat. He would have liked to stay in bed, but he had to preach three times that Sunday at First Baptist Church in Brenham, Texas. Because he was also a professional singer, Miller incorporated music into his messages.

During the first sermon, his voice became raspy. He sang, but he didn't like the sound that came out. For the second service, he left out the song and cut the sermon short.

By the evening service, he couldn't speak—so he asked a deacon friend to fill in for him.

After several days of bed rest, Miller recuperated from the flu, but his throat condition worsened. He consulted with numerous doctors, including a team of 13 specialists at the Baylor College of Medicine in Houston.

One of Miller's doctors videotaped his throat for a symposium of specialists in Switzerland. Those doctors diagnosed his condition as spasmodic dysphonia. They gave him no hope for recovery. The consensus was that he'd probably be mute before too long.

Because he could no longer serve his congregation even after an extended leave of absence, Miller resigned. He struggled because he had to give up what he loved—singing and preaching. The bills piled up, and he couldn't provide for his family. His wife went to work. They returned to Houston, where they had lived before taking the pastorate, and rejoined their home church.

In a *Focus on the Family* interview with Dr. James Dobson, Miller said, "I ran the gamut of emotions. There were times when I was angry with God. There were times when I was in despair." He talked about the well-meaning people who told him that there must be sin in his life, or that if he had sufficient faith his health would be restored.[107]

Miller continued to pray for healing. Friends and family members assured him they felt strongly he would regain his voice. Miller was certain he wouldn't return to the pulpit, and that his public ministry was over. He didn't stop believing that God could heal, but he decided that God had another direction for him.

Prior to taking the pastorate in Brenham, Miller had taught an adult Sunday School class at First Baptist Church in Houston. In the spring of 1992, the teacher for that class resigned, and the Sunday School director insisted that Duane should take the position. "I believe God wants you to teach the class," she said.

Miller wondered who would want to listen to his barely audible, raspy voice for an hour each Sunday. How would they hear him? Would his throat tolerate the strain? Reluctantly, and with the support of others, he agreed to teach. Class members rigged up an ultrasensitive microphone that would pick up the slightest whisper. The windscreen touched Duane's lips when he spoke.

On January 17, 1993, Miller taught the scheduled curriculum and read Psalm 103. Verse 3 says, "[God] forgives all my sins and heals all my diseases." He explained the verses and differing points of view on healing. After Miller had been teaching for about 20 minutes, his throat hurt badly. He strained to get the words out.

Verse 4 says that God "redeems . . . from the pit" (*NIV*). Miller began to speak about "pit experiences." As he did so, his voice grew stronger and stronger. He was shaken and overwhelmed with emotion. Members of the class audience reacted with applause and sang the "Doxology."

That Sunday School class was the only class at First Baptist that recorded the lessons. The audio recording captured Miller's miraculous healing that day—exactly three years to the Sunday from the day when his problems began. The recording serves as a witness to God's amazing power.[108]

When doctors performed a series of tests on Miller's throat, they couldn't find evidence that he had ever had a voice problem. They offered no explanation for why he had no trace of scar tissue.[109]

Freaky Face
(PEGGY CUNNINGHAM)

In 1981, we arrived in Bolivia, South America, to begin our missionary career. We landed with a thump on the short mountaintop airstrip. Our children, then ages 5 and 12, were enjoying every scary detail of this adventure.

My husband, Chuck, became the business manager of a mission station. My primary role was to be a dorm parent for 27 teenage girls. After a four-month initiation into missionary work, the school year ended and our crash course in Spanish began. Not only was I beginning Spanish study, but I also started having symptoms of a mysterious illness.

Each morning, I awoke with a different part of my face swollen. At first, the mission doctor thought the swelling was caused by bites from a *vinchuca*, a parasite insect that carries disease. We fumigated the dorm, but I had no relief.

We finally decided it was an allergy and tried to find the cause. But we were unsuccessful, and my face became distorted from the swelling—I called it a freaky sight. I cringed when I looked at myself; putting on make-up only enhanced the grotesque reflection in the mirror. I was barely recognizable, but I continued to go to class regardless of my appearance.

Five months after arriving in Bolivia, I went to my regular Spanish class. But that day was different; during class, my nose began to run. Chuck looked over and handed me a Kleenex, but I couldn't reach for it.

I was paralyzed. Chuck realized something was wrong and grabbed me. Other missionary students helped him lower me to the floor. I could see and hear, but I couldn't move.

Chuck wrapped me in a blanket and carried me to the school clinic. I was unable to see anything. I knew my husband was on my right side and the nurse on the left. Two friends also flanked my body.

Just then I saw bright lights. *I think I'm dying.* I felt calm and drifted into unconsciousness.

When I awakened, I was in the school clinic—alive, but still paralyzed. My head, packed in ice to reduce the swelling in my brain, was pounding and cold. Chuck was holding my hand, and his tired eyes revealed his concern.

As the swelling in my brain subsided, the movement of my body returned—first one side, then the other. Two days later, the mission plane transported me to a city hospital.

At the hospital, medical personnel injected me with steroids and put me on a strict diet. I improved, but the diagnosis wasn't what we wanted to hear. They said I was allergic to something in the area of the school, and that we would have to leave the area, and possibly Bolivia.

The doctors warned that I would die if we stayed at the school. Should we try to work in another part of Bolivia, only to find I had the same problem there, or should we return to the United States? We loved our ministry. Why would God have prepared us and provided for us to be in Bolivia, just to have us return home after six months?

We asked the leaders of the mission to pray over me and trust God to heal me. They came and prayed. I slept peacefully that night, knowing I was in God's hands.

The next morning, I faced another decision. What did I do next? I had taken a step of faith; now I had to act on it. I asked God to give me the faith to trust and act.

I stopped the injections and the restrictive diet. My taste buds came alive again; everything that touched my tongue was delicious. My face returned to its normal size and image within a week.

I was healed. My allergies never returned. Thirty years later, I'm still alive and living in Bolivia.

Peggy Cunningham and her husband, Chuck, have served since 1981 as missionaries in Bolivia, South America, where they have a children's ministry and two churches. Peggy is a freelance writer and contributes regularly to several Christian publications. See www.peggyjcunningham.com.

A Crippled Deacon

(DR. JAMES B. KEILLER)

My father, the pastor at Gospel Tabernacle in Beloit, Wisconsin, held a Sunday evening service with an emphasis on divine healing. One of his deacons, a construction worker, had fallen off a roof and broken his leg in several places, and he now wore a cast.

After my father gave the invitation for people to come forward for prayer, the deacon hobbled to the front of the church on crutches.

Father prayed for him, and he was immediately healed. The deacon threw down his crutches, tore off his cast, and joyously walked without complications.

"There's No Doubt"

(GENI J. WHITE, RN, MS)

One Tuesday evening in March of 1973, I felt unusually tired, went to bed early, and crawled under my covers.

Late that night I woke. My head felt as if someone had hit me with an ax. My stomach roiled in pain, and I felt worse than if I'd delivered all four of my pregnancies at the same time. Later my husband woke, turned on the bathroom light, and found me leaning against the stool. It was obvious I was quite ill. He called an ambulance.

After the attendants wrapped me in a warm blanket on their stretcher, I felt such comfort. Inside the barely-lit ambulance, the attendant asked, "May I pray for you?" As confused as I was, I nodded, and he prayed.

At the emergency room of Rockford (Illinois) Memorial Hospital, as I lay on the gurney, a doctor examined me. At one point he asked, "Where is the pain?"

"The back of my neck."

I reached my hand behind my neck and felt a line of walnut-sized lymph glands. Those swollen nodes prevented my neck from bending.

The doctor performed a spinal tap, which meant sticking a needle into my lower back to examine spinal fluid. After he finished, he said, "You have encephalitis." Because I'm a nurse, I knew that this was a serious brain infection.

In those days, 20 percent of encephalitis cases were fatal. I'd also known of patients who endured extended convalescences and lifetime problems, such as blindness.

Doctors in the emergency room didn't immediately administer antibiotics as is usually done. One doctor explained the delay in treatment, saying my personal physician would arrive shortly to order the proper medications. (My doctor didn't come that night.)

Around 5:30 in the morning, I was admitted to intensive care. A nurse gave me one aspirin for my headache. My stomach had quieted, probably because draining out spinal fluid had reduced pressure on my brain tissue.

I awakened less than two hours later, feeling so wonderful I couldn't lie still. Thinking I'd crawl out of bed near the foot, beyond the metal rails on each side, I slid on my knees toward the end of the bed, waving my arms and giggling for joy.

Just then, a nurse entered the room. "Stop! You'll fall on the floor."

I laughed, unable to contain my excitement. Only one pea-sized lymph node in the back of my neck hurt, and even that tiny soreness disappeared before my doctor finally arrived.

I'd seen infected tonsils so swollen they nearly closed off patients' throats. (Tonsils are lymph nodes.) In a few days, after antibiotic injections, those tonsils appeared normal. I knew the swelling and infection in the nodes across the back of my neck couldn't disappear in a couple of hours—especially when I'd received no antibiotics.

I hadn't prayed for healing, but the man in the ambulance had prayed for me. That's the only explanation I can figure out.

He was a stranger, and I never saw him again. I don't remember what he looked like.

Because I'd gotten well so quickly, several years later doubts crept in about whether I'd actually had encephalitis.

By then, we had changed doctors. My new physician, Dr. Michael Werkle, shuffled through my medical records while I told him about my experience. He leafed through, read the emergency room and laboratory reports, and said, in a surprised tone, "There's no doubt that you had encephalitis."

There's also no doubt that God healed me.

Geni White and her husband lived in Dubai for eight years before retiring to Oregon. They both taught English at a Chinese college for a year. See http://sam civy.wordpress.com and http://geniwhite.typepad.com.

A Lump and Lighthouse Temple
(Thelma Paslay with Juanita Paslay)

After the death of my father in 1912, our family moved to Eugene, Oregon. We became charter members of the Open Bible Standard Church, Lighthouse Temple, and two of my brothers, Bill and Clyde, attended Open Bible Standard Institute in Eugene. They both became pastors of churches on the west coast.

In the summer of 1980, Clyde's son, Billy, was elected as the pastor of Lighthouse Temple. That was about the time I developed an unusual lump on my neck.

In August, I showed it to my physician, Dr. Dederer. He wasn't initially concerned, yet two months later, the lump remained.

My sister-in-law urged me to return to the doctor. This time, Dr. Dederer ordered blood tests and X-rays and performed a biopsy; the results showed a form of leukemia. He sent me to Dr. Fitzgibbons, a blood specialist, who took more blood tests, re-checked the X-rays, and diagnosed me with nodular lymphoma.

Three weeks later, I had more blood tests and a bone marrow biopsy. A week after that, the doctor reported that cancer cells were in the bone marrow, and recommended that I start chemotherapy.

For financial reasons, I declined taking the expensive treatments and chose to take herbs instead, but they nauseated me, so I discontinued them.

On November 30, 1980, my pastor/nephew, Billy Johnson, invited sick people to come forward for a prayer of healing. I went to the altar with others.

After Billy anointed me with oil, and while he was praying, a shaft of beautiful light came down over my head and shoulders. It felt warm and peaceful, and the fear of cancer left instantly. I knew I was healed.

In July of the next year, friends said I should have the healing verified. So I returned to Dr. Fitzgibbons, who did a complete examination.

"You're healthy and cancer-free," he said, "but I'd like you to return in six months, because cancer often goes into remission."

I returned for another exam on December 17, 1981. As I knew they would be, my blood tests were normal. The lymph glands, spleen and liver all registered normal. Dr. Fitzgibbons found no physical evidence that I had ever had lymphoma.

Mary Thelma Paslay died in 1997 at age 86 from natural causes. Juanita Paslay wrote her testimony from notes she left for the family. Juanita is a member of Gideons International and Toastmasters International, and writes short fiction stories based on Scripture (folks7777@gmail.com).

Wheelchair Singer

An accident with a drunk driver on Christmas day, 1987, paralyzed 25-year-old Delia Roman Knox[110] from the waist down.

On the tenth anniversary of her accident, Knox decided to stop mourning. "From here on, I will worship and use what is productive in my life." She became an international gospel singer and evangelist—from her wheelchair. Her circumstances taught her to walk with God in a way she couldn't have done had she retained the use of her legs.

Although her faith was strong, and she wanted God to heal her, by the end of her twentieth year of paralysis, her hope for healing had wavered. On August 27, 2010, she and her husband, Bishop Levy Knox, attended the Bay of the Holy Spirit Revival in Mobile, Alabama, because the pastor, John Kilpatrick, had asked Levy to give a message at the beginning of the service. Nathan Morris from England would preach.

After Morris's message, people came forward for healing prayer. Delia was ready to go home, because countless past prayers for her healing had left her tired of being disappointed. Before she left, however, parents took their kidney-diseased baby forward. Compassion filled Delia's heart, and she cried for God to touch the child. As she begged God to heal the baby, Morris invited Levy to bring his wife forward for prayer.

Morris, Levy and others prayed for Delia. When Morris laid his hands on her calves, she cried out, "Lord, I allow You to do what You need to do with my life. You are my hope."

Delia *felt* the preacher's hands on her legs. With her left hand on her husband's shoulder and her right hand on Morris's shoulder, she stood. Although wobbly, and still supported on both sides, she took one step after another, back and forth across the front of the large room. As she continued to walk, the crowd of hundreds shouted praise to God.

Delia took unassisted steps for the first time in almost 23 years. She was able to hug her husband in a standing position.

Walking on atrophied legs caused her to be sore the next morning, but it was a blessing to her because she could feel. Gradually she built back the muscle strength in her legs.

Delia and Levy returned to the revival several weeks later, and they went to the platform. Delia walked across the platform in high heels and led the vast audience in praise to God.[111]

Sent Home to Die

Fifteen days before Christmas in 1981, doctors gave Dodie Osteen[112] the devastating news that she had metastatic liver cancer and only a few weeks to live. Medically, nothing could be done for her, so she was sent home to die.

Her husband, John, refused to believe the diagnosis. He told the doctors, "We're going to pray and seek God. We believe in miracles and in the Miracle Worker."

"You'll need a miracle," they said.

Weak and fuzzy-minded from medications, Dodie had relied on other people's prayers and faith during her 20-day stay in the hospital. At various times, Oral Roberts, Kenneth Hagin, Kenneth Copeland, and the T. L. Osborns called and prayed for her. Her Lakewood Church family and others prayed and fasted for her.

Once home, she realized that this was a personal matter between her and Jesus, and she needed to exhibit her own faith. She knew the doctors couldn't do anything to help her; she had to trust in God alone.

The day after she arrived home, Dodie asked John to pray with her. He anointed her with oil, and they lay facedown on the bedroom floor, pouring out their hearts to God. Dodie believes her healing began on that day.

In the days following, she examined her heart and asked God to show her issues she should address. She wrote letters to people she needed to forgive—and letters to people who might need to forgive her. When she was home by herself, her thoughts often overwhelmed her, so she went out and prayed for others. When she focused on others, she felt better.

She tried to keep her thoughts positive by meditating on Jesus day and night. She maintained a running conversation with God. As she performed routine tasks, she prayed. Day by day, little by little, she grew stronger.

Blood drawn two years after Dodie received her death sentence confirmed that a miracle had occurred in her life. The results were normal, and seven liver function tests showed normal readings.[113]

Mild Traumatic Brain Injury

(DICKSON SLATER)

On a Thursday morning in March 2010, I decided to ride an adult-size, standup tricycle down a friend's driveway. I crashed at the bottom, and my head whipped into the pavement. Although shaken up, I thought I was all right and went to work. That afternoon, I felt slightly nauseated, but nothing more. The next morning, I woke early to prepare for a meeting, because my wife, Teresa, and I planned to lead a mission team to Asia two weeks later. The nausea returned and was much worse.

I called two doctors, both of whom suggested that I probably suffered from a mild traumatic brain injury (MTBI). They told me what to watch out for, and both suggested rest. The nausea increased, and with it came intense pressure inside my head. I rested on Saturday. The next day I felt better, so I tried to work again.

By Monday, I could no longer keep track of what I was doing to prepare for our trip. I couldn't focus long enough to complete even simple tasks. A week after the accident, an X-ray revealed a broken rib, which happened when I fell against the handlebars as I went down. A CT scan showed no bleeding in my brain.

The trip to Asia went as scheduled, although I didn't know until two days before the flight if I would be able to go.

On the trip, I texted my doctor from a remote village located 12,000 feet above sea level. I was experiencing altitude symptoms I'd never had before. My symptoms worsened as nausea and pressure headaches became constant. The slightest increase of activity, such as walking fast or gathering materials before leaving home, instantly increased the pressure inside my head.

Within a month, I could no longer fall asleep without medication. I couldn't deal with conflict, and I struggled with depression. I lost the ability to carry on a logical conversation. Even with Teresa, I couldn't discuss the simplest details of life.

I tried to play with our kids, but became frustrated at the slightest provocation. Before the accident, Teresa and I had received frequent compliments on how patient we were with our children, especially with our nine-year-old son, Noah, who was born with Down Syndrome. Repeatedly, Noah asked me to jump on the trampoline with him. I tried, but whenever anything rattled my head, I spent the next several days in bed.

I did everything that I knew to do, both medically and spiritually, but after months, most of my symptoms remained. MTBI symptoms typically resolve within a few months, but mine didn't.

In August of 2011, I went to a clinic that specializes in brain issues. Technicians there performed SPECT scans of my brain function. The doctor said my test results were consistent with someone who had been unconscious for several days after a serious head injury.

The doctor prescribed an anticonvulsant medicine, and within a few days, I noticed some improvement. After two months, I felt somewhat better and stopped taking the medicine. By the next day, however, the symptoms had returned. I started taking the medication again, but I didn't have the same improvement the second time.

On the evening of November 2, 2011—20 months after the accident—I was at the leader's advance at Bethel Church. I stepped out of the worship service.

In the men's room, I stood at the urinal and rested my head against the wall. I felt the presence of God.

About that time, the worship service ended, and a stream of men entered and left the restroom. Two men asked me if I was all right, and I said I was. I felt somewhat self-conscious with men coming through.

I stood there for about 10 minutes. Then I felt my body lean slightly to the left. I lifted my head from the wall and rebalanced both legs. The instant I rested my head back against the wall, my symptoms left.

Just that quickly, I knew I was healed.

The next morning, I was up at 6:30. I told Noah that God had healed me.

"Let's jump!" he said.

We laughed and jumped together on our trampoline until it was time for school.

No pressure, no headaches, no symptoms of any kind.

Yes, God had healed me.

Dickson and Teresa Slater are pastors in Northern California. Dickson previously served for five years as a pastor in the Bethel School of Supernatural Ministry (dicksons@ibethel.org).

A Stroke of Grace
(Kristi Butler)

The snazzy new ringtone startled me as I hurried through the local art supply store. Struggling to balance my armload of purchases, I fumbled through my purse to find my cell phone. My husband, John, was calling to ask me to pick him up at the office.

"I'm not feeling quite right," he said, "I have vertigo or something."

As I hurried to my car, I replayed his words in my head. *Did his voice sound slurred?*

Even though I felt anxious, I kept telling myself: *Stay calm. Be strong.* I prayed as I drove.

The phone rang again. This time it was John's boss, who said, "He doesn't look good. We've called the paramedics."

By the time I reached John's office, an ambulance had already arrived. I reached the door just as the rescue team unloaded their gear. Co-workers ushered me into the room. My 49-year-old husband, who was also a soon-to-be father of the bride, was slumped in a chair, unable to move his left arm or leg. His face was drawn, and he seemed unable to look at me. I kissed him on the forehead and then moved out of the way of the technicians.

One of them knelt by John's side, stroked his arm, and said, "I'm your receptionist's Sunday School teacher. We're going to take good care of you."

His words comforted me.

We assumed that John had had a stroke. The paramedics loaded him onto a gurney and took him away. Those in his office prayed for John. Just before I left, I became aware that the room was filled with people, and all of them were praying—some aloud, others silently.

I called both sets of parents and several friends to ask them to pray as well. I rushed out of the building to follow the ambulance to the hospital.

As I learned later, inside the ambulance a female technician checked John's vitals and used her cell phone to call the hospital and describe his condition to someone in the emergency room.

John said, "I felt a strange sensation flow through my body. Feeling returned to my left side."

As the technician monitored him, she was aware of the change in his status. "This doesn't make sense," she told the ER. She asked my husband, "What's going on?"

John looked up at her. "Did you notice that room full of people as we came out of the building? They were all praying for me. It looks like God answered their prayers."

At the hospital, blood tests, CT scans and an MRI confirmed that John had suffered from a hemorrhagic stroke.

According to research on strokes that occur in that particular area of the brain, John should have faced months of rehabilitation. He had no residual effects.

Kristi Butler is a teacher, speaker and author. She blogs, writes devotions, and enjoys speaking for women's events and writers' conferences. See www.kristibutler.blogspot.com.

"You Don't Need My Services"
(BILL C. CROW WITH RUTH E. CROW)

I'd been healthy and strong, working hard in everything I did. I'd met each responsibility with my greatest effort, including my career as a professional firefighter, as well as playing and coaching sports.

During the fall of 2008, I started losing weight and experiencing shortness of breath. I gradually became too weak to sit at the table for meals. For the first time since early childhood, I relied on someone to help with basic tasks such as eating or getting dressed.

My wife, Ruth, and I asked our loved ones to pray. We regularly visited doctors for tests. Despite that, nothing revealed the source of my problem. At my lowest point, when I felt I was going to die, I completely surrendered to the Lord and knew I was ready to go to heaven.

After more extensive blood tests by a specialist, I was admitted to the hospital for the first time in my life. Along with a bone marrow biopsy and more tests, I received a blood transfusion to improve my blood cell count.

The next morning, our pastor, along with my wife and son, prayed at my bedside. I felt an immediate improvement. Instead of spending the expected week in the hospital, our doctor released me after only one night.

Follow-up visits to the oncologist over the next three months revealed my blood count was within the normal range.

The oncologist was amazed, because she had done nothing that could account for this improvement. I had received no treatment other than the initial transfusion during my hospital stay. "You don't need chemotherapy," she said. "In fact, you don't need my services."

I was healed—and have remained symptom-free.

Bill Crow retired as deputy chief from the Dallas Fire Department after 32 years of service. Ruth E. Crow served for 18 years as an officer in the Dallas Fire Department. Ruth is a graduate of the University of Texas at Dallas (B.A. Political Science with an emphasis on urban studies) and has contributed to six other books, including *Wired That Way* and *Communication Plus* from Regal Books (Ruth@Cumbytel.com).

A Cancer on Her Face

In 1964, Leroy Jenkins started a tent crusade in Pensacola, Florida. Only 75 people showed up for the first meeting in a tent that seated thousands. Members of the Jenkins team thought they should cancel the meetings, but Jenkins refused.

That night, Willie Blackwell, with a bandage covering her right cheek, was present. Jenkins said the Lord had shown him that there was cancer on her face. He told Blackwell to remove the bandage, and an ugly growth was revealed.

Jenkins held a tissue to her face and asked God to let the growth fall off. When he removed his hand, according to an eyewitness, the growth was gone, and Blackwell had an open sore on the side of her face.

After that miracle, people filled the tent.[114]

"I Can See!"

The late Reverend Canon Bill Riesberry, a retired Anglican priest, told about the monthly Bible studies he conducted at a senior citizens' residence.

About a year after these studies began, a man named John brought Russ to one of the meetings. Russ walked with a white cane, and John held a large-print Bible for him.

That night, the group studied the stories of the feeding of the 5,000 and the healing of a blind man. Although that was not his usual way, Bill asked John if they could pray for the return of Russ's sight.

After Russ consented, Bill and John laid hands on him and prayed for him.

"I can see! I can see!" Russ said with tears running down his cheeks.

Then they prayed for a woman named Evelyn. She took off her glasses, and after prayer, she said, "I can see your face."[115]

A Daughter Healed

Although A. B. Simpson embraced healing as a present work of grace, his wife did not. Their young daughter was diagnosed with diphtheria, and Simpson believed that God would heal her. His wife felt that they should seek medical help instead. When Simpson refused, she told him he would be responsible for the consequences.

Simpson cradled his daughter in his arms and committed her to God. Early the next morning, Mrs. Simpson saw the girl but initially refused to believe she could be better. After a few minutes, Mrs. Simpson admitted that every trace of the disease had disappeared. She left the room and, when alone, cried out to the Lord. From that time on, she opened their home to any who were sick.[116]

Simpson tells the story this way: "That night, with a throat as white as snow and a raging fever the little sufferer lay beside me alone. I knew that if the sickness lasted to the following day there would be crisis in my family, and I should be held responsible. . . . With trembling hand I anointed the brow . . . and claimed the power of Jesus' name. About midnight my heart was deeply burdened. I cried to God for speedy deliverance. In the morning her throat was well, and the mother, as she came to see the sick one, gave me one look, when she saw the ulcers gone and the child ready to get up and go about her play, which I shall never forget. From that hour I was never again asked to get a physician in my home."[117]

"My Name Is Richard"
(ROBERT PULEO WITH SALLY PULEO)

"Why don't we see healing miracles in the United States like those in the developing nations?"

My wife and I hear that question often. We give them a simple answer: "When Jesus is all you have, Jesus is all you need."

Sally and I are medical missionary associates with the Assemblies of God, and we travel with a group called Health Care Ministries. After receiving invitations, the organization sends teams of health care professionals around the world.

When we arrived in Zimbabwe in the spring of 2008, the resident missionary said, "The Minister of Health didn't approve your medical licenses, so you can't have a clinic."

That meant we couldn't use medicine to reach out to needy, hurting people. So, we decided to go to their homes and pray for the sick. Stifling heat, flies, dirt, and hopelessness surrounded us. Death clung to wasted bodies of AIDS victims as we prayed for healing and spoke of Jesus the Savior.

After praying for sick and dying people—too many to count—I longed to see a miracle.

The next morning, our team arrived at a local church and a smiling man welcomed me. "My name is Richard," he said. "Do you remember me?"

I did. He was a small man on crutches who moved laboriously toward me. I prayed for him, and he seemed to leave the same way he came.

"Yesterday my right side was paralyzed," Richard said. "Today I am whole."

His name was Richard, and his healing was the first miracle. That same day, a number of others came to the church and testified of restored sight, relief from back pain, cessation of heart palpitations, and paralysis reversed.

God didn't need a clinic or medications.

Robert Puleo and his wife are medical missionaries with the Assemblies of God. Their passion is that all people have access to the compassionate touch of God's love. Recently, their ministry took a new direction through speaking and writing (rspuleo@hotmail.com).

PART 2

QUESTIONS ABOUT

Healing

Does Healing
Happen Today?

The short answer is yes. I (Cecil Murphey) believe you can be healed today. However, there are others—committed and faithful Christians—who do not agree. In Part 1, I mentioned Pastor Olson, who opposed divine healing. I don't blame him for that theological stance. He was only following a long-established tradition. It's easy to trace his position back to the words of Luther and Calvin in the sixteenth century.

The reformers didn't *observe* healing taking place; thus, for them healing was no longer part of the Church's ministry. At least, that's how I see their position. Most leaders of that day and the days that followed insisted, "We have the Bible and the inner witness of the Holy Spirit. We don't need physical healing."

A later, influential scholar, B. B. Warfield (1851–1921), was a professor at Princeton Seminary from 1887 until his death. He wrote that healing and miracles "were part of the credentials for the Apostles as the authoritative agents of God in founding the church. Their function thus confined them distinctively to the Apostolic Church, and they necessarily passed away with it."[1]

Karl Barth (1886–1968), in volume 3 of his *Church Dogmatics*, said he could see no real purpose for the Spirit doing such miracles except to open our minds to understand and accept the original biblical revelation.

One of my seminary professors said to me, "Healing was dismissed by neglect rather than denial." He went on to tell me that after the Christian religion became the official faith of the Roman Empire, such things as healings weren't expected or preached. (That was a good, but partial, answer.)

I suppose that if I lived in a country where there was no television and I had never seen or heard one, I wouldn't believe in the existence of TV. One pastor said, "We don't receive healing today because we don't expect it." He may well have been right.

And yet, if we examine the history of the Church, we learn that healing appears in many writings from the first century to the present. Morton T. Kelsey lists St. Philip Neri, St. Frances de Sales and Jean Francois Regis praying for the sick. After the healing of his niece, Blasé Pascal added to his crest "the symbols of this healing with the words *'scio cui credidi'* (What I once believed, I now know)."[2]

As I'll show in later chapters, throughout human history we've found examples of people being prayed for *and their health is restored.* For example, in our western world, we can easily find records of healing beginning around 1904, slowing down for several decades, and then popping up again in the 1940s, slowing again, followed by a resurgence accompanying the charismatic movement in the 1960s and 1970s. Once again, today there seems to be a general slowing down. However, during the past two decades, the theological temperature has changed from the early definition and praying for the restoration of sick bodies seems to be accepted, believed and sought in many churches. Prayer and belief in physical healing has slowly permeated the thinking of serious, conservative Christians and has become an acceptable practice (if not a doctrine) among many believers.

Probably the force that has done the most to bring about awareness for modern believers has been the charismatic movement. Unlike previous widespread manifestations of the Holy Spirit, the "charismatic renewal" (as it is often called) hit all denominations and united believers as nothing else had done before.

Charis is the Greek word χάρις, which is used more than 150 times in the New Testament, and is most often translated as "grace." Those who call themselves charismatic believe in the current, ongoing supernatural work of the Holy Spirit today.

Healing, along with the ability to prophesy (or declare God's will), as well as speaking in tongues, tended to be part of their theology and experience in the early days when people referred to them as charismatics or neo-Pentecostals.

Modern charismatics seem to downplay speaking in tongues and put less emphasis on prophecy or claiming to declare God's will. They tend to speak of exciting worship styles and healing. One elder said to me, "Our worship style is characterized by a quest for inspired and ecstatic experiences."

I'm a Presbyterian minister and was a pastor for 14 years. I've encountered leaders of various denominations and independent congregations who anoint with oil and pray for the sick, following the instructions of James 5:14-15: "Are any of you sick? You should call for the elders of the church to come and pray over you, anointing you with oil in the name of the Lord. Such a prayer offered in faith will heal the sick, and the Lord will make you well. And if you have committed any sins, you will be forgiven."

Why Do Some Christians Believe We Can't Be Healed?

Here are five basic positions committed Christians hold on the matter of God healing sick bodies.

1. Healing and other miracles *ceased* with the end of the apostolic period.

2. Healing and other miracles *gradually faded* because the Church slowly moved away from belief in miracles and lined up with secular powers, beginning with the Romans in AD 313.

3. Healing and other miracles *ceased* because they were no longer needed as divine proof of the gospel.

4. Because of the sinfulness of Christians, God chose to withhold healing for our physical bodies.

5. Healing and other miracles *have never ceased.*

Many serious Christians have no strong opinion about healing and haven't considered that it might be a divine option. However, in this book we take position number 5—healing and other miracles have never ceased—and we document the ongoing movement of God's healing power.

For the past few months, I've spoken with many people about divine healing. To my surprise, I found more openness about the topic among pastors and lay people than I had expected. Even so, some still offered arguments against the compassionate grace of God. Let's take a look at some of the answers to those arguments.

What Are the Arguments Against Healing Today?

In this chapter, we will look at seven objections put forth about the validity of healing today.

Objection 1: Healing Was a Temporary Gift

This belief states that the healings we see in the New Testament represented a temporary gift God gave to believers to establish the Church. When I argue against this position, the natural response is, "I don't see any healings taking place."

I respond with, "Perhaps you're not in the right place to see them."

The argument that people don't *need* healing and other miracles since the death of the apostles doesn't hold up. Although periods of spiritual activity became intermittent after the apostolic period, by the end of John's exile on Patmos around AD 96, there was widespread persecution. This hostility continued through the time of Diocletian, until Constantine issued the Edict of Milan in 313, which made Christianity an official religion of the empire. So why wouldn't they need the same spiritual power during that period? Every reason for healing being available in the first 30 years of the Church is just as valid two thousand years later.

Objection 2: We Have Faith, So We Don't Need Healing Today

This is the argument I hear most frequently from those who say God used miracles, such as healing, to establish the Church. The belief is that once the gospel had spread throughout the known world, there was no further need for miracles. People believed in the risen Christ, so they didn't need healing or anything supernatural.

I assume that *one* of God's purposes in healing and doing supernatural things was to establish the Church, but what about compassion and God's lovingkindness? Don't we need the same compassion today?

According to Matthew 20:29-34, two blind men wanted healing. Verse 34 as usually translated says that Jesus, "moved with compassion," healed them. Mark 8:2 and Luke 7:13 also speak of Jesus' concern and empathy. There is an unchanging principle at work here. It is this: Jesus loved people, and when they came to Him, He felt compassion for them (see also Matt. 9:35-36; Luke 17:13; John 4:46-53). Has His divine compassion stopped? I don't think so. Hebrews 13:8 says that God never changes.

Objection 3: We Live in a Time of Grace and Don't Need External Signs

This argument adds, "Ours is the higher privilege because we walk by faith and not by sight." Those who believe this way usually point to the words Jesus spoke to Thomas after the resurrection: "You believe because you have seen me. Blessed are those who believe without seeing me" (John 20:29). So, we supposedly share the greater blessings because we believe without seeing any supernatural action by God.

That argument is a way of explaining silence rather than helping us understand why we don't see healing as a common experience within congregations. Because these congregations don't experience healing, or don't offer prayers for the healing of the sick, they don't believe in healing for today. Many congregations pray for God's will to be done or ask the Lord to make people recover quickly; but not many take a bolder step of faith and cry out, "Please heal her by Your Holy Spirit." Their prayers are usually, "Your will be done," which is a nice, safe way to pray. Although I affirm the ultimate answer is God's will, God tells us to ask and to pray without ceasing (see Matt. 7:7; 1 Thess. 5:16).

In *The Ministry of Healing*, A. J. Gordon argues against those who say that miracles, including healing, have ceased:

Why having been once begun should they entirely cease? . . . On the day of Pentecost the Holy Spirit was installed in office to abide in the church perpetually. Exactly as the first disciples were under the personal ministry of Christ we are under the personal ministry of the Comforter. Having begun his miracles at Cana of Galilee, Jesus never permanently suspended them. His last gracious act before he was delivered into the hands of wicked men was to stretch forth his hand and heal the ear of the high priest's servant. And having wrought the first notable miracle after Pentecost by the hand of Peter at "the Beautiful Gate" why should the Holy Ghost in a little while cease from his miraculous works?[3]

Gordon later adds:

Then again the use which was made of miracles of healing as signs seems to argue strongly for their permanency. If the substance remains unchanged why should the sign which was originally chosen to exhibit it, be superseded? . . . The answer given by the majority to this question is "Signs are no longer needed." If reason can be satisfied with this answer, faith cannot. For "faith has its reasons, which reason cannot understand." Among these is this: "Jesus Christ, the same yesterday, today and forever."[4]

After Gordon makes his case for healing today (or in his day), he makes this lengthy summation:

Is it reasonable to conclude that the office of healing through faith, resting on the same apostolic example and held by the same tenure of divine promise and precept as the other functions of the Christian ministry, was alone destined to pass away and disappear within a single generation?[5]

Objection 4: If We Don't Have Faith to Believe in Healing, We Can't Pray for It

That's certainly an honest statement. God wants us to believe, but nowhere does the Bible say *not* to pray if we don't have faith. In fact, Mark records the story of a demon-possessed boy whose father asks Jesus for help: "Teacher, I brought my son so you could heal him. He is possessed by an evil spirit that won't let him talk. And whenever this spirit seizes him, it throws him violently to the ground . . . so I asked your disciples to cast out the evil spirit but they couldn't do it" (Mark 9:17-18).

A little later that father says, "Have mercy on us and help us if you can." To that plea, Jesus says that anything was possible for those who believe. The father instantly cries out, "I do believe, but help me overcome my unbelief" (vv. 24). And Jesus heals the boy.

That story encourages us to pray, whether or not we have faith for healing. If we, or someone we care about, is sick and needs deliverance from illness, isn't that the right time to ask God for healing?

We pray because we care; we pray because we're emotionally touched and see a serious need. That's all it takes and all that God asks of us. If we use the analogy of a parent-child discussion over something the child wants, the argument would be like saying children never ask their parents for anything unless they're positive they'll get what they want. Any parent knows that's not true.

We ask because God tells us to ask. And when we ask, we show faith even if doubt co-exists, as it did with that father mentioned in Mark's Gospel. Would we pray if we didn't believe God exists and *might* give us the answer? It may not be the level of faith some want, but to ask makes it clear that we have some trust in a benevolent God.

In Mark 11:24, Jesus says, "I tell you, you can pray for anything, and if you believe that you've received it, it will be yours." Faith has always been important, but it's not *the* contingent factor. That is, some people such as the lame man in John 5, or the cripple at the Temple on the day of Pentecost recorded in Acts 3, are healed without any evidence of faith.

I point this out because most people who strongly believe in healing stress our role in the healing. "Believe and you'll be healed." The unsaid words are, "Doubt and you won't." The problem with such an approach is that it treats the unhealed as if they are lesser Christians with imperfect faith.

Objection 5: Sickness Is Just Something We Must Endure

This is what I call the martyr-complex response. It's saying that God laid sickness on me and if I do anything about it, I'm fighting against God. And yet individuals who make such statements consult doctors to remove tumors, insert a stint, or have an appendix removed. Are they not then disobeying God by trying to find healing?

Paul had a marvelous experience of being caught up into paradise or the "third heaven" (see 2 Cor. 12:1-10). Afterward, he said that God gave him a thorn in the flesh to keep him humble. He never explains what that thorn was, but most scholars believe it was a physical ailment.

I'd have to ask, "Why would God choose to give *anyone* (Paul or you) a thorn in the flesh?" Paul's thorn was to keep him humble and not brag about his special visit to heaven.

Isn't it more honest to say, "I would like to be healed, but so far God hasn't delivered me"? Is God chastising the person for wrongdoing or for failure to do something? Wouldn't it be wiser—and certainly more spiritual—to confess and ask God to heal?

Objection 6: Only Those with the Gift of Healing Can Pray for the Sick

This argument, which I hear occasionally, is that only those who have a gift of healing can pray for the sick. It's not only a weak argument, but there's also nothing in the Bible to suggest that the Holy Spirit works only through those with such a gift.

Paul's exhortation in Philippians 4:7-8 is that we pray for anything that disturbs or troubles us. First Peter 5:7 urges us to cast *all* our care on him. If I'm unconcerned about someone who is sick, where is my compassion and Christian love if I refuse to ask for his healing?

Objection 7: It Is a Sin to Pray for Those with "Sickness unto Death"

This argument is based on John 11:4 in the story of Lazarus, Jesus' friend who died and was buried. "Sickness unto death" is the way older versions translate the verse. Because of this, people believe it would be sinning to pray for the healing of that person. However, a newer translation of John 11:4 reads, "This sickness will not end in death."

Eventually every human dies, but no one knows when it's God's time to take that person. Isn't it better to pray and let God decide? If it's not a sickness that leads to physical death, perhaps it will please God to heal that person.

I think of the words of Jesus in the Garden of Gethsemane. Luke records the entire story in 22:39-46. Jesus prayed fervently, "Father, if you are willing, please take this cup of suffering away from me" (v. 42). Luke writes, "He prayed more fervently, and he was in such agony of spirit that his sweat fell to the ground like great drops of blood" (v. 44). But Jesus' ultimate prayer was, "I want your will to be done, not mine" (v. 42). Only after importuning and crying out to God did Jesus face the reality that His mission and purpose were to die.

I lived in East Africa for several years among the Luo people, and one thing my mentor-friend Henry Nyakwana used to say has stayed with me: "It does no harm to ask. You might get what you want or receive a promise of something else." That's the principle I use when praying for the sick.

Conclusion

Let's sum up our discussion of why some believe healing is for today and some don't. No matter for whom we pray, ultimately isn't

God the one who heals? Why not pray for individuals who say they want healing? Why not pray with fervency, and let God decide who will live and who won't? By what authority do we take on the responsibility of refusing to pray for healing for a needy person? Shouldn't we rather be focusing on exhibiting the same compassion Jesus showed to people of His time who needed healing?

Years ago, a group of us prayed fervently for the healing of a woman who had been active in our church. After several minutes, Shirley, my wife, said, "As I prayed, I felt God impress on me that she won't survive. God is ready to take her home." We stopped praying for her and focused on asking God to comfort the family. The woman died the next day. In that instance, we did the right thing. We prayed and God answered—not in the way we asked, but it was still an answer.

Does Sickness Happen Because of Sin?

The answer is yes—sometimes. We have to admit that sin certainly brought about sickness. There is no evidence of death before sin entered the world. We can think of diseases and infirmities as part of the divine program that ultimately leads to physical death.

But that's not the real argument. The people who ask the question about sickness being the result of sin usually seek a direct cause-and-effect answer.

Sometimes we can make that connection. If I rush down the street and ignore anything in my path and I fall and scrape my knee, it's obvious that I did something and the skinned knee is the result. If we mistreat our bodies, we can sometimes produce a direct line to illness. Research tells us that if we smoke, it's an excellent way to prepare for lung cancer. If we're obese, we're preparing ourselves for diabetes, hypertension, or heart disease.

It's not always that easy to connect cause and effect of illness. We now know that environmental factors and inherited tendencies toward specific diseases affect even newborns.

Even if we can connect a distinct sin to a sickness, doesn't the Bible give us clear directions on what to do? James 5:13-16 says that the sick should call the elders for prayer. Here are two statements from that passage:

1. "The Lord will make you well. And if you have committed any sins, you will be forgiven" (v. 15).

2. "Confess your sins to each other and pray for each other so that you may be healed" (v. 16).

Consider also these words from David: "When I refused to confess my sin, my body wasted away, and I groaned all day long . . .

Finally, I confessed all my sins to you and stopped trying to hide my guilt. I said to myself, 'I will confess my rebellion to the LORD.' And you forgave me! All my guilt is gone" (Ps. 32:3,5-6).

Psalm 38:3 reads, "Because of your anger, my whole body is sick; my health is broken because of my sins." Jesus sometimes connected sickness and sin; He forgave sin and healed sickness (see Mark 2:5; John 5:14). Psalm 103:3 reads, "[God] forgives all my sins and heals all my diseases."

I suggest that the sick who want prayer should first examine their own hearts and confess any perceived wrongdoing.

Consider Paul's blindness on the Damascus Road. Paul, then called Saul, was struck to the ground and blinded. Reading Acts 9:1-19 makes it clear that *God* struck him blind. Three days later, the Lord sent Ananias to pray for Paul to be healed, and he was. An even clearer case is the story of the sorcerer Elymas, or Bar-Jesus. He tried to prevent the governor Sergius Paulus in Paphos from believing the good news about Jesus Christ:

> Saul, also known as Paul, was filled with the Holy Spirit, and he looked the sorcerer in the eye. Then he said, "You son of the devil, full of every sort of deceit and fraud, and enemy of all that is good! Will you never stop perverting the true ways of the Lord? Watch now, for the Lord has laid his hand of punishment upon you, and you will be struck blind. You will not see the sunlight for some time." Instantly mist and darkness came over the man's eyes, and he began groping around begging for someone to take his hand and lead him (Acts 13:9-11).

In another place, Paul made it clear to the Corinthian Christians that some of them observed the Lord's Supper in an unworthy manner.

> So then, whoever eats the bread or drinks the cup of the Lord in an unworthy manner will be guilty of sinning against the body and blood of the Lord. Everyone ought

to examine themselves before they eat of the bread and drink from the cup. . . . That is why many among you are weak and sick, and a number of you have fallen asleep [died] (1 Cor. 11:27-28,30, *NIV*).

The Sickness/Sin Connection in the Old Testament

The following references are accounts of sicknesses in the Old Testament that point directly to sin:

- Genesis 12:17: Pharaoh's entire household was afflicted with serious diseases because the ruler took Abraham's wife into his palace.

- Genesis 20:18: Abimelech's household became barren when he unwittingly planned to take Sarah as his wife.

- Numbers 12:10: Miriam became leprous for slandering her brother, Moses.

- Numbers 14:11-12,36-37; 17:12-15; 25:3-9,17-18; 31:16: God threatened the people of Israel with pestilence when they were rebelling against Moses and Aaron, struck down many, and later inflicted a plague on them when they turned to Baal.

- 1 Samuel 5:6–6:12: After the Philistines captured the Ark of God, wherever it was taken the people suffered from tumors.

- 1 Samuel 6:19: The 70 sons of Jeconiah were struck down because they did not rejoice at the return of the Ark of the Covenant.

- 2 Kings 1:16: Because King Ahaziah consulted Beelzebub, God refused to heal him.

- 2 Kings 5:26-27: Gehazi contracted leprosy because of his greed and deception.

- 2 Kings 6:18-20: In answer to Elisha's prayer, God struck the enemy blind, but He later restored their sight.

- 2 Kings 19:35; 2 Chronicles 32:21: Sennacharib's army was struck down in the night by the angel of God.

- 2 Chronicles 26:16-20: Because of his pride, King Uzziah became a leper.

- 2 Chronicles 21:14-15: For deserting God, Jehoram was struck down by an incurable disease of the bowels.

The Sickness/Sin Connection in the New Testament

In Acts 5:1-11, we read the story of Ananias and his wife, Sapphira, in the early days of the Christian Church. They sold some property, and Ananias brought part of the price to Peter, claiming he was giving the total amount.

Here are Peter's words of rebuke: "The property was yours to sell or not sell, as you wished. And after selling it, the money was also yours to give away. How could you do such a thing like this? You weren't lying to us but to God!" (v. 4).

The Bible says that "as soon as Ananias heard these words, he fell to the floor and died" (v. 5). Later, Sapphira came to the church, and Peter questioned her. She lied just as her husband had done. After Peter rebuked her for conspiring with her husband, he said, "The young men who buried your husband are just outside the door, and they will carry you out, too" (v. 9).

Luke writes succinctly, "Instantly, she fell to the floor and died" (v. 10). Isn't death the ultimate punishment for sin?

Later, in Acts 19:11-16, we find the account of Paul at Ephesus, where God did amazing miracles and healings through him and cast out evil spirits:

A group of Jews was traveling from town to town casting out evil spirits. They tried to use the name of the Lord Jesus in their incantations, saying, "I command you in the name of Jesus, whom Paul preaches, to come out!" Seven sons of Sceva, a leading priest, were doing this. But one time when they tried it, the evil spirit replied, "I know Jesus, and I know Paul, but who are you?" Then the man with the evil spirit leaped on them, overpowered them, and attacked them with such violence that they fled from the house, naked and battered (vv. 13-16).

The text goes on to say that after the story spread, many people came to Jesus Christ. The deaths of Ananias and Sapphira, the blinding of Saul (Paul) on the Damascus road, and the blinding of the magician Elymas are examples of judgment for sin. The battering of the Jewish exorcists illustrates the danger of attempting to exorcise demons in the powerful name of Jesus without true faith.

Not All Sickness Has a Direct Reference to Sin

Job is the most obvious example of this. In Job 2:4-7, Satan taunted God by saying, " 'But reach out and take away [Job's] health, and he will surely curse you to your face!' 'All right, do with him as you please,' the LORD said to Satan. 'But spare his life.' So Satan left the LORD's presence, and he struck Job with terrible boils from head to foot." Job had done no wrong when God allowed Satan to test him.

The stories are told in the Bible of various women who were barren. Often women were judged as being barren because they had sinned. However, none of them were judged by God of wrongdoing.

The Old Testament generally presents sickness as caused by personal sin or by association with others who have sinned—including groups or nations. Nevertheless, there are more occasions when sickness has no connection at all with sin, except that of being part of the fallen human race. God clearly allows sickness for purposes other than punishment.

God said to Moses, "Who makes a person's mouth? Who decides whether people speak or do not speak, hear or do not hear, see or do not see? Is it not I, the LORD?" (Exod. 4:11; see also Isa. 19:22; 45:7; Jer. 14:19; 30:12-17; Amos 3:6).

In the New Testament, Jesus made it clear that all sickness isn't the result of sin. Several times the New Testament speaks of Satan causing the illness:

- Evil spirits are connected in the Bible with the work of Satan. In Matthew 10:1, "Jesus called his twelve disciples together and gave them authority to cast out evil spirits and to heal every kind of disease and illness."

- Jesus healed a woman on the Sabbath and said, "This dear woman, a daughter of Abraham, has been held in bondage by Satan for eighteen years. Isn't it right that she be released, even on the Sabbath?" (Luke 13:16).

- When Peter preached to Cornelius he said, "And you know that God anointed Jesus of Nazareth with the Holy Spirit and with power. Then Jesus went around doing good and healing all who were oppressed by the devil, for God was with him" (Acts 10:38).

Jesus didn't focus on the cause of the sickness but on healing the afflicted. Several times He also said that their sins were forgiven. He may very well have been saying that for the benefit of the Jewish leaders who attributed every sickness to sin.

John 9:1-5 is the story of a man who had been born blind. When Jesus' disciples asked who had sinned—the man or his mother—they showed the contemporary thinking that God brought the blindness so someone must have been guilty. Jesus' answer makes His position clear: " 'It was not because of his sins or his parents' sins,' Jesus answered. 'This happened so the power of God could be seen in him' " (v. 3).

Does God Cause Sickness?

The next question might well be, "If sickness isn't caused by sin, does God cause sickness?" Throughout the Old Testament the writers present God as the sovereign Lord in absolute control, and nothing happens without His involvement by direct actions or by granting divine permission. For example, God:

- Created all things
- Gave Adam and Eve life
- Selected Abraham to be the father of Israel
- Chose Isaac over Ishmael and Jacob over Esau, despite their not being the firstborn
- Selected the younger Joseph to be the deliverer rather than one of his ten older brothers
- Passed over seven of Jesse's sons and chose David, the youngest

The Old Testament attributes all matters of life and death to God. Sickness and health, prosperity and poverty, victory and defeat—nothing happens without God being actively involved, for He is sovereign.

The first mention of disease occurs in Genesis 12:17: "But the LORD sent terrible plagues upon Pharaoh and his household because of Sarai, Abram's wife."

In Leviticus 26:15-26, God tells the Israelites about future punishments if they don't obey. He mentions physical affliction such as "wasting diseases and burning fevers that will cause your eyes to fail and your life to ebb away" (v. 16).

Through Moses, God declared to Israel, "There is no other God but me! I am the one who kills and gives life; I am the one who wounds and heals" (Deut. 32:39). Throughout the Old Testament, God blesses with health but sends sickness, misery, misfortune and even death as punishments.

Today we have trouble saying God causes or permits anything negative such as sickness. Perhaps we feel we must defend God or explain the divine actions. My response is that I'm not intelligent enough or wise enough to attempt to do that. My belief in a sovereign God means absolute sovereignty.

The writers of the Old Testament frequently referred to God sending or causing bad things to happen. For me, it's a matter of

faith. All through the Bible, God's people were able to accept that
God caused or sent troubles.

What Is the Gift of Healing?

The Bible speaks about healing from two perspectives. As James 5:14 points out, elders should pray for the sick that they will be healed. Although James doesn't specifically state the fact, the implication here and in other places in the New Testament is that elders and all believers without any kind of specific gift or ability can pray for the sick. Nothing in the Bible suggests that such prayer for the sick is limited to a specific class or group.

There are also *gifts* of healing mentioned in 1 Corinthians 12:4 (it's a plural noun in Greek, though translated as singular in most English Bibles). As we prepared Part 1 of this book, we were aware that some people who have amazing results in praying for sick people also have limited success. That is, some seem gifted to pray for the deaf and the mute; others have amazing results by praying for broken arms and legs; and still others in praying for those with any type of heart disease.

On a national Christian talk show, one woman said, "I have had great success in praying for people with cancer. That seems to be my special anointing." She said she had witnessed other healings through prayer, but she was most successful in praying for any of the 200 types of cancer.

Paul writes to the Corinthians about spiritual gifts in 1 Corinthians 12. Most people who believe in and exercise spiritual gifts today affirm that it's a gift and not a possession. That is, those with a gift of healing sometimes pray for the sick and God heals them—but not always. This position considers healing a function of the Church as a *corporate entity*; that is, spiritual gifts function within the Christian fellowship for the good of everyone.

There is a distinction between believers praying for the sick and those with the gift of healing. Compassion for the afflicted is always open to believers, and many times God answers sincere prayers. Beyond that, in 1 Corinthians 12 Paul lists various spiritual gifts given to the Church that are administered through individuals.

He begins with these words: "There are different kinds of spiritual gifts, but the same Spirit is the source of them all" (v. 4). Verse 7 reads, "A spiritual gift is given to each of us so we can help each other." He lists several of them, including the power to perform miracles: "to someone else the one Spirit gives the gift of healing" (v. 9).

Near the end of the chapter, the apostle points out that God gives specific gifts to certain people and that no one has all of them. "Do we all have the power to do miracles? Do we all have the gift of healing? Do we all have the ability to speak in unknown languages? Do we all have the ability to interpret unknown languages? Of course not!" (vv. 29-30).

Did Only Apostles Heal During the Time of the Early Church?

The answer is an emphatic *no* as we mentioned in the previous chapter. Here is the evidence.

Acts 8 records what happens after Christians were persecuted and scattered from Jerusalem: "All the believers except the apostles were scattered through the regions of Judea and Samaria" (v. 1). Verses 4 through 8 describe the ministry of Philip, who was *not* an apostle. In Acts 6, we learned he was one of seven men chosen to make sure the Greek-speaking widows in Jerusalem weren't slighted in the daily distribution of food.

We read the account of Philip going to Samaria and preaching: "Many evil spirits were cast out, screaming as they left their victims. And many who had been paralyzed or lame were healed" (Acts 8:7). Although it doesn't specifically mention healing, we can infer from the text and the activity within the Early Church that God used another table-waiter (or deacon) named Stephen to heal. "Stephen, a man full of God's grace and power, performed amazing miracles and signs among the people" (Acts 6:8). *Signs* is one of the ways the biblical writers refer to healing.

No place in the New Testament does it state that only apostles could heal. Paul points out in 1 Corinthians 12, "A spiritual gift is given to each of us so we can help each other" (v. 7). He lists many spiritual gifts after that, including the gifts of healing (see v. 9).

The obvious conclusion is that God provides abilities (*charisma*) for the Church to minister to human needs. Paul says all of us have gifts because the Holy Spirit provides them. The ability to heal the sick is only one of those gifts. But nowhere does it say that only those so gifted can pray for the sick.

Are There Certain Conditions for Healing to Occur?

Several promises for healing and health appear in the Old Testament. We often read and claim them without being aware of the historical context in which God spoke. The promises are true, but God offers healing and health *only* to those who obey Him. Below we quote the promises in their context to make this clear.

Exodus 15:25-26

Shortly after the Israelites left Egypt under Moses' leadership, they arrived at a place called Marah. They couldn't drink the bitter water and complained. God told Moses to throw a piece of wood into the water. After that they were able to drink. That's when God promises to heal—but it's conditional. It was there at Marah that the Lord set before them the following decree as a standard to test their faithfulness to him: "If you will listen carefully to the voice of the LORD your God and do what is right in his sight, obeying his commands and keeping all his decrees, then I will not make you suffer any of the diseases I sent on the Egyptians, for I am the LORD who heals you."

Exodus 23:25-26

During the years in the wilderness, God again promises healing to the Israelites and also sets up the condition: "You must serve only the LORD your God. If you do, I will bless you with food and water, and I will protect you from illness. There will be no miscarriages or infertility in your land, and I will give you long, full lives."

Deuteronomy 7:12-15

Just before the former Egyptian slaves entered into the Promised Land, we read another promise: "If you listen to these regulations and faithfully obey them, the LORD your God will keep his covenant of unfailing love with you, as he promised with an oath. . . . He will love you and bless you, and he will give you many children. . . . None of your men or women will be childless, and all your livestock will bear young. And the Lord will protect you from all sickness. He will not let you suffer from the terrible diseases you knew in Egypt, but he will inflict them on all your enemies!"

Psalm 103:3

This verse reads, "[God] forgives all my sins and heals all my diseases."

Isaiah 33:24

This verse is a promise to the people of Israel after their defeat by the armies of Assyria. "The people of Israel will no longer say, 'We are sick and helpless,' for the LORD will forgive their sins."

Isaiah 53:5

This is one of the great promises of the Old Testament that foretells the coming of Jesus, the Messiah. "But he was pierced for our rebellion, crushed for our sins. He was beaten so we could be whole. He was whipped so we could be healed." We could argue this refers only to spiritual healing, but if we think about the first people who read this verse, it seems obvious that they would have assumed the literal interpretation of healing for their bodies.

Hosea 6:1

In this passage, written by the prophet about 30 years before the destruction of the northern kingdom, he calls for the people to repent. This is figurative language. The two verses may not be a literal promise for physical healing, but many who believe in divine healing quote them: "Come, let us return to the LORD. He has torn us to pieces; now he will heal us. He has injured us; now he will bandage our wounds."

Malachi 4:2

This is another figurative passage and sets up the coming of Elijah (i.e., John the Baptist). "But for you who fear my name, the Sun of

Righteousness will rise with healing in his wings. And you will go free, leaping with joy like calves let out to pasture."

Other Verses

Here are some other verses that *may* refer to physical healing:

My child, pay attention to what I say. . . . Don't lose sight of them . . . for they bring life to those who find them, and healing to their whole body (Prov. 4:20-22).

"Lord, help!" They cried in their trouble, and he saved them from their distress. He sent out his word and healed them, snatching them from the door of death (Ps. 107:19-20).

O Lord my God, I cried to you for help, and you restored my health. You brought me up from the grave, O Lord. You kept me from falling into the pit of death (Ps. 30:2-3).

Is Demon Possession an Illness?

Demon possession occurs in biblical accounts. The biblical writers spoke of the activity of evil spirits or demons. Jesus and the apostles cast out demons or cleansed people from such spirits. Today we call this action "exorcism."

Matthew 12:22-26 tells the story of a demon-possessed man whom Jesus healed so that "he could both speak and see" (v. 22). Although the people were amazed, the religious leaders cried out, "No wonder he can cast out demons. He gets his power from Satan, the prince of demons." Jesus countered with, "If Satan is casting out Satan, he is divided and fighting against himself. His own kingdom will not survive" (vv. 24,26).

Today, most people would call demon possession mental illness. An obvious example is the naked man who lived among the tombs and beat up people. Mark 5:1-20 tells the story of the man's deliverance and ends with these words: "So the man started off to visit the Ten Towns of that region and began to proclaim the great things Jesus had done for him, and everyone was amazed at what he told them" (v. 20). So, regardless of whether we call it demon possession or mental illness, Jesus and His disciples healed them.

When we examine the records of the Early Church fathers, they spoke of those possessed by evil or unclean spirits.

A Biblical View of Demons

Here are New Testament verses that call the sickness the work of various spirits.[6]

- Matthew 12:22-28: Blindness and muteness caused by a demon (Greek *daimonizomenos tuphlos kai kophos*), which Jesus healed by driving out the demon.

- Matthew 9:33: Muteness caused by a demon (*anthropon kophon daimonizomenon*).
- Mark 9:17,25: Mute and deaf spirit (*pneuma alalon /to alalon kai kophon pneuma*).
- Luke 11:14: Demon of muteness (*daimonion . . .kophon*).
- Luke 13:11: Refers to a spirit of sickness (*pneuma astheneias*).
- Acts 16:16: Spirit of divination (*pneuma puthona*).
- Romans 11:8: Spirit of stupor (*pneuma katanuxeos*).
- 1 Timothy 4:1: Deceiving spirits (*pneumasin planois*).

Jesus Exorcized Demons from People

Exorcisms show a different approach. Although Matthew and Luke also record deliverance from demons, here are the four mentioned in the Gospel of Mark:

Mark 1:21-28

Jesus attended the synagogue at Capernaum. "Suddenly, a man in the synagogue who was possessed by an evil spirit began shouting." In this account, the man, possessed by an evil spirit, recognizes Jesus, fears Him, talks to Him and addresses Jesus as "the Holy One sent from God." The Lord commands, "Be quiet! Come out of the man." After that, "the evil spirit screamed, threw the man into a convulsion, and then came out of him."

Mark 5:1-20

This is the most famous of the demon-possession stories, and is also recorded in Matthew and Luke. The possessed man lives among the burial caves and is quite violent. Even when chained, he breaks free. He wanders in the hills, howling and cutting himself with sharp stones.

When confronted, the demon reacts much like the one in Capernaum. He tells Jesus his name is Legion—a reference to a band of Roman soldiers that numbered between 3,000 and 6,000 men—to imply that there are many of them. When this demon leaves it doesn't convulse the man.

Mark 7:24-30

This story is quite different from the other three. A gentile woman asked Jesus to free her daughter who is possessed by an evil spirit. The daughter is at home, and Jesus tells the woman, "Now go home, for the demon has left your daughter." The story concludes by telling us that when the mother returns home, "she found her little girl lying quietly in bed, and the demon was gone."

Mark 9:14-29

This recounts the story of a father who brings his son to Jesus. "He is possessed by an evil spirit that won't let him talk. And whenever this spirit seizes him, it throws him violently to the ground" (vv. 17-18). Jesus "rebuked the evil spirit. 'Listen, you spirit that makes this boy unable to hear and speak,' he said, 'I command you to come out of this child and never enter him again!' Then the spirit screamed and threw the boy into another violent convulsion and left him. . . . Jesus took [the boy] by the hand and helped him to his feet, and he stood up" (vv. 25-27).

How Does God's Will Play a Part in Times of Healing?

To ask about the decline of healing is one way to look at divine healing, but the question is misleading in that it implies or suggests that healing has not only declined but also disappeared. That's the wrong question.

The answer usually comes out that Christians turned away from God, became less concerned about total commitment, or lived in such a way that God no longer blessed the Church.

Those who start with the question and the precluded answer usually find the solution they sought. Even though there's a better way to ask about the decline, those are certainly serious possibilities.

We don't see them as the *cause*. We suggest a better reason. It's not as much what people do or don't do as it is the will of God to give and to withhold as *He* chooses.

There are special times when God's Spirit works mightily among humans; during other periods, God chooses not to manifest widespread healing. (We don't believe healing ever disappears in any period, but that's as unprovable as saying that God stopped healing.)

The word "recrudescence" helps to explain the phenomenon of healing. This unfamiliar word refers to a breaking forth or a popping out of a dormant stage such as when a dormant volcano suddenly springs to life and explodes. God chooses the times when healing, revival, or spiritual awakening explodes upon a culture.

We humans can't make the Holy Spirit work. We can pray according to the words God said to King Solomon when He spoke of the times of plagues and grasshoppers ruining crops (and it was an agrarian culture): "Then if my people who are called by my name will humble themselves and pray and seek my face and turn from their wicked ways, I will hear from heaven and will forgive their sins and restore their lands" (2 Chron. 7:14).

Jesus' words to Nicodemus also state this position: "The wind blows wherever it wants" (John 3:8). He compares the wind to the work of the Spirit. It reminds us that we can't control God or make miracles happen, but we can be open to them when they come.

We'll explain recrudescence by starting with some biblical accounts. If we look at the entire biblical record from Genesis to Revelation, we see that God poured out miracles (including healing) at *three* significant times.

The First Miracle Period

The first miracle period occurred during the time of Moses, beginning in the book of Exodus. Here's a list of the miracles. Note that it's difficult to distinguish all of them as healings—for instance, do we say the plagues God sent to the Egyptians became healings when they stopped? This list of the miracles probably fits under the category of healings from the time of the Egyptian captivity until the Israelites enter the Promised Land.

- Exodus 7:14-25: The waters of the Nile become blood.
- Exodus 8:1-15: Moses smites the borders of Egypt with frogs.
- Exodus 8:16-19: Moses smites the dust of the earth and it becomes lice.
- Exodus 8:20-31: A plague of flies covers the land.
- Exodus 9:1-7: The Egyptians' cattle die, but the Israelites' cattle don't.
- Exodus 9:8-12: God afflicts the Egyptians with boils.
- Exodus 9:13-35: The plague of hail ruins crops and hurts and kills livestock.
- Exodus 10:1-20: The plague of locusts destroys the crops of the Egyptians.

- Exodus 10:21-29: For three days, darkness covers the land where Egyptians live but not that of the Israelites.
- Exodus 11:1-10: The Lord said through Moses, "At midnight I will pass through the heart of Egypt. All the first-born sons will die in every family in Egypt, from the oldest son of Pharaoh, who sits on his throne, to the oldest son of his lowliest servant girl who grinds the flour. Even the firstborn of all the livestock will die" (vv. 4-5).
- Exodus 14:15-31: The Israelites come to the Red Sea and God stops the waters so they cross on dry land. Pharaoh and his army chase them. The waters return and they're all drowned.
- Exodus 15:22-27: The water at Marah was undrinkable. "Moses cried out to the LORD for help, and the LORD showed him a piece of wood. Moses threw it into the water, and this made the water good to drink" (vv. 24-25).
- Exodus 16:1-16: The Israelites had no food, so God sent quail to feed them. "When the dew evaporated, a flaky substance as fine as frost blanketed the ground. . . . And Moses told them, 'It is the food the LORD has given you to eat'" (vv. 14-15).
- Exodus 16:35: God continued to provide daily manna for the entire 40 years the Israelites stayed in the wilderness.
- Exodus 17:1-7: God made water come out of a rock.
- Numbers 12: God afflicted Miriam, the sister of Moses, with leprosy because she had sinned and rebelled against Moses. "So Moses cried out to the LORD, 'O God, I beg you, please heal her'" (v. 13). God healed Miriam in answer to Moses' prayer.

The Second Miracle Period

The second great period incorporates the overlapping ministries of Elijah and Elisha. We read of specific healings through Elijah and even more through his pupil, Elisha. Although there aren't many healings mentioned, we're aware of the power and work of the Holy Spirit in Israel in that era.

The emphasis by the writers is on miracles, and few directly focused on healing. God has always been at work in the world and among His people, but this is the second special time when divine activity and healings were intensified and an observable phenomenon flourished.

Peter, on the day of Pentecost, exhorted the people, "Now repent of your sins and turn to God, so that your sins may be wiped away. Then times of refreshment will come from the presence of the Lord" (Acts 3:19-20). That was certainly a time of great refreshing.

As in the Exodus period, the miracles are mixed with healing experiences. The following is a list of supernatural events during the life and ministry of the two prophets.

Elijah and the Widow's Son (1 Kings 17:8-24)

At Zarepath, a widow opened her home to Elijah and he stayed with her. "Some time later the woman's son became sick. He grew worse and worse, and finally he died" (v. 17). She cried out to the prophet. He took the boy and prayed, "O Lord my God, why have you brought tragedy to this widow who has opened her home to me, causing her son to die?" (v. 20). The Bible says Elijah stretched himself over the child three times and prayed, "Please let this child's life return to him" (v. 21). God healed the boy and Elijah took him to the woman and said, "Your son is alive!" (v. 23).

Elisha and the Barren Woman from Shunem (2 Kings 4:8-36)

Whenever Elisha passed through the town of Shunem he stayed with a wealthy woman and her husband, and they even built a room for him when he came. Later, Elisha, aware of her barrenness, visited her and said, "Next year at this time you will be holding a son in your arms!" (v. 15).

The woman did bear a son. "One day when her child was older, he went out to help his father, who was working with the harvesters. Suddenly he cried out, 'My head hurts! My heart hurts!'" (vv. 18-19).

The boy died, and his mother hurried to the prophet. He accompanied her to the house and prayed for the boy. "The boy sneezed seven times and opened his eyes!" (v. 35).

The Healing of Naaman the Leper (2 Kings 5:1-19)

This is one of the best-known healings in the Bible. Naaman, the commander of the army of Aram, "was a mighty warrior, he suffered from leprosy" (v. 1). A slave girl sent him to Elisha and the prophet told him, "Go and wash yourself seven times in the Jordan River. Then your skin will be restored, and you will be healed of your leprosy" (v. 10).

Although Naaman resisted, one of his officers talked him into obeying the word of the prophet. He did as Elijah commanded him, "and his skin became as healthy as the skin of a young child's, and he was healed" (v. 14).

Healing from Elisha's Bones (2 Kings 13:20-21)

The strangest miracle is recorded in this passage: "Then Elisha died and was buried. Groups of Moabite raiders used to invade the land each spring. Once when some Israelites were burying a man, they spied a band of those raiders. So they hastily threw the corpse into the tomb of Elisha and fled. But as soon as the body touched Elisha's bones, the dead man revived and jumped to his feet!"

The Third Healing Period

The third healing period is recorded in the New Testament. Beginning with Jesus' healing on the Sabbath in Luke 6 (the man with the withered arm), we read of healings all through the book of Acts. Jesus promises the first disciples that they would do even greater things that He did (see John 14:12), and the record certainly implies that.

Healings by Jesus

The healings Jesus did are listed in biblical order, starting with Matthew's Gospel. Some healings are recorded in more than one gospel, so I've tried to put them together.

- Matthew 4:23: "Jesus traveled throughout the region of Galilee, teaching in the synagogues and announcing the Good News about the Kingdom. And he healed every kind of disease and illness."

- Matthew 8:2-3: A man suffering from leprosy "approached [Jesus] and knelt before him. 'Lord,' the man said, 'If you are willing, you can heal me and make me clean.' Jesus reached out and touched him. 'I am willing,' he said. 'Be healed!' And instantly the leprosy disappeared" (see also Luke 17:12-14).

- Matthew 8:5-13: Jesus heals the son of a Roman army officer.

- Matthew 8:14-15: Jesus heals Peter's mother-in-law of a fever.

- Matthew 9:1-8: A group of men carry a paralyzed man to Jesus. "Jesus turned to the paralyzed man and said, 'Stand up, pick up your mat, and go home!' And the man jumped up and went home!" (vv. 6-7).

- Matthew 9:20-22: A woman "who had suffered for twelve years with constant bleeding came up behind [Jesus]." Jesus healed her. This is also recorded in Luke 8:43-49.

- Matthew 12:9-14: A man with a deformed hand asks for healing. "Then [Jesus] said to the man, 'Hold out your hand.' So the man held out his hand, and it was restored, just like the other one" (v. 13).

- Matthew 9:29-30; 20:34; Mark 8:23-25; 10:51-52; John 9:7: These are several accounts of Jesus healing the blind.

- Matthew 17:14-18: A man comes to Jesus to beg for the healing of his son. "He has seizures and suffers terribly"

(v. 15). Verse 18 tells us, "Then Jesus rebuked the demon in the boy and it left him. From that moment the boy was well."

- Mark 7:31-37: The story of a man with a speech impediment and who was apparently also deaf. "Jesus led him away from the crowd so they could be alone. He put his fingers into the man's ears. Then, spitting on his own fingers, he touched the man's tongue. Looking up to heaven he sighed and said, '*Ephphatha*,' which means 'Be opened!' Instantly the man could hear perfectly, and his tongue was freed so he could speak plainly" (vv. 33-35).

- Luke 7:1-10: A Roman officer asks for the healing of his slave, and Jesus heals him (see also John 4:52-53).

- Luke 7:11-17: Jesus sees a funeral procession carrying the only son of a widow. "When the Lord saw [the widow], his heart overflowed with compassion. 'Don't cry!' he said. Then he walked over to the coffin and touched it, and the bearers stopped. 'Young man,' he said, 'I tell you, get up.' Then the dead boy sat up and began to talk!" (vv. 13-15).

- Luke 8:40-56: The leader of the synagogue named Jairus begs Jesus to heal his daughter. She has just died, but Jesus "took her by the hand and said in a loud voice, 'My child, get up!' And at that moment her life returned, and she immediately stood up!" (vv. 54-55).

- Luke 13:10-13: "One Sabbath day as Jesus was teaching in a synagogue, he saw a woman who had been crippled by an evil spirit. She had been bent double for eighteen years and was unable to stand up straight. When Jesus saw her, he called her over and said, 'Dear woman, you are healed of your sickness!' He touched her, and instantly she could stand straight. How she praised God!"

- Luke 14:2,4: "There was a man whose arms and legs were swollen . . . Jesus touched the sick man and healed him and sent him away."

- Luke 22:50-51: When soldiers try to arrest Jesus, "One of [His disciples] struck at the high priest's slave, slashing off his right ear. But Jesus said, 'No more of this.' And he touched the man's ear and healed him."

- John 5:1-15: The story of a man who had been lame for 38 years. Jesus heals him.

- John 11:1-44: Jesus' friend Lazarus dies. Jesus arrives at the home in Bethany after Lazarus has been dead for four days and buried in a cave. Jesus tells them to roll away the stone. "Then Jesus shouted, 'Lazarus, come out!' And the dead man came out, his hands and feet bound in graveclothes, his face wrapped in a headcloth. Jesus told them, 'Unwrap him and let him go!'" (vv. 43-44).

Healings by Peter

The book of Acts records the beginning of the Church, and it began on the Jewish Day of Pentecost, 50 days after Passover (and the death of Jesus). God had promised to pour out His Spirit. On that historic date the assembled believers were filled with the Holy Spirit. From then on miracles of various types took place.

The Healing of a Lame Man (Acts 3:1-11)

The healing of a lame man was the first miracle of healing of Peter's ministry. The account says that Peter and John go to the Temple to participate in a prayer service. "As they approached the Temple, a man lame from birth was being carried in. Each day he was put beside the Temple gate . . . so he could beg from the people going into the Temple" (vv. 1-3).

He asks the two apostles for money "and Peter said, 'Look at us!' The lame man looked at them eagerly, expecting some money" (vv. 4-5). Peter says he has no money, "'But I'll give you what I have. In the name of Jesus Christ the Nazarene, get up and walk!' Then Peter took the lame man by the right hand and helped him up. And as he did, the man's feet and ankles were instantly healed and strengthened. He jumped up, stood on his feet and began to walk!

Then walking, leaping and praising God, he went into the Temple with them" (vv. 6-8).

Two important points are worth noting. First, the man was born paralyzed. His healing was not a gradual restoration but instantaneous and complete. Of special notice is that the man doesn't ask for or expect to be healed. His healing is a complete surprise. Second, the healing occurs in public view. "All the people saw him walking and heard him praising God. When they realized he was the lame beggar they had seen so often at the Beautiful Gate, they were absolutely astounded" (vv. 9-10).

The next day the council of rulers in Jerusalem have Peter and John arrested. "They brought in the two disciples and demanded, 'By what power, or in whose name have you done this?' Then Peter . . . said to them, 'Rulers and elders of our people, are we being questioned today because we've done a good deed for a crippled man? Do you want to know how he was healed? Let me clearly state to all of you and to all the people of Israel that he was healed by the power of the name of Jesus Christ the Nazarene'" (Acts 4:7-10).

So not only does the healing take place in public and even the leaders acknowledge it, but Peter makes it clear that Jesus healed the man. One more thing to point out is that many make healing a matter of faith—that the sick person has to believe. This is an example of someone being healed without asking or believing. Another example is when Jesus heals a man at the pool of Bethsaida (see John 5:1-13) and the man neither asks nor believes. It is totally the work of Jesus Christ.

Luke records another healing in Acts 5:12-16. Among other things it reminds us that the healing of the lame man in Acts 3 was not a one-time event. This is such an important passage of Scripture that I'm quoting it in its entirety:

The apostles were performing many miraculous signs and wonders among the people. And all the believers were meeting regularly at the Temple in the area known as Solomon's Colonnade. But no one else dared to join them, even though all the people had high regard for them. Yet more and more people believed and were brought to the Lord—crowds of both men and women. As a result of the apostles' work, sick people were brought out into the streets on beds and mats so that Peter's shadow might fall across some of them as he went by. Crowds came from the villages around Jerusalem, bringing their sick and those possessed by evil spirits, and they were all healed.

I don't understand the statement about Peter's shadow, although I accept it as a fact because the Bible records it. Some believe that Luke doesn't say they were healed by Peter's shadow, but I think that's an argument from silence. The implication is that they were healed. How else can we interpret "they were all healed" in verse 16?

The Healing of Aeneas (Acts 9:32-35)
Peter travels from place to place and he stops at Lydda. A man named Aeneas had been "paralyzed and bedridden for eight years" (v. 33). There is no asking for or expecting healing. We read only this: "Peter said to him, 'Aeneas, Jesus Christ heals you! Get up and roll up your sleeping mat!' And he was healed instantly" (v. 34).

The account ends with these words: "Then the whole population of Lydda and Sharon saw Aeneas walking around, and they turned to the Lord" (v. 35). This is much like the healing in Acts 3:5, where Peter and John encounter a lame man at the Temple on the Day of Pentecost.

The Healing of Dorcas (Acts 9:36-43)
This is a healing-and-raising-from-the dead story. Dorcas (also called Tabitha) was kind to the poor, but she becomes ill and dies. Believers send for Peter to come, apparently after her death. After he arrives, he asks the others to leave the room. "He knelt and prayed. Turning to the body he said, 'Get up, Tabitha.' And she opened her eyes! When she saw Peter, she sat up! He gave her his hand and helped her up" (vv. 40-41). Luke records the response

that the news spread through the whole town and many believed in Jesus Christ.

Paul's Healing Ministry in Acts

Paul is the major figure in the Acts of the Apostles and there are, naturally, more explicit healings recorded during this ministry. In several of them, Luke, the writer of the book, is evidently present and refers to "we" when he writes the accounts.

Paul and Barnabas in Iconium (Acts 14:1-7)

Although Luke records no specific healing, we can certainly infer it from other accounts in Acts. Verse 3 says that Paul and Barnabas stayed there a long time, preaching boldly about the grace of the Lord. And the Lord proved their message was true by giving them power to do miraculous signs and wonders.

Paul Heals a Lame Man (Acts 14:8-10)

Although this story is similar to the one in Acts 3, here the element of faith comes into the account. Paul and Barnabas were in Lystra and "came upon a man with crippled feet. He had been that way from birth, so he had never walked" (v. 8). The man listened to Paul's preaching, and the apostle realized that the crippled man "had faith to be healed. So Paul called to him in a loud voice, 'Stand up!' And the man jumped to his feet and started walking" (vv. 9-10).

This is one of the few places where healing happens because the sick person has the faith for healing. This isn't the usual or expected response.

Healing of the Fortune Teller (Acts 16:16-18)

As I have pointed out previously, delivering people from evil spirits or demon possession comes under the heading of healing. At Philippi, Paul and Silas "met a demon-possessed slave girl. She was a fortune-teller who earned a lot of money for her masters" (v. 16). She followed them and shouted, "These men are servants of the Most High God, and they have come to tell you how to be saved" (v. 17).

In exasperation, Paul turned "and said to the demon within her, 'I command you in the name of Jesus Christ to come out of her.' And instantly it left her" (v. 18).

Unusual Healing by Paul (Acts 19:11-12)

In these two verses, we learn "God gave Paul the power to perform unusual miracles. When handkerchiefs or aprons that had merely touched his skin were placed on sick people, they were healed of their diseases and evil spirits were expelled." This is as strange as people being healed by Peter's shadow, but it's also in the Bible.

Notice that Luke calls them "unusual miracles." Miracles are, by nature, out of the ordinary, so why the redundant terminology? It's not used elsewhere in Acts, either. In Acts 28:2, the same Greek word is used to describe the people of Malta after Paul and others got safely to the land after the destruction of their ship: "very" kind. I assume Luke meant it to stand out as unique and to show that wasn't a common occurrence.

The Story of Eutychus (Acts 20:7-12)

At Troas, Paul preaches until midnight in an upstairs room. "As Paul spoke on and on, a young man named Eutychus, sitting on the windowsill, became very drowsy. Finally, he fell sound asleep and dropped three stories to his death below" (v. 9).

Paul hurries down, bends over the young man "and took him into his arms. 'Don't worry,' he said, 'he's alive!' " (v. 10). The account ends by saying that people take Eutychus home and he is unhurt.

The Healing of Publius (Acts 28:7-10)

Publius was the chief official of Malta. His father "was ill with fever and dysentery. Paul went in and prayed for him, and laying his hands on him, he healed him" (v. 8).

Some commentators point out that as the Acts of the Apostles continues, the healings and miracles become fewer. That's possible, but an unprovable assumption. We can just as easily assume that the supernatural events continued, but they have been covered so well, why not take for granted that they continued?

We could use the same argument against tithing (giving a tenth). Some modern church people speak against the practice because it's not specifically commanded in the New Testament. While what they say is true, perhaps the New Testament may not speak of tithing because the godly had been taught from antiquity to give a tenth of their income to the Lord.

We can see no reason for the decrease of miracles and healings because the gospel continues to go forth and people turn to Jesus Christ. (We show in other chapters there was no total disruption of healing and other miracles.)

Stephen's Healing Ministry (Acts 6:8)

Stephen is one of the seven men chosen to oversee the food served to Grecian widows (see Acts 6:1-6). Although the word "healing" isn't used, it's implied: "Stephen, a man full of God's grace and power, performed amazing miracles and signs among the people."

Philip's Healing Ministry (Acts 8:4-8)

Philip was also one of the men who served food to the widows (see Acts 6:5). He went to a city in Samaria and preached about Jesus the Messiah. "Crowds listened intently to Philip because they were eager to hear his message and see the miraculous signs he did. Many evil spirits were cast out, screaming as they left their victims. And many who had been paralyzed or lame were healed" (vv. 6-7).

This passage makes clear that the apostles were not the only ones God used to heal the sick. It's also one more passage that shows the common appearance of healing during the early days of the Church. Even those who don't accept physical healing from God today agree that the Holy Spirit did such acts to impress unbelievers and to bring them to faith.

Miracles in Other Times

Miracles and healings take place in other times, but they don't seem widespread. For instance:

- Genesis 11:30: Sarah was barren and received the ability in old age to conceive.

- Genesis 20:17-18: Another time, "Abraham prayed to God, and God healed Abimelech, his wife and his female servants, so they could have children. For the LORD had caused all the women to be infertile."

- Genesis 25:21-22: Rachel was unable to conceive and "Isaac pleaded with the LORD on behalf of his wife, because she was unable to have children. The LORD answered Isaac's prayer, and Rebekah became pregnant with twins."

- Judges 13:5-25: Another healing-fertility account is the healing of Manoah's wife, who later bore Samson.

- 1 Samuel 1:1-20: Hannah prayed for the ability to have children, and she did.

- 1 Kings 13:4-6: "When King Jeroboam heard the man of God speaking against the altar at Bethel, he pointed at him and shouted, 'Seize that man!' But instantly the king's hand became paralyzed in that position, and he couldn't pull it back. . . . The king cried out to the man of God, 'Please ask the LORD your God to restore my hand again!' So the man of God prayed to the LORD, and the king's hand was restored and he could move it again." (If the godly man hadn't prayed, I assume Jeroboam's hand would have remained paralyzed.)

- 2 Kings 20:4-5: Hezekiah was sick and God told Isaiah the prophet, "Go back to Hezekiah. . . . Tell him 'This is what the LORD . . . says, I have heard your prayer and seen your tears. I will heal you.'"

In addition to these incidences of individual healing there are *occurrences of corporate healing* in response to prayer.

• Numbers 14:4-50: By offering incense and making atonement for the people of Israel, Aaron stopped the plague, which had killed 14,700 people.

• Numbers 21:4-9: This passage tells of the venomous snakes God sent among the rebellious Israelites "and many were bitten and died. Then the people came to Moses and cried out, 'We have sinned by speaking against the LORD and against you. Pray that the LORD will take away the snakes.' So Moses prayed for the people. Then the LORD told him, 'Make a replica of a poisonous snake and attach it to a pole. All who are bitten will live if they simply look at it.' So Moses made a snake out of bronze and attached it to a pole. Then anyone who was bitten by a snake could look at the bronze snake and be healed" (vv. 6-9).

• 2 Samuel 24: King David sinned by insisting that Joab, his commander, count the number of troops. Nine months later, they recorded a total of 1.2 million. As punishment, "The LORD sent a plague upon Israel that morning and it lasted for three days. A total of 70,000 people died throughout the nation" (v. 15). David pleaded for God to stop. God told him to build an altar and "the LORD answered his prayer for the land, and the plague on Israel was stopped" (v. 25).

These are the exceptions to widespread healing. We don't read much about God doing outstanding things. They seem rare. Consider the words in 1 Samuel 3:1 that precede the calling of young Samuel: "Now in those days messages from the LORD were very rare, and visions were quite uncommon.

Why Did the Apostles Heal the Sick?

If Jesus healed and did signs and wonders to show His authority and reveal His role as the Messiah or Savior, some suggest that should have been the end of such spiritual manifestations. We contend that Jesus' healings were for more than proving His messiahship. They were also acts of human empathy and care.

> [Jesus] healed every kind of disease and illness. When he saw the crowds, he had compassion on them because they were confused and helpless, like sheep without a shepherd (Matt. 9:35-36; Mark 6:34 records the same account).

> Jesus saw the huge crowd as he stepped from the boat, and he had compassion on them, and healed their sick (Matt. 14:14).

> A leper comes to Jesus and kneels before Him. " 'If you are willing, you can heal me and make me clean,' he said. Moved with compassion, Jesus reached out and touched him. 'I am willing,' he said. 'Be healed!' Instantly the leprosy disappeared and the man was healed" (Mark 1:40-42).

Certainly the first reason the apostles healed was to obey Jesus. He sent them out and they did what they saw Him doing. Especially in light of John 14:12 or 20:21, we would expect this. Luke tells us that Jesus sent out 72 disciples, and after they returned they said, "Lord, even the demons obey us when we use your name" (10:17). Jesus says, "I have given you authority over all the power of the enemy, and you can walk among snakes and scorpions and crush them. Nothing will injure you. But don't rejoice because evil spirits obey you; rejoice because your names are registered in heaven" (vv. 19-20). As followers of a compassionate Christ, would they not also yearn to see bodies healed?

Matthew records Jesus sending out the Twelve and telling them to announce that the Kingdom of Heaven is near and to "heal the sick, raise the dead, cure those with leprosy and cast out demons" (10:8). If the first disciples had that command from Jesus while He was still with them, why wouldn't they continue healing the sick, raising the dead, curing those with leprosy and casting out demons?

Although some authorities dispute the last 12 verses of Mark's Gospel, the command to heal and cast out evil spirits is there. Even if those statements aren't in the original text, healing must have been significant enough for those words to have found their way into the sacred text.

Here is part of what we find: "These miraculous signs will accompany those who believe: They will cast out demons in my name . . . they will be able to place their hands on the sick, and they will be healed" (Mark 16:17-18). Yet even without the words of Mark 16, the apostles would have been obeying what they saw Jesus do.

The apostles seem indiscriminate in praying for the sick. They don't ask, "Should we pray for this person?" They prayed for all. They don't seem to worry if someone wasn't healed. They went on praying for others.

Mark 9:18 tells of a failure with an epileptic boy that happened while Jesus was still with them. It's reasonable to expect that they had failures, but Luke writes nothing about them.

The early disciples lived in close contact with God. Several times it says the Holy Spirit spoke, and they heard Him. We assume they heard by a message impressed on their hearts, and perhaps by the voice of one of the prophets, as in Acts 13:2-3, when the leaders of the church prayed and fasted: "One day as these men were worshiping the Lord and fasting, the Holy Spirit said, 'Dedicate Barnabas and Saul for the special work to which I have called them.' So after more fasting and prayer, the men laid their hands on them."

In the four Gospels, only Jesus and the apostles heal. In Acts, ordinary non-apostles such as Philip have the ability to heal the sick. In Acts 3, as we previously noted, Peter and John see a crippled man who asks for alms. They have no money but they have the healing power of the Spirit, so they heal him.

Again, in 1 Corinthians 12, Paul stresses that all believers have spiritual gifts and all gifts come from the Holy Spirit. He lists many of those gifts: "To someone else the one Spirit gives the gift of healing. He gives one person the power to perform miracles. . . . It is the one and only Spirit who distributes all these gifts. He alone decides which gift each person should have" (vv. 9-11).

In this passage Paul makes it clear that the Holy Spirit chooses the recipients and provides gifts by divine choice. He also makes it clear that all of us have gifts because we are part of the mystical body of Christ.

It's interesting that those who claim we no longer need or have the ability to heal don't deny *all* the gifts listed. Paul lists the offices of teachers, and "those who can help others, those who have the gift of leadership" (1 Cor. 12:28). Who are we to decide which gifts God bestows on Christians today and which ones are withheld?

Did Healing Continue After the Biblical Accounts?

Although some insist that the ability to heal stopped (based on their lack of information or personal knowledge), the truth is God never stopped healing during the next 2,000 years. In fact, human history, after the Bible, is akin to human history during the biblical period. If we look objectively at the records, we can see the recrudescence of healing. This seems to be a pattern throughout history, and not only during the three biblical periods.

In the following chapters, we'll point out the concentrated periods of healing throughout the ages since the apostles. As A. J. Gordon wrote, "Witnesses who are above suspicion leave no room for doubt that the miraculous powers of the apostolic age continued to operate at least into the third century."[7]

Gordon quoted those words from Dr. Gerhard Uhlhorn and says that anyone who has read his words "will not doubt his eminent fitness to judge of such a question."[8] If there were still miracles (which included healing) in the second century after Christ, Gordon insists, there should be no reason why anyone would not expect them in his time (the nineteenth century).

We have records of many accounts of healing around the turn of the twentieth century. Many people know the beginning of the modern Pentecostal movement that began as an outbreak of revival (and healing) at Azusa Street in Los Angeles. But there was also an outbreak in India and the Philippines around the same time. The Welsh Revival (1904–1905) is lesser known, but historians referred to it as the greatest revival ever recorded in Wales.

Another argument that deserves consideration is that several times (e.g., John 14:12, Acts 1:8) Jesus said there "would be an augmenting rather than a diminishing of supernatural energy after his departure." A. J. Gordon went on to add that Jesus made no provision for stopping "the stream of divine manifestations which he started, either in the next age or in a subsequent age."[9]

Healing probably did decline over time, although we can go only on the written records left behind. There was also a major shift in theological thinking in which the worldview of Aristotle replaced Platonic thinking. That resulted in a more rational acceptance and left little direct contact between God and humanity, with no major theologians advocating healing.

Along with that, however, was the belief among those deemed uneducated who held to an uncritical belief (some called it superstition) in miracles. As time went on some of those views became more far-fetched and bizarre, and it was almost impossible to discern the true from the fanciful.

During this period, the most gifted and notable theologian was St. Thomas Aquinas (1225–1274), who championed Aristotelian thought. He argued that if we know God primarily through our intellect and not experience, there is little place for any gifts of the Spirit.

Largely because of his influence, the medieval Church took a strong stand that past revelation and human reasoning were all that was needed. There was no need for God to "break through" and intervene in human lives.[10]

Despite that, healings continued throughout the period. Someone said of the Western church that it had an Aristotelian head and a Platonic heart—and they don't function together.

That's one reason no one can be declared a saint in the Roman Catholic Church without showing healings in their life and ministry. Healings also took place during the time of trade in relics and pilgrimages to shrines, as writings circulated of amazing (and strange) miracles during that period. The 1885 publication of E. Cobham Brewer's *A Dictionary of Miracles, Imitative, Realistic and Dogmatic* records many such beliefs.

Although the Protestant Reformation changed many aspects of the Church's life, it didn't stand against the Aristotelian understanding.

From the Acts of the Apostles to Emperor Constantine

The reason people turned to Jesus Christ in the first wave of the Church's expansion wasn't the teaching or the theological explanations. It was the *proof*—what the people saw and experienced. Hardly anyone disputes that, and many verses back up those words.

For example, Acts 8:4-24 tells us about Philip's ministry in Samaria, and he says, "Crowds listened intently to Philip because they were eager to hear his message and see the miraculous signs he did" (v. 6). The account goes on to explain those miraculous signs: "Many evil spirits were cast out, screaming as they left their victims. And many who had been paralyzed or lame were healed. So there was great joy in that city" (vv. 7-8).

Simon the sorcerer witnessed the exploits—healings and miracles—and he wanted to buy the power to do the same thing. "He began following Philip wherever he went, and he was amazed by the signs and great miracles Philip performed" (v. 13).

The message of the early proclaimers said, in effect, to people everywhere, "We serve the God who created the universe. We can do powerful things that your so-called gods can't do."

The miraculous events, though different in nature and purpose, remind us of the days of Moses. When he asked who would believe that the Lord had sent him, he knew the problems he'd face if he simply announced to Pharaoh and the Egyptian slave owners that he was the Lord's servant. But he convinced Pharaoh and the people of Egypt, and even the resistant Israelites, because he performed acts of power. (Read Exodus 3 and the chapters that follow.) The people believed *not because of Moses' words*, but because of the signs and wonders.

Early Belief in Healing

We can document that the early post-biblical Christians believed in healing. As much as it may offend our modern sensibilities, the approach in the Early Church was very simple. Just as Jesus attracted crowds by His miracles and sent His disciples out two by two to heal and cast out evil spirits, so, too, the early Christians emphasized healing and exorcism as the chief instruments of conversion.

The earliest Christian writers such as Justin Martyr, Irenaeus, Cyprian and Tertullian all say this. For instance, Irenaeus (c. AD 130–202) asserts that "Some people *incontentestably and truly* drive out demons, so that those very persons often become believers."[11]

Theophilus (died c. AD 181), who was called the patriarch of Antioch, said he himself had witnessed healings and "that demons were sometimes exorcised and confessed their demonic nature."[12]

In several places, Justin Martyr (AD 100–165) tells of Christians healed in the name of Jesus Christ, driving out demons and various evil spirits. Writing about the *charismata*, the gifts God pours upon believers, he calls attention to the power to heal as one of the particular gifts that was being received and used. Justin Martyr wrote:

> For numberless demoniacs throughout the whole world and in your city, many of our Christian men, exorcising them in the name of Jesus Christ, who was crucified under Pontius Pilate, have healed, and do heal, rendering helpless and driving the possessing devils out of the men, though they could not be cured by all the other exorcists and those who used incantations and drugs.[13]

Tertullian (c. AD 160–225) and Cyprian (died c. AD 258), both of Carthage in North Africa, were apologists who wrote into the third century. (We call them apologists not in the sense of apologizing for their faith but giving evidence or explanations for what they believed.) Clement of Alexandria (AD 150–215) and Origen (c. AD 184–254) belong in that group. Some might consider the first apostles as intellectually naïve, which they weren't, even though they didn't have quality education of their day. But these men who followed were of outstanding intellect and highly respected throughout the Roman Empire.

Early Evidence of Healing in the Post-biblical Period

The apologists wrote about various healing experiences (among other things) to show that God acted *and continued to act* in the lives of believers. Those experiences included healing and the ability to free people from demon possession.

In *Against Celsus,* Origen wrote that Christians "expelled evil spirits, and performed many cures," and that he had witnessed many of them himself. "The name of Jesus can still remove distractions from the minds of men, and expel demons, and take away diseases."[14] He made a number of similar comments to pagan leaders.

In *Epistle* 75:15, Cyprian wrote that baptism was sometimes the means by which people received healing from serious illnesses and many Christians surrendered their lives to the church because of such an experience.[15]

Godly leaders such as Justin Martyr, Tatian (AD 120–180) and Theophilus provide evidence of exorcism and healing in the second half of the second century, but their comments also suggest there were differences of opinion within the Church as to whether one should seek healing simply by trusting God or by using medical means.[16]

In book 5 of *Against the Heresies,* Irenaeus is particularly concerned to rebut the Gnostic disparagement of the body and to show that God intends it, like the human soul, for eternal salvation. He emphasizes that Jesus healed the blind and restored a withered hand and brought the dead back to life.[17]

The literature of the Church's healing activities in the second century is plentiful and varied. That the Apostolic Fathers pass over the subject virtually in silence may well be due to their not finding it relevant to the matters about which they were writing. Marginal sources indicate that healing miracles were taking place in the first half of the century both at baptism and through the exercise of gifts of healing. Justin Martyr is our primary witness for the powerful continuance of exorcism in the name of Christ, bettering both Jewish and pagan counterparts.

The writers of the Church in the first half of the third century refer to healings, *charismata* and particularly exorcisms performed by Christians. By the mid-century physical healings seemed to be less frequent.[18]

The writings of Tertullian provide valuable sources of information about the continuing ministry of the Church in exorcism and healing into the early third century. His writings indicated that Christian exorcism was well-known and free of charge. He argued for the supremacy of Christ over the gods of the State.

Of pagan parentage, the well-educated Novatian (c. AD 200–258) fell seriously ill, but on receiving clinical baptism he recovered. The third section of Novatian's work on the Trinity contains the following passage about the work of the Holy Spirit: "This is he who places prophets in the Church, instructs teachers, directs tongues, gives powers and healings, does wonderful works, counsels and orders and arranges whatever other gifts there are of *charismata;* and thus makes the Lord's Church everywhere, and in all, perfected and completed."[19]

St. Augustine's Admission

Augustine's (AD 354–540) early writings claimed that healing had ceased in the Church and was no longer necessary—and scholars still quote him. However, they don't mention that Augustine wrote a book called *Retractions* in 427, three years before he died. In that book, he admitted he had been wrong.

Experiences in his own life changed his mind because, in his own diocese, nearly 70 attested miracles took place in a period of two years. He not only retracted his earlier position but described the miraculous cures he had witnessed.

> I also said, *These miracles are now allowed to continue in our time, lest they should always require things that can be seen, and by becoming accustomed to them mankind should grow cold toward the very things whose novelty had made men glow with fire.*

Too many stop there without quoting, "But what I said should have been taken as understanding that no miracles are believed to happen today in the name of Christ. For at the very time I wrote this book. . . ."[20]

Augustine's change started two weeks before Easter in 424. A brother and sister came to Hippo, North Africa, where Augustine was the bishop. Both were suffering from convulsive seizures. Each day they prayed for healing. Easter morning the brother fell down as if he had died. People rushed to him, but he stood up, totally cured.

Augustine mentioned the healing in his Easter sermon but didn't emphasize it. Three days later, the prelate asked the siblings to sit down while he talked about the healing. He was interrupted by the sister who, like her brother, had been instantly healed.[21]

Kelsey tells of other healings and adds, "Just before his death Augustine himself . . . became a healer of others who came to him. . . . His biographer Possidius mentions how [Augustine] prayed with tears and supplications for certain demoniacs, and they were freed from possession."[22]

One further account in Kelsey's book says that a man brought a sick relative to Augustine and asked the bishop to lay hands on him so that the man would be cured. Augustine said he had no such power but the visitor said that, in a vision, God had spoken to him, "Go to Bishop Augustine that he may lay his hand upon him, and he will be healed." Augustine did as the man said and the sick person was healed.[23]

Defending the Christian Message

In the years following the end of the event of Acts, Christian leaders began to write to defend the Christian message.

Quadratus of Athens (died AD 130) was one of the earliest apologists. It's generally agreed that he wrote between 110 and 130. He stated that the works of the Savior had continued to his time and that the continued presence of men who had been healed left no question as to the reality of physical healing.[24]

Irenaeus says, "Wherefore also those who are in truth the disciples receiving grace from him do in his name perform miracles so as to promote the welfare of others, according to the gift which each has received from him."[25] After listing various spiritual gifts, he continues, "Others still heal the sick by laying their hands upon them, and they are made whole."[26]

Tertullian of Carthage writes that an evil spirit often threw a clerk to the ground, and through prayer he was set free from his affliction. He also mentions the healing of a relative and also of a boy. "And how many men of rank, to say nothing of the common people, have been delivered from devils and healed of disease."[27] He identified individuals who had been healed and "testified to their great number and the wide range of physical and mental diseases represented."[28]

Theophilus of Antioch wrote about various healings he had witnessed. In the *Acts of Eugenia,* he writes of a woman who was so close to God that she could cast out devils. There is also the account of a noblewoman of Alexandria who was healed of a recurring fever after Eugenia prayed for her.[29]

Origen says, "And some give evidence of their having received through their faith a marvelous power by the cures which they perform, invoking no other name over those who need their help than that of the God of all things and of Jesus, along with a mention of his history. For by these means we too have seen many persons freed from grievous calamities and from distractions of mind and madness, and countless other ills which could be cured neither by men or devils."[30]

Clement of Alexandria (c. AD 150–215), in giving directions for visiting the sick and afflicted, wrote, "Let them, therefore, with fasting and prayer, make their intercessions, and not with the well arranged and fitly ordered words of learning, but as men who have received the gift of healing confidently, to the glory of God."[31]

A. J. Gordon quotes a Dr. Waterland who says the miraculous gifts continued at least through the third century. In a footnote he cites the source of the quotation.[32] Gordon also quotes the translator of Cyprian who states there is evidence of healings until the age of Constantine. Gordon picks up on that statement and stresses how the Church changed after the emperor "legalized" the Christian faith. There are other sources that say they can document miracles after 313, but they certainly became more rare so it's a significant date to use for what he calls the "termination of miracles."

After Constantine, the Church stopped depending on the Lord and began resting "in the patronage and support of earthly rulers and ceasing to look ever for the coming and Kingdom of Christ as the consummation of her hopes."[33]

Conclusion

Jesus brought healing and life to the people He encountered. He also showed that His power was greater than Satan's by His victory on the cross. Many of the Early Church fathers believed that when the Spirit of God gained complete control over the world, such forces would be destroyed completely *and illness will disappear.*

Another well-documented fact is that members of the primitive Church sought out the sick to care for them and heal them, just as it sought out sinners and tried to convert them. They believed that healing their bodies was rescuing men and women from the domination of the enemy.

The prevailing acceptance of healing as normal in the Early Church appears from many sources. *The Shepherd of Hermas,* although never part of the New Testament, was around during the Early Church and is still available today. One reference is to those who did *not* undertake to relieve illness and distress in the Christian way. "He therefore," Hermas wrote, "that knows the calamity of such a man, and does not free him from it, commits a great sin and is guilty of his blood."[34]

Healing of physical illness was seen in this period as evidence that the Spirit of Christ worked among Christians. Since both bodily and spiritual illness were to them signs of domination by the devil, the power to heal disease was prime evidence that the opposite spirit—the Spirit of God—was operating through the healer. Thus the healing of "demon possession" was often spoken of in conjunction with curing illness from other causes.

What Healings Have Occurred Since the Time of the Early Church Fathers?

Healing in Medieval Times (600–1400)

Saint Bede, or Venerable Bede, was an English monk (c. 672–735). Because of his famous *Ecclesiastical History of the English People,* Bede is often referred to as the father of Church history.

In chapter 17, Bede tells of an incident in which demons were expelled. Chapter 18 records the story of a man and wife who brought their 10-year-old blind daughter for healing. A priest named Germanus prayed for her and she was instantly healed.

In Book 2, Bede records another story of a blind person being healed. In Book 5 is an account of a bishop named John who heals a mute. In the same book he tells of the healing of a young woman, the resuscitation of the servant of an earl as well as the resuscitation of his own clerk.

Morton Kelsey cites eyewitness accounts of healings by Bishop John of Beverley. The wife of an earl was quite ill for a month. John came to consecrate a nearby church. When he heard of the woman's illness, he sent holy water for her to drink and with the rest of it to wash herself in the most painful places. That evening, John visited the earl's estate and the woman, completely healed, served the bishop.[35]

In another instance, Bede records where Bishop John took a scab-covered mute boy to live with him during Lent. One day John told the boy to stick out his tongue and the bishop made the sign of the cross on it. He asked the boy to say "yea." "The boy's tongue was immediately loosed and the bishop had him repeat letters, then syllables and words; during the rest of the day he hardly stopped speaking."[36]

The Crusades started in 950 and extended to 1350. During the last of the Crusades, the Western Church established the Inquisition to crush heresy. In so doing, they persecuted small groups, such as the Albigensians in Southern France and the Bogomiles in Bulgaria, who emphasized a personal experience with God.

Kelsey says, "About the year 1100 several of the most illustrious saints of the Middle Ages made their appearances. Around each of these . . . appeared the same kind of miraculous events, usually healings."[37]

There are documented healings in the lives of Bernard of Clairvaux (1090–1153) and Saint Dominic (1170–1221), who began the Dominican order. Healing miracles are claimed for lesser-known saints such as Malachy of Ireland, St. Francis's disciple Antony of Padua (1195–1231), England's Thomas of Hereford (1218–1282), Edmund of Canterbury (1175–1240), and Richard of Chichester (1197–1253).[38] St. Francis of Assisi (1181–1226), founder of the Franciscan Order, had an amazing healing ministry.[39]

The Waldensian Community began in northwest Italy around 1179, and the Church began to persecute them. They believed in an evangelical obedience to the gospel, a rigorous asceticism, an aversion to recognizing the ministry of unworthy-living priests, a belief in visions, prophecies and spirit possession. A. J. Gordon quotes the following doctrine of the Waldensians:

> Therefore, concerning this anointing of the sick, we hold it as an article of faith, and profess sincerely from the heart that sick persons, when they ask it, may lawfully be anointed with the anointing oil by one who joins them in praying that it may be efficacious to the healing of the body according to the design and end and effect mentioned by the apostles; and we profess that such an anointing performed according to the apostolic design and practice will be healing and profitable.[40]

Healing During and After the Reformation Period (1500–1800)

The sixteenth century ushered in a religious unrest in which belief in the existence of spiritual realities received rebirth and the reformers sought to purify Christianity. Although not new, the effort to rid the church of superstition and distrust of the traditional had never been so widespread.

Martin Luther (1483–1546), in his commentary of John's Gospel, stated that the day of miracles was past and contended that the purpose of the Holy Spirit was to enlighten Scripture. John Calvin (1509–1564) followed him and said that the gift of healing disappeared along with other miraculous powers. His position was that healing and miracles were needed in the Early Church to amplify the preaching of the gospel.

However, here's something Morton Kelsey points out when detractors either don't know or ignore when they list Luther:

> Luther, who had denied the gift of healing for his time, lived to see his friend Melanchthon visibly brought from the point of death through his own prayers. Five years later in 1545, the year before he died, when asked what to do for a man who was mentally ill, Luther wrote instructions for a healing service based on the New Testament letter of James, adding, "This is what we do, and that we have been accustomed to do, for a cabinetmaker here was similarly afflicted with madness and we cured him by prayer in Christ's name."[41]

Morton Kelsey adds, "Like the two great saints of the church before him—Augustine and Aquinas both—[Luther] seems to have learned in his mellower years to value, rather than to disregard this gift from God."[42]

John Calvin, in referring to the healing miracles of Jesus in the New Testament, "explained them as manifestations of Christ's divine glory, not events that Christians should expect to see continued through history. Christ's human form did not reveal his divinity; miracles did . . . These miracles ended with the deaths of the apostles who witnessed and conveyed his glory."[43]

Despite the emphasis on reformation, healing did take place, especially in the years following Luther and Calvin.

David Robertson writes in his article "From Epidauros to Lourdes: A History of Healing by Faith" about Valentine Greatlakes (d. 1683), a Protestant Irishman in Ireland who fled to England. In 1661, he discovered he could pray for people and they could be healed from diseases such as epilepsy, paralysis, deafness, ulcers and nervous disorders.[44]

George Fox and the Quakers (Society of Friends) began around 1640. They trace their origins back to English Puritanism. The first leader was George Fox (1624–1690). A Quaker meeting was characterized by the people waiting for the Spirit to speak through them and people "quaked" as God moved among them.

Fox knew the power of God to heal and recorded facts all through his journals. He also wrote a volume called *Book of Miracles* that wasn't published and today the title, index and a few notes about his experiences are all that remain.

John Wesley (1703–1791) described healing miracles, many through his own prayers. In one account he was on his way to preach when his horse, without warning, became lame. He placed his hand on the animal and prayed. When he was ready to go the animal was well.[45]

In a journal entry for December 1742, Wesley wrote that he prayed for a man whose doctor had said the patient was beyond hope. After prayer by Wesley, the man recovered. Wesley added, "What does all this prove? Not that I claim any gift above other men, but only that I believe that God now hears and answers prayer even beyond the ordinary course of nature."[46]

Healing in the Nineteenth and Twentieth Centuries

We find various healing accounts in the 1800s. For example, shortly after Prince Alexander of Hohenlohe (1794–1849) became a priest in 1815, there was an epidemic in Germany. He realized that when he touched the sick and asked God to heal them, they were healed.[47]

Dorothea Trudel (1813-1862), who ran a home factory in Zurich, learned that several of her workers were sick. Their illnesses worsened and seemed hopeless. Trudel thought of the words of James 5:14-15, where Christians are to call on the elders of the church for prayer. She knelt by their bedsides and prayed for them. Every one of them recovered.

Trudel's reputation spread and other sick people came to her. She prayed for healing and many recovered. Although reluctant at first, so many came that she bought two more houses and eventually they became a hospital.

In 1842, Johann Christoph Blumhardt (1805-1880), a pastor near Germany's Black Forest, prayed for a girl who was physically ill and apparently with "frightening psychic phenomena," and she regained her physical and mental health. After that, people came to him for prayer for confessing of their sins. Many of them received physical healing. In 1846, although Church authorities forbade him praying for the sick, he said he couldn't stop healings from taking place. They allowed Blumhardt to continue his ministry.

Smith Wigglesworth (1859-1947), an uneducated British evangelist, made healing a large part of his ministry. The popular press as well as a Pentecostal magazine followed his work. He was widely known for his healing ministry.

The Azusa Street Awakening (1906) in Los Angeles is probably the best-known revival or awakening in the United States. It's also the birth of the modern Pentecostal movement and many would say the Charismatic renewal that came half a century later. The story is probably one of the most written-about events of the early twentieth-century, and the accounts of salvation and healing are well documented. One book, *Azusa Street: They Told Me Their Stories,* is highly anecdotal, and the author tells personal stories rather than recounting the history of the event.[48]

The Healing Revival of 1947–1958

The Healing Revival, better known among its followers as Latter Rain movement, which came out of Sharon Bible College in North Battleford, Saskatchewan, Canada, was probably an offshoot of William Branham's (1909–1965) meetings in Vancouver, British Columbia, in 1947. "Some of the teachers from the Bible College had attended his meetings and were impressed by Branham's demonstration of the word of knowledge and by the miraculous healings they observed. . . . On February 12, 1948, they experienced an unusual demonstration of God's presence and power."[49]

The Wrights go on to say that within a short time, North Battlefield became *the* place, much like Azusa Street of half a century earlier. They also point out that many of the things that took place there were similar to those of Azusa Street.

The name of the movement comes from Joel 2:16-32. In older translations, the prophet speaks of the former rains (which came around August or September) and the latter rains (March or April). The latter rains lasted longer and farmers depended on them for their crops.

The Latter Rain advocates especially quoted verses 28 and 29: "Then . . . I will pour out my spirit upon all people. Your sons and your daughters will prophesy. Your old men will dream dreams, and your young men will see visions. In those days I will pour out my spirit even on servants—men and women alike." They connected that prophecy with the words of Peter in Acts 2:16, when the apostle quoted Joel and said, "What you see was predicted long ago by the prophet Joel."

By the early 1950s, healing evangelists filled tents and auditoriums around the country and reported healings and other miracles. In 1950, more than 1,000 healing evangelists gathered at a Voice of Healing convention.

Gordon Lindsay was the founding editor of *The Voice of Healing*, with his friend Jack Moore and Jack's daughter, Anna Jean Moore. Some of the healing evangelists specialized in foreign evangelism, but many of the independent ministers of the 1950s conducted crusades outside the United States, attracting hundreds of thousands to healing revivals in Latin America, Africa and Asia. *The Voice of Healing* magazine published reports of scores of extraordinary foreign revivals led by evangelists such as Tommy Hicks and Tommy L. Osborn. Later, Lester Sumrall and Morris Cerullo became well-known names in world evangelization and healing.

Most people agree that the renewal hit its peak around 1957, but its influence extended into the next two decades and its main message and ministry became absorbed by the ever-increasing Pentecostal and charismatic churches.

The Charismatic Movement (1960s)

This movement began around 1960, and many called it neo-Pentecostalism. Like Pentecostals, they believed in being "filled with" or "baptized into" the Holy Spirit as a second or subsequent experience after salvation. In 1962, American Lutheran minister Harald Bredesen (1918–2006) coined the term "charismatic" from the Greek *charismata* (ἁρισμα) to describe what was happening inside mainline historic churches.

After World War II, which ended in 1945, two major national movements revitalized the American church. One was the evangelical movement spearheaded by Billy Graham (1918–), and the other was the healing revival represented by William Branham (1909–1964), Oral Roberts (1918–2009) and other lesser-known ministers like A. A. Allen (1911–1970) and Jack Coe (1918–1956). This second group, which flourished from 1947 to 1958, emphasized spiritual gifts, especially healing and deliverance from demons.

The movement revitalized American Pentecostalism, popularized the doctrine of divine healing and spawned organizations such as the Full Gospel Business Men's Fellowship International (FGCBMI), with Demos Shakarian (1913–1993) as its founder.

To the surprise of many, the American Episcopal Church was the first Protestant denomination to feel the impact. Father Dennis Bennett (1917–1991), rector of St. Mark's Episcopal Church in Van Nuys, California, preached Easter Sunday in 1960 and recounted his charismatic experience. His message was controversial, and he received wide coverage. Three years later Bennett wrote his experience in *Nine O'clock in the Morning* —a reference to Peter's speech on the Day of Pentecost that took place at that time.[50] From Van Nuys, the movement spread into mainline churches. Many historic denominations began holding healing services.

Many consider the FGCBMI as the spiritual father of the modern charismatic movement that bridged almost every denomination. Reports from FGCBMI claim that thousands were healed, tens of thousands were converted, and droves of missionaries went to unevangelized areas and planted churches. "Soon many mainline denominations, including Lutherans, Baptists, Methodists [Reformed Church of America sic.] and Roman Catholics were set on fire."[51]

The Catholic Charismatic Renewal traces its beginning to 1967, at Duquesne University in Pittsburgh, Pennsylvania. Even though Pentecostals shared little with Roman Catholics (and many did not consider them as true Christians), the charismatic renewal forged a relationship among Roman Catholic charismatics and their brothers and sisters in the historic Protestant denominations.

In the United Kingdom, Colin Urquhart, Michael Harper and David Watson led similar developments. "Key figures in this incredible outpouring were Harald Bredesen and David du Plessis. David was called by many 'Mr. Pentecost' because of his tireless energy and desire to see the Holy Spirit poured out on the whole Church."[52]

"Charismatic" is a broad term to describe the movement, although there is great variation. A renewed belief in miracles (which includes healing) seems to be only one major factor in the modern charismatic development.

Many in the charismatic movement distanced themselves from Pentecostalism for cultural and theological reasons. Foremost among theological reasons is the Pentecostals' insistence that speaking in tongues is always the initial sign of receiving the fullness of the Holy Spirit. They also varied in style of worship and music.

Presbyterian J. Rodman Williams (1918–2008) held a PhD from Columbia University and was professor of theology of the School of Divinity at Regents University, Virginia Beach, Virginia. In 1996, he published *Renewal Theology: Systematic Theology from a Charismatic Perspective*.[53] The back cover of the book, a three-volumes-in-one book, declares that it "deals with the full range of Christian truth from within the charismatic tradition."

One major reason for the systematic theology was the accusation that charismatics had no united theological position, other than beliefs in the present work of the Holy Spirit. Despite Rodman's book, the complaint is still valid.

Peter Wagner believes the conservative branch of the Church began to embrace the charismatic movement around 1985. He referred to this shift as the "third wave of the Holy Spirit." Separate denominations (such as the Vineyard Movement) have formed in the United States as part of that third wave.

Here are examples of three historic denominations changed by the charismatic movement:

1. Lutherans: Larry Christenson did much in the 1960s and 1970s to interpret the charismatic movement for Lutherans. A large annual conference was held in Minneapolis during those years. Charismatic Lutheran congregations in Minnesota became especially large and influential. The next generation of Lutheran charismatics clustered around the Alliance of Renewal Churches.

2. Reformed Churches: Reformed Churches had many who embraced the renewal. The Presbyterian Charismatic Communion was formed in 1966, it began with four Presbyterian ministers and grew to include lay people. Generally, reformed charismatics distance themselves from movements that display over-emotional tendencies.

3. Roman Catholics: Since 1967 the charismatic movement has been active within the Roman Catholic

Church in the U.S. In the early days, the Catholic
Charismatic Renewal focused on individuals such as
Kevin Ranaghan at the University of Notre Dame in
Notre Dame, Indiana. Father Matt Linn and his
brother Dennis were leaders in spreading the message
among Roman Catholics.

Duquesne University in Pittsburgh, founded by the Congregation of the Holy Spirit, a Catholic religious community, began
hosting charismatic revivals in 1977. In a foreword to a 1983 book
by Cardinal Léon Joseph Suenens, Cardinal Joseph Ratzinger (now
Pope Benedict XVI) stated that there was a new experience of the
Holy Spirit that had burst forth.[54]

Who Were the Healers of the Twentieth Century?

In the pages that follow, we present brief biographies of the major names in the healing movement from the late 1800s until the latter part of the twentieth century.

A. A. Allen (1911–1970)

A. A. Allen grew up with poverty, hard work, a heavy-drinking father, and a mother who lived with several different men. In 1934, he began his ministry. Always controversial, he was one of the first healing evangelists to go on national television and pray for the sick and the demon possessed.

In 1958, he started the Miracle Valley Bible College with an emphasis on healing. His followers say he helped start more than 400 churches.

F. F. Bosworth (1877–1958)

Fred Francis Bosworth was born in Nebraska, and became a believer when he was sixteen years old. Later he developed lung problems that lasted for eight years until he was prayed for by a Methodist evangelist named Mattie Perry. He moved to Zion, Illinois, and became bandleader for the Zion City Band. He personally witnessed many miracles of healing.

Under the influence of Charles Parham, a pioneer in the Pentecostal movement, Bosworth left Zion, and became pastor of the First Assembly of God Church in Dallas.

He taught people about healing and prayed for them, but his most important work was evangelism. With his brother Burt (B. B.) in the 1920s, they held evangelist-healing campaigns all over the United States and Canada.

Bosworth wrote a book in 1924, still in print, called *Christ the Healer*. He was also a pioneer in radio. He retired in 1947, but a year later, he met William Branham, and joined him. The two men traveled extensively. One source says that Bosworth's most successful campaign was a trip to Africa at age 75. He and Branham witnessed an extremely large number of conversions and healings. He also received greater press coverage in Africa than any other time in his ministry.

William Branham (1909–1964)

Branham, like many healing evangelists of the past hundred years, was born in a poor family and he had little religious training. He became seriously ill, and that's when he turned to God. He visited a church where they anointed him with oil and prayed for him. He said many times that he was instantly healed.

When he was 24 years old, he began preaching and holding tent meetings. As early as 1933, he began having visions against the evils of Nazism and communism. He became the founding pastor of a church in Jefferson, Indiana. He also married and had two children. When invited to join a Pentecostal group as a traveling evangelist, he felt it was God's will but others talked him out of it.

His wife and children were drowned in the record-breaking flood of the Ohio River in 1937. He felt it was divine judgment for failing to do what he was supposed to do.

In May 1946, he had a vision in which an angel said he was a prophet and would have two distinct signs. First, he would be able to detect illness in people, and second, he would be able to point out sins in others' lives. That's when he began his healing ministry.

Branham worked with Gordon Lindsay and the Voice of Healing from 1947 through the 1950s. By the late 1950s his ministry had begun to diminish. Although he lived a simple lifestyle, he kept poor business records and got into trouble with the IRS.

Worse, as many of his friends said, he became unbalanced and began to think of himself as Elijah, who was heralding the end of life, although others said he never made that claim.

In 1964, Branham had a vision by which he understood that he would die soon. The following year, a drunk driver hit his car, and Branham died on Christmas Eve, 1965.[55]

Jack Coe (1918–1956)

The son of a gambler and alcoholic, Coe was one of seven children. Their mother left when they were young, and Coe was raised in an orphanage from age nine to seventeen. He became an alcoholic like his father.

Coe developed ulcers and an enlarged heart and a doctor told him he would die unless he quit drinking. He stopped drinking for a time but started again and became ill.

God spoke to him and said, "This is your last chance." The following week, Coe went to a Nazarene church and became a believer.

He felt called to the ministry and attended Southwestern Bible Institute but left in 1941 to join the army. In 1944, Coe became ill with malaria and was sent home because the doctors said they couldn't help him. He prayed and was healed.

In 1945, he went to Texas and announced in a church that God had called him to heal the sick. One woman received her sight that night and Coe's ministry began.

Coe was controversial and often hit, jerked, or pulled people out of wheelchairs. He claimed that God would strike dead those who stood against him. He was anti-medicine and preached against going to doctors.

In 1950, he began his own magazine, *Herald of Healing*. Within six years, his readership was more than 350,000. He raised money to start an orphanage and bought 200 acres outside of Dallas.

In 1952, he went on radio and 100 stations carried his program. He started his own church in Dallas in 1953, and opened a faith home a year later where needy people could stay for extended periods of time to receive prayer for healing.

In 1956, he was arrested for practicing medicine without a license and it brought him national attention—negative and positive.

He was acquitted. Coe was obese, and in 1956, he became paralyzed because of bulbar polio and died the same year.

John Alexander Dowie (1847–1907)

Dowie was born in Scotland and his family moved to Australia. He later became a pastor of a Congregational church. In 1876, several members of his congregation became sick and died. Dowie said God spoke to him and told him to resist sickness. He prayed and from that day on, none of the members was affected by the disease that plagued the area.

In 1890, Dowie attended the Chicago World's Fair and held healing meetings outside the fairgrounds. They were so successful, the front wall of the meeting was covered with paraphernalia left by those who had been healed. He started a church and began publishing a magazine called *Leaves of Healing* to promote the ministry of healing.

Dowie preached against the medical profession and eventually moved 40 miles north of Chicago to found the city of Zion. In its early days, Zion was a "holy" city where it was against the law to drink or smoke within the city limits. They also observed Jewish dietary laws and no store in the city carried pork or other biblically unclean products.

Many thousands claimed healing from Dowie and his people in Zion. Among the prominent people influenced by Dowie were John G. Lake, F. F. Bosworth, Raymond T. Rickey and Martha Wing Robinson.

Lorne Fox (1911–1988)

Fox, a pastor in Calgary, Alberta, Canada, wanted to protect his members from the healing evangelist Charles S. Price. He attended the meetings himself so he could denounce the fraud; however, because he was pastor, Price asked him to sit on the platform.

"What he saw that day changed his life. He saw healings and miracles he knew that no one but God could do."[56] Fox and his congregation became sponsors of Price's ministry while he was in their area.

When Price laid his hands on Fox's father and sister, they were healed. Fox suffered from a number of physical ailments, including trouble with his heart. Price prayed for him as well and he was "dramatically healed within moments."[57]

In 1947, Fox began holding meetings in Oregon and other places on the west coast and reported outstanding results. He started his own magazine, *The Healing Word,* and became associated with the Voice of Healing organization.

Fox ministered alongside other well-known evangelists at the time, including William Branham. He traveled to many foreign countries and healings were regular events at his meetings.

W. V. Grant Sr. (1913–1983)

Walter Vinson Grant, one of thirteen children, was born in 1913, in Arkansas to a poor family. He was a sickly child. His mother taught the children Bible stories and referred to W. V. as her "preacher boy." He had little schooling.

His mother had fainting spells and heart troubles but went to a healing meeting and was healed.

Grant rebelled and by nineteen was an alcoholic, and his stomach was in bad shape. Shortly afterward, he straightened out his life, sought God and was healed.

In 1945, he became an Assembly of God minister and witnessed many people being healed. He went to a Voice of Healing meeting and became an evangelist in 1949. He attended a meeting held by Oral Roberts and the evangelist prayed for him.

In the early 1950s, Grant became a tent evangelist and saw remarkable healings. He also developed a radio ministry and held "Faith Clinics." He wrote more than 600 booklets about healing, miracles and deliverance. He also regularly wrote for the *Voice of Healing* magazine.

He didn't spare himself and prayed for people, sometimes until 3:00 in the morning or even all night. In 1956, his health broke and he retired from traveling. He became vice president of the Voice of Healing organization. In 1962, he started his own magazine,

Voice of Deliverance, which reached a circulation of two million. In 1964, he organized a church in Dallas and by the time of his death in 1983, the attendance had grown to 2,500 people.

Kathryn Kuhlman (1907–1976)

Born in Missouri, she was one of four children. She claimed her mother showed no love or affection, but her father did. Converted at age 14 in a Methodist church, she left high school after tenth grade to join her married sister as an itinerant evangelist. Although Kuhlman had planned to stay only for the summer, she remained with them for five years.

One time when the evangelist missed a meeting, Kuhlman preached in his place. The pastor of that church encouraged her to step out in her own ministry. In 1933, she went to Colorado and began the Denver Revival Tabernacle two years later. She saw great success and began a radio show called *Smiling Through,* and inviting speakers from around the country. Phil Kerr, one of her guests, taught on divine healing.

In 1938, she met evangelist Burroughs Waltrip, whom she married and with whom she bore two sons. Waltrip left her and the sons and divorced her in 1947. Everything seemed to go wrong for her, including losing the church. In 1948, Kuhlman held meetings in Carnegie Hall in Pittsburgh and moved there two years later. She continued to hold meetings there until 1971—they were her best years.

She was flamboyant and her miracle services filled the auditorium in Pittsburgh every time she spoke. The records say that hundreds were healed in her meetings and many were set free from sicknesses while listening to her on radio or television.

Diagnosed with a heart problem in 1955, she kept a busy schedule but her heart became enlarged. She died after open-heart surgery in 1976.

John G. Lake (1870–1935)

Born in Canada as one of 16 children, his parents moved to Michigan when he was young. Lake studied to become a Methodist minister.

Physical illness remained a common problem in his family: one brother was an invalid, one sister had cancer, and another suffered from severe bleeding. Lake's wife had heart disease and tuberculosis.

In 1899, the family went to Chicago to hear John Alexander Dowie. The invalid brother was healed and so were both sisters. After prayer, Lake's wife also reported being healed.

Lake joined Dowie's organization and served in a branch church in Sault Ste. Marie. He later moved to Spokane. Over a five-year period reports say that 100,000 people were healed. He started healing rooms in other cities on the West Coast.

J. Gordon Lindsay (1906–1973)

James Gordon Lindsay was raised in an atmosphere of healing in Zion, Illinois. His parents were disciples of John Alexander Dowie, the famous healing evangelist who founded the city of Zion. Lindsay was converted during a meeting led by Charles G. Parham of Topeka, Kansas. He also developed a relationship with John G. Lake, who started the Divine Healing Missions in Spokane, Washington. He traveled with Lake, but eventually became a pastor in the early 1940s.

He heard William Branham preach on healing, resigned his church, and became Branham's campaign manager. Lindsay felt there was a need for literature that covered history, theology and the experience of healing and started the *Voice of Healing* magazine in 1948. He wrote 250 books and pamphlets, as well as making regular contributions to his own magazine. Lindsay also sponsored an international mission campaign and a radio program.

Lindsay died unexpectedly in 1973. His wife and daughter Carole continue the work he began.

Aimee Semple McPherson (1890–1944)

Her first husband, Robert Semple, died in 1910, while they served as missionaries in China. She married Harold McPherson two years later. In Canada, she joined the Pentecostal movement and was even then a flamboyant evangelist. In Los Angeles, her ministry reached its peak. With her dramatic appeal, she was able to build a 5,000-seat church, debt free, which she called Angelus Temple. Later McPherson started a Bible school, the Lighthouse of International Foursquare Evangelism and began radio evangelism in 1924.

Aimee Semple McPherson was well known for an incredible healing ministry. John Wimber (of the Vineyard Church) once remarked that his visit to Angelus Temple caused his heart to hunger after a healing anointing as he saw all the crutches, wheel chairs and other medical equipment left behind by people who had been healed by the meetings she held.[58]

Many of the physical healings that occurred at Angelus Temple were so well documented, in fact, that the American Medical Association officially approved of her work.[59]

Her ministry was extraordinary, and some said resembled stage productions with a brass band, costumes and elaborate sets. But even her critics admitted that she reached people who wouldn't have gone to a church.

There are an amazing number of reports of people for whom she prayed who walked without crutches, regained their eyesight, had broken bones healed and hundreds left their wheelchairs. She had many critics, but she gained the attention of newspapers like the *Los Angeles Times* and the *New York Times*.

Her Foursquare movement grew and churches appeared across the States. Her novelty as a female religious leader was heightened through the use of radio, which expanded her access to the public's attention: she was a featured performer on various Los Angeles stations in 1923 and became a radio station owner in 1924. By the late 1920s she was preaching 20 times a week.

Andrew Murray (1828–1917)

The writings of Andrew Murray, a pastor in the Reformed Church of South Africa, were extremely influential in his time and have had resurgence in recent years. Between 1858 and 1917, Murray wrote 240 books. Many are considered classics and are still in print or have been reprinted.

In 1879, he became ill and lost his voice, which took him to a period he referred to as two "silent years." During that time, he surrendered everything to God.

In 1881, he went to London to meet with a faith healer, W. E. Boardman. Murray was healed and never again had trouble with his throat. After that he began to teach and write that the gifts of God were for believers of his day.

David O. Nunn (1921–2003)

Nunn grew up in an Assembly of God church and while quite young, God healed his foot. His healing ministry began in 1949 when he prayed for a girl whose face was paralyzed and God healed her. He continued to pray for the sick in his church.

In 1950, Nunn felt God tell him to go into other cities and heal the sick. He bought a tent and founded the Bible Revival Evangelistic Association, which he oversaw for 42 years. He became a member of the Voice of Healing and was an international radio speaker. He held many international crusades and authored 20 books.

T. L. Osborn (1923–)

Tommy Lee (T. L.) Osborn was converted at age 13. His family became friends with Oral Roberts, then the pastor of a small church. In the mid-1930s, Osborn helped Roberts in evangelistic meetings.

Osborn and his wife, Daisy, went to India as missionaries and returned after a year. He prayed fervently for God's guidance and empowerment. In 1947, Osborn had a vision that changed his life. After that, he attended meetings held by William Branham and witnessed the healing of many people. He was often quoted about what he saw: "The blind saw, the deaf heard and the crippled walked."

Osborn said publicly many times that God spoke to him and promised that "no demon, no disease, or no power can stand before you all the days of your life." The Osborns started healing services in their church. The first miracle was a woman who had been injured in a car accident and was on crutches. After Osborn prayed for her, she was healed.

Healings continued and the Osborns felt the need to go to for-eign lands. He affiliated with The Voice of Healing organization in 1949, and later appeared with William Branham, F. F. Bosworth and Gordon Lindsay. That affiliation threw him into national attention.

In 1953, Osborn founded the Association of Native Evangel-ism to raise up national pastors to plant churches. Wherever Os-born went not only did thousands turn to Jesus Christ, but there were dramatic healings.

Charles F. Parham (1873–1929)

Parham was born with a clubfoot. While still an infant, he con-tracted a viral infection that left him weak and later came down with rheumatic fever. His mother died when he was twelve, which devastated him. Determined to see her in heaven, he became a be-liever and joined the Methodist church. By age 15, Parham was holding evangelistic meetings.

In 1890, rheumatic fever hit him again and he thought he might die. He prayed and God not only healed him of his rheu-matic fever but also of his clubfoot. From then on, he studied healing and holiness teaching. By 1895, he was an independent minister, teaching about healing and praying for the sick.

Parham visited John Alexander Dowie and the man so im-pressed him that he founded a "healing faith home" in Topeka, Kansas. He and his wife published a magazine, *Apostolic Faith*.

In 1903, Mary Arthur asked him to pray for her and she was healed of several infirmities, including blindness in one eye. She in-vited him to preach in her home in Galena, Kansas. He stayed sev-eral months and a thousand people claimed healing.

Although he died at age 56, he spent the last 20 years of his life as a preacher and faith healer.

Charles S. Price (1887–1947)

Born in England, Price went to Wesley College and later moved to Canada. He became a Congregational pastor for twelve years and was quoted as saying he was one who was "spiritually blind, leading his people into a ditch."

After moving to California in 1921, he attended a revival led by Aimee Semple McPherson. After investigating her work, Price became a Pentecostal. He gave his testimony and saw many people healed in his church. He left the pastorate a year later.

He traveled all over Canada and the United States and witnessed many healings. In 1923, Lorne Fox and his entire family were healed. Shortly after that, Fox and his sister began their own evangelistic and healing ministry.

In 1926, Price started a magazine, *Golden Grain*, and told the story of many healings and conversions. Two years later, he bought a tent and called it the Kanvas Kathedral. There were reports of miraculous healings.

Despite the Great Depression of the 1930s, when most evangelists stopped or slowed their ministry, he continued to draw large crowds. He traveled through Europe and the Middle East. By 1939, Price estimated that he had traveled more than a million miles doing evangelistic work. He often spoke two or three times a day and prayed for individuals for healing well into the night. In a six-month period in 1940, he preached 218 times and held 35 healing services.

Price also published books, spoke extensively on radio and taught at the Southern California Bible College.

Oral Roberts (1918–2009)

Oral Roberts is probably the best-known of all modern healing evangelists. Born Granville Oral Roberts, his parents were members of the Pentecostal Holiness Church. His mother regularly prayed for the sick. Oral stuttered badly as a child, but his mother assured him that one day God would heal him and he would speak to multitudes.

When he was 16, he rebelled, left home, and turned from God. After he contracted tuberculosis, Roberts repented and his sister assured him that God would heal him.

Roberts' older brother took him to meetings conducted by a healing evangelist named George Moncey. Roberts told his story several times on television. He was on the way to the meeting when God spoke to him. God said that he would be healed and he was "to take my healing power to your generation." God also told him that he would one day build a university.

At the meeting, Roberts was too sick to go forward, so he waited until the evangelist came to him. Moncey prayed for him and he was instantly healed. His stutter was also gone. After that, Roberts traveled the evangelistic circuit for a time.

After Roberts married, he became a pastor and also went to college. He never lost his belief in healing, and one story Roberts often told was that he prayed for a church member with a crushed foot and the man was instantly healed. As Roberts continued to study, and especially to read his Bible, he was convinced that Jesus was the healer and he was to proclaim that message.

In 1947, Roberts began an itinerant ministry. A number of outstanding healings took place. He received widespread notice when a man unsuccessfully tried to shoot him to death. The man was convicted, and the incident brought Roberts into the spotlight.

Roberts bought a tent that held 3,000 people and later bought one that held 12,000. He established the Oral Roberts Evangelistic Association in 1948, and traveled extensively. Like many other healing evangelists, his meetings were interracial and that sometimes brought serious criticism. In Melbourne, Australia, he was physically attacked and driven out of the city because he prayed for the sick.

In 1954, Roberts began playing his sermons on radio, filming his crusades, and airing the crusade tapes during television prime time. He established an around-the-clock prayer service. In the 1950s and 1960s, his name appeared on the lists of the nation's most respected leaders.

In his later years, Roberts shifted from healing meetings to television and to Oral Roberts University.

Martha Wing Robinson (1874–1936)

Although converted at eight years of age, Robinson suffered from many physical ailments, having problems with her stomach, liver and kidneys. Her joints swelled and she experienced excruciating headaches. A family friend connected her with John Alexander Dowie, who was then in Chicago. Dowie prayed for her and she later said she was partially healed.

In 1901, Dowie ordained her as a minister of the gospel. Many healings took place under her ministry. One time she prayed for a woman who was paralyzed by a stroke. After prayer, the woman got out of bed and walked fourteen blocks.

Robinson lived in Zion, Illinois, the city started by Dowie. She and her husband opened the Faith Homes (which still operate today in Zion), where people could come for teaching, prayer and for healing. Healings became a regular occurrence. She continued to minister in the Faith Homes until her death in 1936.

Agnes Sanford (1897–1982)

Agnes White (later Sanford) was the daughter of missionary parents to China. She returned to the United States at age 15, and finished her education.

At one point she had surgery and during the surgery momentarily died or had a near-death experience. From then on, she grasped the difference between the physical and the spiritual. A family friend had epilepsy and she committed herself to pray for years for his healing. He was eventually healed.

At age 21, she had earned her college degree and returned to China to be with her parents. But she wasn't happy. She developed a sensitivity to others' emotional well-being. While teaching in China, she met and married Ted (Sandy) Sanford. They returned to the United States and she bore three children. After the third birth, she became seriously depressed.

An Episcopalian priest and friend, Hollis Colwell, visited the Sanfords. One of the Sanford children was ill. Colwell prayed for the boy, who was immediately healed. Mrs. Sanford then asked

Colwell to pray for her, and when he laid hands on her, her depression left.

He urged her to write and to pray for the sick herself. She began to pray for the sick and many claimed healing. Her first book, *The Healing Light,* covered emotional and physical healing. She was a forerunner of those who stressed inner (or emotional) healing. Her husband also prayed for the sick and saw visible results.

Agnes prayed for people at a distance and not just those on whom she could lay hands. During World War II, she went to veteran's hospitals, prayed for the sick and often witnessed remarkable healings.

The Sanfords started the School of Pastoral Care where they taught people how to pray and care for the sick. Her husband died of a heart attack, and she carried on until she was 85. She never spoke to large crowds, but her writing and teachings went everywhere and some consider them classics.

A. B. Simpson (1843–1919)

Simpson was born to Christian parents in Western Canada and they prayed for him to become a minister. At age fourteen, he was in college, suffered from a complete breakdown, and thought he might die. He became a believer, finished college and became pastor of a 1,200-member church. Simpson remained there for eight years and they added 750 members during his tenure.

Simpson still battled personal health problems and moved to Louisville, Kentucky, for five years and then on to New York City in 1879. In 1881, a woman with a son in a coma asked Simpson to pray for him. He prayed for the son and the boy awakened, totally healed.

That summer, Simpson and his family went to Maine, where Charles Cullis spoke at a convention. Simpson had little interest in the meetings, preferring to rest, but he heard many stories of physical healing. He went into the forest alone to pray and asked God to show him the truth about healing. He himself was healed.

After that experience, Simpson preached about divine healing. He left his prestigious position and started the Gospel Tabernacle in New York City, as an independent congregation.

In 1883, he conducted healing services and declared his house a "home for faith and physical healing." Later Simpson created two organizations that later joined together to form the Christian and Missionary Alliance.

Charles Haddon Spurgeon (1834–1892)

C. H. Spurgeon was a British Baptist preacher. Scholars estimate that he spoke to about ten million people in his lifetime. He became pastor of a once-prestigious Park Street Baptist Church in London at age 20, revitalized the congregation, and eventually moved to the Metropolitan Baptist Church where he remained until his death at age 57.

Spurgeon was a prolific writer and his Sunday sermons were transcribed and printed every Monday. Many of his writings and sermons are still in print.

Lester Sumrall (1913–1996)

Sumrall came from a home with a mother who prayed fervently. While he was still a boy, his mother was diagnosed with breast cancer. Many prayed for her and God healed her.

When Lester's grandfather suffered a stroke and was paralyzed, his mother's friends prayed for him. The old man got out of the wheelchair, walked and moved his arms. He lived another 15 years.

Lester drifted from the faith, dropped out of school at age 16, and later was diagnosed with tuberculosis—in those days TB was a death sentence. On Lester's seventeenth birthday, the doctor said he was going to die and even prepared the death certificate.

That night, Lester had a vision with a Bible on one side of his bed and a coffin on the other. He believed God showed him that either he would preach or die. He told God he would preach. The next morning he was healed.

With no formal training, Sumrall preached and gathered enough people to start a church. Two years later, he met Bible teacher Howard Carter, and they traveled the world together. Sumrall told of remarkable healings taking place as well as conversions.

In 1940, he met a missionary, Louise Layman, and married her. They made South Bend, Indiana, their home base. In 1950, they went to the Philippines and nothing much happened, until he prayed for a girl who was demon possessed. The account was so dramatic that newspapers across the world carried the story.

After that, a famous actor, unable to walk, was healed, and that gave Sumrall even more publicity. A lawyer, who had been on crutches for 12 years, was healed.

Sumrall returned to the United States and was one of the first evangelists to embrace television as an evangelistic medium. He started Lesea Broadcasting Network and oversaw the operation of the station until his death in 1996.

John Wimber (1934–1997)

As a young man, Wimber helped form the musical group the Righteous Brothers, and played the keyboard. After a conversion experience in 1963, he became a Quaker and joined the staff of a Yorba Linda, California, church in 1971. Three years later he became the founding director of the Department of Church Growth at Fuller Institute of Evangelism and Church Growth.

In 1977, Wimber affiliated with the Calvary Chapel organization and established his own congregation in Yorba Linda. A year later, Wimber witnessed his first healing. He later left Calvary Chapel and joined the Vineyard Church organization, and in 1982, he became the head of Vineyard churches.

Wimber continued to be involved with Fuller Seminary. In 1984, he took a class on the road and taught his students how to pray for the sick. He focused on every-member ministry within the congregation and taught that they could expect healing. Wimber's health deteriorated and he died of a massive brain injury caused by a fall.

ENDNOTES

Part 1: Stories and Testimonies of Healing

1. A. J. Gordon, *The Ministry of Healing* (Houston, TX: The Full Gospel Advocate, 1882), p. 1, emphasis added.
2. Adapted from an interview with Amy DiBiase on April 11, 2005, "BarlowGirl Strikes Back," http://www.jesusfreakhideout.com/interviews/BarlowGirl.asp; Amy Hammond Hagberg, "Features: BarlowGirl," Soulshine, January 21, 2008, http://www.soul shine.ca/features/featuresarticle.php?fid=285; and "BarlowGirl Shares About Struggle with RSD," ShareYourStory, http://www.youtube.com/watch?v=DVC_GfUTGPY.
3. Reverend Russell H. Cornwell, *The Life of Charles Haddon Spurgeon* (Philadelphia, PA: Edgewood Publishing, 1892).
4. This account is taken from a report in the September 14, 2005, issue of the newsletter of Iris Ministries (http://www.irismin.org), an organization started by Rolland and Heidi Baker.
5. Edmund Goerke, "The Gift of Healing in the Life of George Fox," part 1, Quaker info.com. http://www.quakerinfo.com/healing1.shtml.
6. Ibid, quoting George Fox, *The Journal of George Fox*, vol. 1 (Cambridge, MA: 1911), p. 199.
7. Henry J. Cadbury, editor, *George Fox's "Book of Miracles"* (Cambridge, MA: 1948), p. 147.
8. Ibid., p. 124.
9. Ibid., p. 108.
10. Goerke, "The Gift of Healing in the Life of George Fox," part 1.
11. Ibid.
12. Ibid.
13. Don Stewart, *Only Believe: An Eyewitness Account of the Great Healing Revival of the 20th Century* (Shippensburg, PA: Destiny Image, 1999), p. 75.
14. Reported by Carey Cramer of the Randy Clark Ministry Team on January 26, 2005, and condensed from *Global Awakening Report*, January 31, 2006.
15. "Testimonies," Bethel Church, Redding, California, August 16, 2012. http://www.ibeth el.org/testimonies/2012/08/16/a-girl-can-hear-in-partially-formed-ear.
16. The accounts in this section come from "Healing in the Medieval Period 600–1400," *The Voice of Healing*. http://www.voiceofhealing.info/02history/medieval.html.
17. Stewart, *Only Believe: An Eyewitness Account of the Great Healing Revival of the 20th Century*, p. 164.
18. "Kathryn Kuhlman," God's Generals. http://www.godsgenerals.com/person_k_kuhlman.htm.
19. This story received wide publicity. See T. G. S. Hawksley, "Kateryn Kuhlman 1907–1976, 'I Believe in Miracles, Because I Believe in God,'" Sternfield Thoughts, April 6, 2009, http://sternfieldthoughts.blogspot.com/2009/04/kathryn-kuhlman.html; and Linda Josef, "The Miracle Healing of Delores Winder," And the Truth Shall Set You Free, May 24, 2008, http://lumel1962.blogspot.com/2008/05/miracle-healing-of-delores-winder.html.
20. Nick Ittzes, "GOD, Not Program!" taken from *The Psalmist Magazine*, June/July, 1988. http://www.angelfire.com/oh2/spiritsong/notprogram.html.
21. "Testimonies," Bethel Church, Redding, California, June 6, 2012. http://www.ibeth el.org/testimonies/2012/06/06/gallstones-gone.
22. Ibid., May 18, 2012. http://www.ibethel.org/testimonies/2012/05/18/healed-of-a-blood-disorder.

23. Marcus Brotherton, *Teacher: The Henrietta Mears Story* (Ventura, CA: Regal Books, 2006), pp. 37-40.

24. "The International Order of St. Luke the Physician." http://orderofstluke.org/.

25. A different form of this article appeared in *Sharing Magazine*, March/April 2010, p. 6. Used with permission.

26. For the full account of this story, go to http://www.oslregion8.org/testimonies.htm#freddie.

27. Gordon Lindsay, compiler, "Facial Paralysis Healed by David Nunn," excerpt from *Men Who Heard from Heaven*, 2004 Digital Press. http://www.branham.it/joomla/evangelisti/document_davidnunn.pdf.

28. Rufus Elbert Davidson, "Healed of Cancer," *Voice of Healing*, January 1962, p. 2. http://www.branham.it/joomla/documenti/thevoiceofhealing/1962_GENNAIO.pdf.

29. "Testimonies," Bethel Church, Redding, California, June 28, 2011. http://www.ibethel.org/testimonies/2011/06/28/bilateral-renal-artery-stenosis.

30. Civilla D. Martin and Charles H. Gabriel, "His Eye Is on the Sparrow" (1905).

31. For more information see http://www.ibethel.org/bethel-school-of-supernatural-ministry.

32. Testimonies," Bethel Church, Redding, California, April 26, 2012. http://www.ibethel.org/testimonies/2012/04/26/deafness-healed-again-and-again.

33. "Equipping the Saints," *Healing and Revival*, 2004. http://healingandrevival.com/BioJWimber.htm.

34. "Alan Davies," Naracoorte Uniting Church. http://naracoorteuca.org.au/index.php?option=com_content&view=article&id=55&Itemid=61.

35. John Wimber, "Signs, Wonders, and Cancer," *Christianity Today*, October 7, 1996, vol. 40, no. 11. http://www.christianitytoday.com/ct/1996/october7/6tb049.html?start=2.

36. Gordon, *The Ministry of Healing*, pp. 171-172.

37. "The Man Who Believed God," Biography for Dr. Charles Cullis, Healing and Revival. http://healingandrevival.com/BioCCullis.htm.

38. "Apostle of Healing," the biography of Dorothea Trudel, Healing and Revival. http://healingandrevival.com/BioDTrudel.htm.

39. Jeff Doles, *Miracles and Manifestations of the Holy Spirit in the History of the Church* (Seffner, FL: Walking Barefoot Ministries, 2007), p. 236.

40. Agnes Sanford, *Sealed Orders: The Autobiography of a Christian Mystic* (Alachua, FL: Bridge-Logos, 1972), pp. 204-207.

41. Alice Marshall, "John Alexander Dowie," *The News-Sun*, August 28, 1996. http://www.dowie.org/john_alexander_dowie.htm.

42. John Alexander Dowie, *American First-Fruits* (San Francisco: Leaves of Healing, 1889), p. 5. http://play.google.com/books/reader?id=IyiSXeN1RkEC&printsec=frontcover&output=reader&hl=en.

43. Ibid., pp. 10–11.

44. Roberts Liardon, *God's Generals: The Healing Evangelists* (New Kensington, PA: Whitaker House, 2003), pp. 279-280. Liardon's account comes from the Hunters' book *Since Jesus Passed By*, pp. 139-140.

45. Ibid., p. 281. Liardon's account comes from *Since Jesus Passed By*, p. 115.

46. Ibid., pp. 281-282. Liardon's account comes from *Since Jesus Passed By*, p. 115.

47. Doug and Becky Neel serve on the Global Resource Team of The Mission Society.

48. Becky Neel, "God Shoulders Our Burdens: Rheumatoid Arthritis Healed," The Mission Society. http://www.themissionsociety.org/learn/multimedia/unfinished/issue-templ/mag-templ/god-shoulders-our-burdens.

49. United Methodist missionaries, Martin and Tracy Reeves serve with the Mission Society in Trujillo, Peru.

50. "God Knows Our Needs: Unborn Baby Is Healed, The Mission Society. http://www.the missionsociety.org/learn/multimedia/unfinished/issue-templ/mag-templ/god-knows-our-needs.

51. Stewart, *Only Believe: An Eyewitness Account of the Great Healing Revival of the 20th Century*, pp. 1-2.

52. Liardon, *God's Generals*, p. 64. Liardon's account comes from *Since Jesus Passed By*, pp. 139-140.

53. Thomas S. Kidd, *The Great Awakening: The Roots of Evangelical Christianity in Colonial America* (New Haven, CT: Yale University Press, 2007), pp. 162-163.

54. "The Man of Reckless Faith," God's Generals. http://www.godsgenerals.com/person_j_coe.htm.

55. Pauline Young, "Cancer Cured," *The Voice of Healing*, August, 1951, p. 10, http://www.gods generals.com/PDF/1951_AUGUST.pdf#Page=10.

56. "John G. Lake," Reference.com, http://www.reference.com/browse/john_g._lake; "John G. Lake—A Man of Faith and Works," Christian Assemblies International, http://www.cai.org/bible-studies/john-g-lake-man-faith-and-works.

57. "Louise Reinbold Testimony," John G. Lake, overseer, The Church at Spokane, May 20, 1918. http://johnglake.org/content/spokesman-review-sunday-may-26-1918.

58. "John G. Lake," God's Generals. http://www.godsgenerals.com/person_j_lake.htm.

59. "John G. Lake—A Man of Faith and Works," Christian Assemblies International. http://www.cai.org/bible-studies/john-g-lake-man-faith-and-works.

60. Audra Smith, "Kimberly Funk: See What God Can Do," *The 700 Club*, October 25, 2010. http://www.cbn.com/700club/features/amazing/Kimberly-Funk-102510.aspx.

61. Shawn Brown and Zsa Zsa Palagyi, "Mike Fisher's Miracle," *The 700 Club*. http://www.cbn.com/700club/features/amazing/WOK154_Mike_Fisher.aspx.

62. Tom Welchel, storyteller, *Azusa Street: They Told Me Their Stories* (Dare 2 Dream, 2006), p. 15.

63. Ibid., p. 34.

64. Ibid., pp. 44-45.

65. Ibid., p. 45.

66. *Early Christian Biographies* (Washington, DC: The Catholic University of America Press, 1952), p. 255.

67. This story was taken from a DVD from the Lester Sumrall Legacy Archive: "Luzon Headhunter," a presentation by the Lester Sumrall Evangelistic Association (LeSEA), Inc., South Bend, Indiana.

68. Lester Sumrall with J. Stephen Conn, *Miracles Don't Just Happen* (Plainfield, NJ: Logos International, 1979), pp. 52-53. http://www.scribd/com/doc/89105660/

69. Ibid., pp. 53-56.

70. Ibid., pp. 56-57.

71. Ibid., pp. 62-67.

72. "Amazing Healing Testimonies," Choices for Living. http://www.choicesforliving.com/spirit/part4/healing3.htm.

73. Thomas W. Miller, "Testimony 'From Out of the Past,'" Dr. Charles S. Price Testimony, http://www.earstohear.net/price/testimony.html; see also "Goitre Healed Through Prayer," Christian Assemblies International, http://www.cai.org/bible-studies/goitre-healed-through-prayer.

74. Miller, "Testimony 'From Out of the Past,'" http://www.earstohear.net/price/testimony.html.

75. "New Organs Created," excerpt from *Golden Grain* magazine, 1942, edited by Charles S. Price. http://healingandrevival.com/CSPrice1.pdf. Digital Copyright © 2004 by Healing and Revival Press.

76. This is taken from the foreword Don Piper wrote for *When You Need a Miracle: How to Ask God for the Impossible* (Grand Rapids, MI: Revell, 2012) by Linda Evans Shepherd, p. 11.

77. "F. F. Bosworth: A Healing Evangelist of Power and Spiritual Integrity," Mel Montgomery Communications International. http://www.brothermel.org/audio-video/74.

78. Liardon, *God's Generals: The Healing Evangelists*, p. 38.

79. Ibid., pp. 13-15.

80. Eunice M. Perkins, *Joybringer Bosworth: His Life's Story* (Dayton, OH: John J. Scruby, 1921), p. 162, quoted in Liardon, *God's Generals*, pp. 31-33.

81. Liardon, *God's Generals*, pp. 34-36.

82. Ibid, pp. 43-44.

83. Bill Hybels, *Too Busy Not to Pray* (Downers Grove, IL: InterVarsity Press, 2008), p. 55.

84. "A Man of Notable Signs and Wonders," God's Generals. http://www.godsgenerals.com/person_w_branham.htm.

85. Ibid.

86. "Congressman Upshaw," BelievetheSign.com. http://en.believethesign.com/index.php?title=Congressman_Upshaw.

87. "William David Upshaw," Wikipedia.org. http://en.wikipedia.org/wiki/William_D._Upshaw.

88. "'Miracle' Sets Boy Walking Normally," *The Voice of Healing*, March 1952, pp. 14-15. http://www.godsgenerals.com/PDF/1952_MARCH.pdf#Page=14.

89. "Reports from South Africa: Part One," The William Branham Home Page. http://www.williambranhamhomepage.org/visitsa1.htm.

90. Stewart, *Only Believe: An Eyewitness Account of the Great Healing Revival of the 20th Century*, p. 131.

91. Ruth Carter Stapleton, *In His Footsteps: The Healing Ministry of Jesus—Then and Now* (San Francisco: Harper & Row, 1979), p. 4.

92. Ibid., p. 47.

93. *The Voice of Healing*, February 1952. http://www.godsgenerals.com/PDF/1952_FEBRUARY.pdf.

94. Ibid., p. 8.

95. Ibid., p. 9.

96. Ibid., p. 18.

97. "Sister Aimee Begins Her Healing Ministry," The Foursquare Church, October 20, 2009. http://www.foursquare.org/news/article/sister_aimee_begins_her_healing_ministry.

98. Ibid.

99. Aimee Semple McPherson, "Doubters Believe When Sister Aimee Is Healed," The Foursquare Church, January 26, 2010. http://www.foursquare.org/news/article/doubters_believe_when_sister_aimee_is_healed.

100. Dr. Raymond L. Cox, "Revival in Denver." http://www.oocities.org/heartland/7707/denver.htm.

101. "The Miracle Man," God's Generals. http://www.godsgenerals.com/person_a_allen.htm.

102. "A. A. Allen Miracles: REPLACED RIBS and LUNG Proven by X-RAY!" excerpt from *Miracle Magazine*, vol. 4, no. 7, April 1959, pp. 1,14. http://www.miraclevalley.net/gpage23.html. Several sources cite this healing, including Don Stewart's *Only Believe* (pp. 175-176).

103. A longer version of this story was published in the *Pentecostal Evangel*, May 12, 2002.

104. A longer version of this story appears in the *Pentecostal Evangel*, March 15, 1987, p. 21.

105. James Hammonds, "Totally Blind Eye," The Voice of Healing, February 1952, p. 11. http://www.godsgenerals.com/PDF/1952_FEBRUARY.pdf.
106. "The Father of Pentecost," God's Generals. http://www.godsgenerals.com/person_c_parham.htm.
107. "Breaking the Silence—Duane Miller Ministry Videos," GodTube, © 1989, 1997 Focus on the Family. http://www.godtube.com/watch/?v=922C0MNU.
108. Listen to Miller's healing moment on his website www.nuvoice.org.
109. You can read Duane Miller's complete story in his book Out of the Silence (Nashville, TN: Thomas Nelson Publishers, 1997).
110. Known as Lady Delia to her congregation at Living Word Christian Center in Mobile, Alabama, Delia Roman Knox co-labors with her husband, Bishop Levy Knox. She has ministered around the world in person and on TV. See http://www.lwccim.com.
111. To watch what happened the night Delia Knox was healed, see http://bit.ly/R0xvy5. To hear Delia's testimony about her healing, see http://bit.ly/nOfgY1.
112. Dodie Osteen and her late husband, John, co-founded Lakewood Church in Houston, Texas, in 1959. Her son, Joel Osteen, is now Lakewood's senior pastor. After her dramatic and miraculous healing, God called Dodie Osteen into a special ministry of prayer.
113. Dodie Osteen, Healed of Cancer (Houston, TX: John Osteen Publications, 1986).
114. Stewart, Only Believe, p. 124.
115. The late Reverend Canon Bill Riesberry was an Anglican Church of Canada minister.
116. Albert Edward Thompson, The Life of A.B. Simpson (New York: Christian Alliance Publishing Company, 1920), p. 112.
117. Reverend A. B. Simpson, The Gospel of Healing (New York: Christian Alliance Publishing Company, 1890), Chapter 7: "Testimony of the Work." http://www.cmalliance.org/resources/archives/downloads/simpson/the-gospel-of-healing.pdf.

Part 2: Questions About Healing
1. B. B. Warfield, Counterfeit Miracles (Edinburgh, UK: Banner of Truth Trust, 1983), p. 6.
2. Morton T. Kelsey, Healing and Christianity (New York: Harper & Row, 1973), p. 234.
3. A.J. Gordon, The Ministry of Healing (Whitefish, MT: Kessinger Publishing, 2006), p. 45.
4. Ibid., pp. 46,51.
5. Ibid., p. 56.
6. This material in this section comes from The Kingdom and the Power, edited by Gary S. Greig and Kevin N. Springer (Ventura, CA: Regal, 1993), pp. 413-415.
7. Gordon, The Ministry of Healing, quoting from Dr. Gerhard Uhlhorn, Conflict of Christianity with Heathenism (New York: Charles Scribner's Sons, 1908), p. 58.
8. Ibid.
9. Gordon, The Ministry of Healing, p. 59.
10. Morton T. Kelsey provides persuasive evidence for the shift from Platonic to Aristotelian in Encounter with God: A Theology of Christian Experience (Mahwah, NJ: Paulist Press, 1972).
11. Francis MacNutt, Healing (Notre Dame, IN: Ave Marie Press, 1974, 1999), p. 46, quoting Dr. Ramsey MacMullen of Yale's book Christianizing the Roman Empire: AD 100–400 (New Haven, CT: Yale University Press, 1984).
12. Kelsey, Encounter with God: A Theology of Christian Experience, p. 149.
13. Gordon, The Ministry of Healing, p. 60.
14. Origen, Against Celsus, I. 46 and 67, as quoted by Morton T. Kelsey, Encounter with God: A Theology of Christian Experience, p. 136.
15. Ibid.

16. Andrew Daunton-Fear, *Healing in the Early Church* (Eugene, OR: Wipf & Stock, 2009), p. 55.

17. Ibid.

18. Ibid., p. 68.

19. Ibid., p. 90.

20. In *Healing and Christianity,* Morton T. Kelsey quotes from *Retractions* (New York: Harper & Row, 1973), p. 185.

21. Kelsey (and others) tell this story. *Healing and Christianity,* pp. 185-186.

22. Ibid., p. 187.

23. Ibid., pp. 187-188.

24. Kelsey, *Healing and Christianity*, p. 149.

25. Gordon, *The Ministry of Healing,* p. 60.

26. Ibid.

27. Ibid., pp. 60-61.

28. Kelsey, *Healing and Christianity,* p. 149.

29. Ibid., p. 150.

30. Gordon, *The Ministry of Healing,* p. 61.

31. Ibid.

32. Ibid., p. 62.

33. Ibid., pp. 62-63.

34. Kelsey, *Healing and Christianity,* pp. 148-149, translated by William Wake (1900), 1:299, *Shepherd of Hermas,* III.X.4 in the *Apostolic Fathers.*

35. Kelsey, *Healing and Christianity,* p. 229.

36. Ibid.

37. Ibid., p. 231.

38. Ibid., pp. 231-232.

39. For examples, see Part 1, pages 39-40.

40. Gordon, *The Ministry of Healing,* p. 65.

41. Kelsey, *Healing and Christianity,* p. 233.

42. Ibid.

43. Amanda Porterfield, *Healing in the History of Christianity* (New York: Oxford University Press, 2005), p. 99.

44. "Healing in the Reformation Period 1400–1700," The Voice of Healing. http://www.voiceofhealing.info/02history/reformation.html.

45. Kelsey, *Healing and Christianity,* p. 235.

46. Porterfield, *Healing in the History of Christianity,* p. 167.

47. These accounts appear in Kelsey, *Healing and Christianity,* pp. 235ff, but they are also recorded several other places.

48. Tom Welchel, storyteller, *Azusa Street: They Told Me Their Stories* (Dare2Dream, 2006). See Part 1, pages 101-102 for several accounts.

49. Fred and Sharon Wright, *The World's Greatest Revivals* (Shippensburg, PA: Destiny Image, 2007), p. 187.

50. Dennis J. Bennett and John Sherrill, *Nine O'clock in the Morning* (Alachua, FL: Bridge-Logos, 1970).

51. Wright, *The World's Greatest Revivals,* p. 189.

52. Fred and Sharon Wright, *The World's Greatest Revivals* (Shippensburg, PA: Destiny Image, 2007), pp. 189-190.

53. J. Rodman Williams, *Renewal Theology: Systematic Theology from a Charismatic Perspective* (Grand Rapids, MI: Zondervan Publishing House, 1996).

54. Cardinal Léon Joseph Suenens, *Renewal and the Powers of Darkness* (London, UK: Darton, Long and Todd Ltd, 1983), pp. ix-xv.

55. A personal note from Cecil Murphey: I attended two meetings in Mansfield, Ohio, in 1960 and heard William Branham. I saw his gifts at work. Both nights Branham preached a long, rambling sermon that lasted about an hour. After he stopped, he started his healing-and-prophetic ministry. I had been skeptical of him, so I sat fairly close to the platform both nights. I witnessed an amazing number of healings. I was convinced that the healings and the sins he pointed out in several people were authentic.

56. "Healed to Be a Healer: The Biogrpahy of Lorne Fox," Healing and Revival Press. http://healingandrevival.com/BioLFox.htm.

57. Ibid.

58. Wright, *The World's Great Revivals*, p. 184.

59. Adapted from Aimee Semple McPherson, *Aimee: Life Story of Aimee Semple McPherson* (International Church of the Foursquare Gospel, 1979).

ACKNOWLEDGMENTS

Cecil Murphey:
Steven Lawson, then an editor at Regal, took me to dinner at a writers' conference. As we talked, I told him about my wife's healing after the doctor gave me no hope.

Months later, the topic of healing came up at an editorial meeting at Regal. They decided to do a book about divine healing. Steve suggested me to write it.

That conversation was the beginning. This book is the result.

When I told my agent, Deidre Knight, about the project, she was highly enthusiastic—and I've learned to trust her instincts.

Twila Belk, who is also my assistant, provided invaluable help in soliciting and writing some of the stories.

Gail Smith helped me with her insightful Internet searches.

Stan Jantz stepped into the project and moved it along, and for that I'm grateful.

I promised Mark Weising that I wouldn't tell anyone how much he helped to make this a better book.

Twila Belk:
Thanks to the Regal team for allowing us to do a book that brags on God. That's my favorite thing to do.

Deidre Knight (agent extraordinaire), I appreciate your wisdom and friendship.

Gail Smith, you wear the Wonder Woman title well. Thanks for your help with research and tracking down details.

Stephen, I love you. Thanks for all you do to help me do what I do. Working on this book helped me believe in healing all the more for you.

Great is the Lord and most worthy of praise!